—9388(4)

PLANNING AND ACCOMPLISHING SCHOOL-CENTRED EVALUATION

To my dear friend Amadou

PLANNING AND ACCOMPLISHING SCHOOL-CENTRED EVALUATION

KEITH MORRISON

Director of Higher Degrees
School of Education, University of Durham

PETER FRANCIS PUBLISHERS

Peter Francis Publishers
The Old School House
Little Fransham
Dereham
Norfolk NR19 2JP

**A CIP catalogue record for this book
is available from the British Library**

ISBN 1-870167-27-9

Printed and bound in Great Britain by Biddles Ltd,
Guildford and King's Lynn.

Contents

List of Figures   vi
Preface   vii
Acknowledgements   viii

1   Introducing Evaluation   1
2   How Do I Plan an Evaluation?   14
3   Instruments for Collecting Data   59
4   Sampling   112
5   What Can I Do with the Data?   128
6   Achieving Reliability and Validity   162
7   How Do I Report an Evaluation?   175
8   The Management and Ethics of Evaluation   181
9   Conclusion   190

Appendix A: Costing an Evaluation   193
Appendix B: A Sample Interview Schedule   195
Appendix C: Calculating the Chi-Square (χ^2) Statistic 196
Appendix D: Calculating the Spearman Rank Order
            Correlation Co-efficient   199
Appendix E: Calculating the Standard Deviation of
            a Set of Scores   201
Appendix F: Calculating Z-Scores   202
Appendix G: The T-Test of Significance   204
Appendix H: Calculating the Pearson Product Moment
            Correlation Co-efficient   208

Bibliography   210
Index   213

List of Figures

2.1: Key Elements of an Evaluation 18
2.2: A Matrix for Planning an Evaluation 21-28
2.3: Stages in Planning an Evaluation 30
2.4: Using Models to Organize Evaluation Approaches ... 55-56
3.1: A Sample Extract from a Questionnaire 76
3.2: A Structured Observation Schedule 82
3.3: A Matrix for Timing the Data Gathering Process ... 107
3.4: A Matrix for Planning the Data Gathering 108
3.5: A Summary Matrix for Planning the Data Gathering ... 109
4.1: Determining the Size of a Random Sample 116
4.2: A Matrix for a Random Stratified Sample 120
4.3: A Sampling Matrix which Indicates Proportions
     of the Population 124
5.1: A Contingency Table 2×3 132
5.2: A First Graph Indicating Position of the Mean
     and Distributions 143
5.3: A Second Graph Indicating Position of the Mean
     and Distributions 144
5.4: A Third Graph Indicating Position of the Mean
     and Distributions 144
5.5: Using Statistics to Answer Particular
     Evaluation Questions 149
5.6: The Early Stages of a Cognitive Map 157

Preface

A little over a hundred years ago the German philosopher Nietzsche wrote a short but corrosive account of scholars, commenting that they 'sit in the cool shade: they want to be mere spectators in everything and they take care not to sit where the sun burns upon the steps. Like those who stand in the street and stare at the people passing by, so they too wait and stare at thoughts that others have thought'. A hundred years later the comment is just as pertinent even though the context has altered.

Perhaps as never before the educational community is both vilified in the media and subject to intense political intervention; teachers, scholars and educationists in all spheres are being forced to sit in the cool shade whilst politicians take decisions for them. At national and international levels there is a thirst for assessment, testing, evaluation, appraisal, measurement and monitoring of performance which is barely slaked by the battery of instruments which have been developed to comment on every aspect of students' and teachers' lives.

This book has two purposes; the first of these is to introduce readers to issues in evaluation so that they might develop their understanding of this topical issue. Secondly it takes readers step-by-step through key elements of planning, implementing and reporting evaluations in such a way that they can come out of the cool shade and become involved in evaluation themselves as active rather than passive participants. This book takes the view that such knowledge is empowering.

Evaluation is an intensely political activity whose profile has been raised over the last decade - witness the millions of pounds and dollars that are being spent on it annually by governments. On a much smaller but perhaps no less political scale teachers, curriculum leaders, curriculum co-ordinators, project leaders, faculty heads, local authority officers, students on courses of both initial and post-initial teacher education are being involved in all sorts of evaluations. This book is a timely, concise and practical introduction to the field of evaluation. It is set out in such a way that it enables readers to undertake evaluations fully aware of their important features and how these might be addressed, giving worked examples and practical advice together with suggestions for further reading. This book will enable readers to become evaluators, however embryonic, empowered to plan and carry out evaluations from a position of informed awareness of its elements, implications and practicalities.

Readers can use this book in its entirety if they wish to gain an overall insight into evaluation; alternatively, they may use it selectively to focus on particular features of evaluation. Though it is in some respects a manual, it is much more than this, for it directs attention to the underlying rationales and issues in evaluation. Its expressed intention is to provide both an overview of and a practical introduction to this field. Come out of the cool shade and begin evaluating!

ACKNOWLEDGEMENTS

Acknowledgements are given as follows for permission to reproduce material in this volume: *Educational and Psychological Measurement*, G. Thomas (ed.) for R.V. Krejcie and D.W. Morgan, Determining Sample Size for Research Activities; Pasternak: *Fifty Poems* by Boris Pasternak, translated by Lydia Pasternak Slater and Unwin Hyman, an imprint of Harper Collins Publishers Limited, for short quotation from *It Is Not Seemly*; *Thus Spake Zarathustra* by Friedrich Nietzsche, translated by R.J. Hollingdale (Penguin Classics, 1961), copyright R.J. Hollingdale, short quotation reproduced by permission of Penguin Books Ltd., Harmondsworth; W.B. Yeats *Selected Poetry*, edited by A.N. Jeffares, copyright Macmillan and Co. Ltd and A. Norman Jeffares (1962). Lines from "News for the Delphic Oracle" are reprinted by permission of Macmillan Publishing Company from THE POEMS OF W. B. YEATS: A NEW EDITION, edited by Richard J. Finneran. Copyright by Georgie Yeats, renewed 1968 by Bertha Georgie Yeats, Michael Butler Yeats, and Anne Yeats.

Keith Morrison
University of Durham

1 Introducing Evaluation

WHAT IS EVALUATION?

Mention the word 'evaluation' to many teachers and they recoil, believing it to be an arcane, mysterious activity carried out by a few elite professional cognoscenti. It is seen as an enterprise veiled in mystique, being complex, unclear, difficult and, significantly, done by someone else. Evaluation is believed to be important but in ways which are uncertain. We know that it is called for by a range of parties - e.g. government ministers, education officers, curriculum promoters, headteachers, senior management and curriculum co-ordinators. We also know that it somehow affects policy making, that it can promote or reduce the impact of a piece of policy. Yet for many people evaluation has a status which is born out of a strange secrecy of knowledge of how it works, what it is for, who does it and who uses it. If it is unclear, it must be hard; if it is hard, it must be important; if it is important, it ought to be done by a specialist!

Nothing need be further from the truth. Every day of our lives all of us make evaluations and judgements about our own lives and the lives of those whom we meet - what to eat, whom to meet, where to go, what to say, how to react, what to plan, how to behave. As teachers we make hundreds of evaluations every day - what David needs to do next, how to help Gemma, whether Susan needs to read book X or book Y, how has Narinder coped with the mathematics problems, whether we need a quiet atmosphere in this lesson, whether several activities can take place at once for the next hour, whether the science lesson was worthwhile, etc. What we are doing is calling to mind some information, weighing it and reaching a decision for action. We would not be able to function satisfactorily, nor would children be able to learn if constant evaluation were not taking place; it is the stuff of our interpersonal behaviour and personal growth.

If evaluation is an everyday and necessary occurrence why, then, is it cloaked in secrecy and confusion? The answer to the problem probably lies in the fact that 'evaluation' suffers from untidiness of definition. It is a 'catch-all' term which embraces vastly different activities. For some it smacks of inspection, monitoring, appraisal, accountability and review; for others it involves gathering information, collecting data, compiling 'evidence'; for others it concerns assessment, testing, measuring pupil performance; for others it means making judgements - moral judgements,

judgements about the value or worth of an activity, judgements about the desirability of a project; for others it is about making informed choices, decision-making, management, action planning. It is little wonder, then, that its amorphous nature gives rise to it being seen as that which is only understood, and hence undertaken, by a select few.

The truth of the matter is that it is some or all of these things; what separates it from the everyday judgements which we routinely make is simply the level of formality with which it is imbued. One carries out, undertakes, implements or does an evaluation, implying that such an enterprise involves a certain degree of planning, systematization and structure which leads to a definite, and often visible, outcome. In fact the different conceptions outlined *above* introduce us to the main elements of evaluation:

- evaluations answer specified questions;
- they concern gathering information in a variety of ways;
- information informs judgements about the objects of the evaluation;
- such judgements concern value and worth;
- judgements inform decision-making;
- decision-making serves a variety of political purposes - to persuade, to support, to undermine, to critique, to promote.

Evaluations are intended to answer questions, to be useful and to be used. These key elements (1) answering specific, given questions, (2) gathering information, (3) making judgements, (4) taking decisions and (5) addressing the politics of a situation are the central elements of evaluation. A working definition of 'evaluation', then, would be: *the provision of information about specified issues upon which judgements are based and from which decisions for action are taken.* Seen like this it is easy to see how evaluation is part-and-parcel of everyday activities. It is how one interprets this definition that gives rise to the several different conceptions of evaluation, for the definition itself permits a spectrum of different kinds of evaluative activity to be undertaken. What is unavoidable but nevertheless attractive about evaluation is that it is linked to decision-making; for teachers this will necessarily bring them into contact with the politics of the institution, situation or objects of the evaluation. Evaluation by teachers accords high status to their professionalism and judgement.

HOW IS EVALUATION POLITICAL?

On an everyday basis teachers and other educationists engage in a vast range of interpersonal behaviours, some of them by dint of their position or role in the institution, others by dint of formal and informal contacts that they have with colleagues. As a matter of course we all behave differently in different contexts. Sometimes we are friendly; other times we are more guarded. What we are doing, consciously or not, is 'reading a situation' - judging and responding to the politics at play in it, i.e., we are *evaluating* a situation, comment, conversation, observation, behaviour, for example: 'Is it advisable to speak out about X? Should I pass on to the headteacher a comment which I received from Mrs Y? Should I tell the school staff about proposed cutbacks now or in a month's time? Shall I volunteer to join this new curriculum team?'

Human contact is infinitely rich, complex, subtle, discriminating and negotiable; involvement in, or appreciation (or evaluation) of that richness draws on our awareness of the politics involved. Just as evaluating a situation is central to participating in it so judging the politics of the situation is central to that evaluation. This is both attractive and problematic. Involvement in the politics of a situation can be comfortable *and* uncomfortable. This carries an important message for evaluation. It is this: evaluations cannot be politically or ideologically innocent; they cannot be clean, antiseptic activities - that is both their attraction and their difficulty.

Evaluation is prone to both internal biases and external biases - they are inescapable because they involve people. Internal biases figure in the way that evaluations are constructed - very easily they can distort (wittingly or unwittingly) the reality they are attempting to capture. External biases figure in the way that they are used by the recipients of the evaluation or indeed the wider public, ways which may or may not have been intended when the evaluation was undertaken. Often evaluations are brought into the service of wider educational purposes, be it within the internal politics of the school, the local politics of an education authority, or the national politics of government agencies. It is perhaps this latter point which leads many to regard evaluation with a mixture of excitement and suspicion.

If one wishes to attach status to an area of the curriculum, then one evaluates it, witness the evaluation-as-assessment in the national curriculum for England and Wales, where the importance of certain high status subjects (for example, Mathematics, Language and Science) is reinforced not only by the high level of formal assessment of pupils in those subjects but also by the fact that these were the *first* subjects out of all of the national curriculum to develop their assessment instruments. In the field of curriculum innovation the first round of the government sponsored Technical and Vocational Education Initiative (TVEI) was accompanied by a mandatory requirement to have its implementation, uptake and results evaluated. With money specifically set aside for these evaluations their effect was to draw attention to TVEI as a major government-driven educational innovation that had to succeed (Brown and Morrison, 1990). The act of subjecting something to evaluation seems to infer on that something an increased status - it must be important if it's worth evaluating!

This scenario may be familiar to students of national, large-scale evaluations. Large scale evaluations have been used to further the implementation of policies for social reform; evaluation activity has been increasingly used in the service of centralized policy making and controlled through the sponsoring (or non-sponsoring) of contracts for evaluation by the central government (Norris, 1990).

At local or institutional levels evaluations can be used politically. Take the example of a science teacher who is a junior member of a science department being asked to evaluate the science curriculum in what she knows is an under-resourced area of that school. If she finds the science teaching acceptable, then this might indicate that the science department can manage in a climate of lack of resources. This might then steer money away from the science department into another area of the school curriculum. What effect would this have on her own career prospects and interpersonal relations with colleagues in the department?

If she finds the science teaching unacceptable then this might have the effect of bringing more money into the science department, or it might have the effect of suggesting that the quality of the science teachers was suspect - a very dangerous issue if it came to the attention of parents and/or governors who could exert power to terminate employment. What effect would this have on others in the department - and what effect would this have on her own career prospects and interpersonal relations with colleagues in the department? It could be a no-win situation. Indeed if the curriculum area were not deemed necessary, for example the teaching of Spanish in a modern language department, then a negative evaluation might have the effect not of bringing resources into the Spanish department but of closing down that department.

It is difficult to overstate the politically charged nature of evaluation; to commit yourself to an evaluation, in the same way as to commit yourself to an innovation, is to court excitement as well as possible danger. Evaluation carries risks whether it runs smoothly or whether it goes wrong, whether its results are favourable or unfavourable; it is a high profile activity, the outcomes of which may bring benefits to individuals, curricula or evaluators or may generate hostility. Whether it be positive or negative an evaluation may be used in ways which may or may not have been anticipated. Evaluation is the high wire balancing act of education, balancing political allegiances with objectivity. To commit yourself to an evaluation is to risk gaining or losing prestige, status, promotion, co-operation, credibility and legitimacy. It is an invitation both to opportunity and to danger, opportunity to be involved in a complex interplay of personalities and danger from putting one's hand into the fire which both warms and burns.

WHAT IS THE BACKGROUND TO EVALUATION?

Evaluation is a political enterprise which in turn serves political decision-making. This comment also indicates the hybrid pedigree of evaluation for, just as evaluation serves a variety of political purposes so it comes out of a range of different backgrounds. On the one hand it can be seen as an index of the new managerialism of schools and the control of teachers and curricula in response to the demands for accountability. Here school inspections, curriculum review, teacher appraisal, performance indicators, the publication of school level data on truancy and examination results in the United Kingdom, and formal reporting of pupils' achievements to parents all indicate how evaluation-as-judgement of worth has been distorted into the view of evaluation-as-assessment and pressed into the service of measuring school effectiveness and total quality management. The drive for numbers and statistics as a palliative for the concerns about falling standards of education in our schools is supposed to be served by the production of a host of measurements, as though the effectiveness of the education service can be evaluated in the same way as one measures a length of cloth. The quantitative approach to evaluation, so loved in the industrial sector with its appeal to 'scientific management', is being exported from the natural sciences and imported into the human sciences, of which education is one. On the other hand evaluation can be seen as stemming from a much longer liberal tradition, stretching back to ancient Greece, of deliberative, valuative, qualitative judgement about the worth, purposes and desirability of curricula and education. Here is a different scenario where moral debate, weighing the arguments about educational worth, in short adopting a less instrumental view of education, all contribute to a view of evaluation as a debate about value.

On a professional level the notion of evaluation has been promoted in the interests of curriculum improvement and development. Here evaluation is an inescapable prerequisite to rendering more effective the curricular and pedagogical diet available to students. One evaluates the current state of affairs in order to know what improvements and developments are necessary and where they need to be made. The need for the inclusion of evaluation as an integral element of curriculum development and innovation has been recognized since the inception, in its own right, of the discipline of curriculum theory and practice in the early part of the twentieth century. Evaluation was initially viewed as necessary to gauge students' achievements of pre-specified objectives (Bobbit, 1918; Tyler, 1949) - a move which struck sympathetic chords in the psychometric movement earlier in this century and the attempts to categorize and classify learning taxonomically in the work of Bloom (1956), Krathwohl (1956) and Harrow (1984).

More recently evaluation has been seen as an ongoing process of monitoring student experiences in schools as well as the outcomes of those experiences against given criteria. In the last decade evaluation has been set in the context of the enhancement of teacher behaviour, curriculum effectiveness and school improvement, thus developing the concept of the 'reflective teacher' (Pollard and Tann, 1987), which is itself an outgrowth of the 'teacher-as-researcher' movement documented so clearly by Stenhouse (1975). In this latter context the work of Eisner (1985) has made a fascinating contribution to the role - or art - of evaluation in the development of educational connoisseurship. Just as one develops and sensitizes one's palate for wine by careful tasting and evaluation, Eisner argues that through the process of self-criticism and self-disclosure one can develop and sensitize one's educational palate and thereby refine one's sensibilities about teaching. Evaluation as connoisseurship, despite its possibly elitist overtones, commends itself to teachers as experienced professionals whose judgement and accumulated wisdom one should both respect and utilize.

Hence evaluation is seen not as something which is 'done' to individual children, teachers or curricula but as a process of developing critical insights into educational practice. In this context an evaluation is seen as a debate in which interested parties interrogate aims, content, pedagogy etc., in order to improve the quality of the experiences offered to students and the quality of the teachers who facilitate those experiences. Evaluation here is concerned with the growth and development of people through critical reflection on experience.

HOW DO I BALANCE ALL THE BACKGROUND ISSUES IN EVALUATION?

How are these potentially incompatible contexts bound together in the activity of evaluation? Evaluation is a multi-faceted activity, the implications of which are several. At one level evaluators will need to be clear on exactly what the style, the nature, the purposes of the evaluation are, what agenda they are serving. At another level evaluators have to consider their political allegiances very carefully before undertaking an evaluation. At a third level evaluators will have to go into evaluations 'with their eyes open' - fully aware of the nature of the activity and how it may be used. The maxim that 'knowledge is power' serves to show that knowledge derived from evaluations can be used for all sorts of purposes; it also signals the need for evaluators to be apprised of the ways in which evaluations can be planned so that they are as free from bias as possible.

Whilst recognizing the likelihood of the politicization of evaluation, however, this book takes the view that this should not stifle local and institutional evaluation initiatives which will promote educational rather than political purposes, rather it should invite readers to become participants in this process. Whilst recognizing an indissoluble link between the two it is in the spirit of promoting teacher effectiveness, professional decision-making and educational improvement that this book is written. To be aware of all possibilities is to be in a more secure position when devising evaluations, it is not to suggest that they should not be undertaken.

If evaluation is to be undertaken by 'knowledgeable' people, if it is to be seen as the property of all those affected by it and those concerned with education, then there is a need for it to be demystified. This book attempts to do this in a practical way, setting out an introduction to the fields of such evaluation knowledge. How can this be done?

HOW CAN I APPROACH EVALUATION?

Whether one takes large-scale, complex evaluations or small-scale evaluations in one or two schools the organizing principles facing the evaluator are straightforward and similar - it is only in their interpretation that different levels of complexity lie. With the expressed intention of enabling practitioners to develop evaluative skills this book introduces topics that will enable small scale evaluations to be undertaken, though it will be seen throughout how the issues are addressed at wider levels. At heart an evaluation plan addresses two fundamental questions:

- What questions do I wish the evaluation to answer?
- What kind of evaluation will I need which will furnish me with answers to these questions?

From these flow a range of subsidiary questions which can be used to organize an evaluation:

- What do I need to focus on in the evaluation (what will give me answers to the questions which the evaluation asks)?

- What are the purposes of the evaluation?
- What style of evaluation do I need?
- What kind of sample do I need?
- What kind of information do I need?
- What instruments do I need (how will I acquire the information)?
- How will I process and present the data?
- How will I achieve validity (what steps can I take to render the evaluation less biased)?
- How will I achieve reliability (how can I ensure confidence in my results)?
- What timing and time scales do I need?
- What costs are involved?
- How will I judge the data?
- What ethical considerations must I address?
- How will I report the evaluation (who is the evaluation for)?
- Who will do the evaluation?

It is in the answers to these 'organizing' questions that the structure or formalization of an evaluation lie. What is the novice evaluator to make of this list? At first blush it seems perhaps overwhelming, but taken in response to the areas (1) to (5) *above* set out as key elements of evaluation and it becomes more manageable. Each of the five elements discussed *above* draws on one or more of this list of questions, as follows:

(1) Answering Specific, Given Questions

- What do I need to focus on in the evaluation (what will give me answers to the questions which the evaluation asks)?
- What are the purposes of the evaluation?
- What are the actual evaluation questions?

(2) Gathering Information

- What style of evaluation do I need?
- What kind of information do I need?
- What instruments do I need (how will I acquire the information)?
- How will I process and present the data?
- How will I achieve validity (what steps can I take to render the evaluation less biased)?
- How will I achieve reliability (how can I ensure confidence in my results)?

- What timing and time scales do I need?
- What costs are involved? (*see* Appendix A);
- What ethical considerations must I address?

(3) Making Judgements

- How will I judge the data?
- How will I report the evaluation (who is the evaluation for)?
- Who will do the evaluation?

(4) Taking Decisions

- What ethical considerations must I address?
- What are the purposes of the evaluation?
- What style of evaluation do I need?

(5) Addressing the Politics of a Situation

- What are the purposes of the evaluation?
- How will I report the evaluation (who is the evaluation for)?
- Who will do the evaluation?

These areas set the scene for evaluation, they provide the framework, indeed these areas and questions are taken up repeatedly through the book. Subsequent chapters explore issues raised by such questions in more detail, exposing their problematic features and exploring possible solutions to these problems.

HOW WILL THE ELEMENTS OF EVALUATION BE ADDRESSED IN PRACTICE?

Issues (1) to (5) may become clearer if an example of them is provided. Suppose the governing body of a primary school asks the headteacher 'are standards of mathematics rising or falling in our school?' One response to this could be 'I'll carry out an evaluation of this and report back to you'. What might such an evaluation entail?

With regard to issue (1) - the *specific questions of the evaluation* - there would be a need to 'operationalize' the main evaluation question which is 'are standards of mathematics rising or falling in our school?'. 'Operationalizing' the purposes of an evaluation is the translation of purposes of an evaluation into concrete questions, the answers to which will yield data. The evaluator would have to ask 'what are the component elements of these purposes and what data do I need to answer these questions? What behaviours must I observe, what opinions must I gather, what factual information do I need, what test scores do I need in order to provide answers to the evaluation questions which, in turn, will answer the purposes of the evaluation?' This would entail a discussion of what was meant by 'standards', of 'rising' and 'falling', a clarification of the time scale over which comparisons were being made and an indication of whether the question referred to the school in a crude, holistic, aggregated way or whether it referred to specific groups of children - maybe very able children or children with a history of difficulties in mathematics, and so on. The main evaluation question could then be broken down into sub-questions like:

- What do we mean by 'standards'?
- What elements make up a standard?
- Do we wish to measure each element separately or aggregate them all together?
- What constitutes a rise or fall in standard?
- Will a rise or a fall in standards be constituted by an *overall* rise or fall or a *specific* rise or fall in named elements of mathematics? If it is the former how can this be measured, if it is the latter how can this be measured?
- Over what time scale are we to judge a rise or fall?
- Is a rise or fall to be judged by comparing a score now against a score once in the past (if so, when) or against a series of scores in the past (if so, over what time scale)?
- At what point does a rise or fall begin to be, or cease to be, significant? How will we judge 'significance' - statistically, educationally (the two not necessarily being the same)?
- Is a rise or fall to be judged in regard to the *whole* school population or in regard to *specific* year groups, or in regard to *specific groups* of children (e.g. very able, children with special educational needs, children experiencing difficulty in mathematics)?
- Is it possible to compare like with like over time, or has the mathematics curriculum altered over time?
- Have teaching methods altered over the given time scale?

With regard to (2) - the *gathering of information* used to answer the evaluation questions in the notion of 'rising' and 'falling' - there is a clear implication that there should be some comparison. What style of evaluation would enable comparison of like with like to be made? Here there is a suggestion that test scores might be a useful indicator - i.e. a quantitative set of data - figures and marks rather than words and impressions. There is an assumption that test scores could be obtained on the same groupings of children on the same type of mathematics over time, so that one can have a firm measure of confidence in the results, that they display a measure of consistency and that they actually measure what is required to be measured (i.e. so that the results are valid and reliable).

Alternatively, if the teaching staff in the school has been stable over time, with teachers teaching the same age or ability groups in mathematics it might be helpful to enquire of the teachers their opinions (backed up with evidence) of a decline or elevation of standards over time. This would mean that an evaluation would use both words and numbers - leaning towards qualitative and quantitative data respectively. Scores, rating scales and frequencies are the stuff of quantitative analysis, whilst words, opinions, perceptions are the stuff of qualitative analysis.

With regard to (3) - the *making of judgements* based on the information - it is clear that when the appropriate data have been assembled, the criteria against which 'standards', 'rising' and 'falling' are to be assessed, the time scales and groups of children to be represented (i.e. the parameters of the judgements), and the type of assessment required, it is possible to come to some judgement about whether standards are rising and falling in the school.

With regard to (4) - the *taking of decisions* - there are two main types of decision-making in the example given. The first is the amount of information to be made available to given audiences (*see* the discussion *below* of the politics of the situation). The second is the action which will be recommended by the governing body on the basis of the information and judgements about it which have been provided by the headteacher. This is an example of where the decisions on the evidence are taken by those who receive the evaluation; in this case the sponsors are not the same people as those who are carrying out the evaluation. In many school-level evaluations this would not be the case - those undertaking the evaluation are the same people as those who are involved in the teaching.

With regard to the *politics of the situation* - clearly the headteacher will need to clarify where the results of the evaluation will go - to the governors or beyond to the parents, the education authority, the local inspectors, the teachers, the local secondary schools, the local press? This has major implications for how the evaluation might appear.

For example the staff of the school might deliberately withhold information which could be used against them; the headteacher might gather very full information but withhold the negative aspects of it from the governors, keeping the remainder for 'internal consumption' only. On the other hand staff may wish to 'tell everything' so that it was made public that the mathematics was going very well and that they ought to be applauded, or that the staff were working very hard even though the results might not be favourable. The headteacher, recognizing perhaps that the staff might be more willing to yield data to someone other than the head-teacher, might ask the mathematics co-ordinator to carry out the evaluation and report back to him. Here the mathematics co-ordinator might gather full information but only present the headteacher with a summary or a partial presentation of evidence in order to protect interests. He or she might deliberately expose a weak teacher who had been giving trouble to colleagues for some time, and might present an evaluation which pointed to the need for far more resources to be invested in the school. There is clearly a tension between the governors' and other interested parties' rights to know and the individual's right to privacy. How this is resolved is a matter for discussion in each instance.

In this example it can be seen that the five areas (1) to (5) outlined earlier as the key elements of an evaluation can be used to formalize the evaluation process. This is the starting point. As has been shown there are very many issues and practices embedded in each element. The worked example has assumed, for instance, that the evaluation is a single event, a *summative* evaluation which reports on the end stage of the collection of data. Alternatively an evaluation might be *formative* - a series of staged data gathering and reporting exercises over time which feed into the decision-making about a particular programme. A formative evaluation is particularly useful in piloting a new programme or programme materials, as it enables the programme designers and implementers to monitor and refine the innovation as it is being developed and introduced. This, of course, can be an intensely political activity as it cedes considerable power to the evaluators to make recommendations and criticisms both in public and in private.

The remainder of the book attempts to unpack these issues accessibly and in an uncomplicated style. The list of questions which were contained in the five main areas provides the topics for subsequent chapters. Each chapter will address key issues and provide worked examples and guide-lines for practice, so that by the end of the book the reader will not only have been introduced to main features of evaluation but will be encouraged to undertake the stimulating activity which is evaluation.

RECOMMENDED READING

Adelman, C. (1984) *The Politics and Ethics of Evaluation*. London: Croom Helm.

Cooper, K. (1976) Curriculum Evaluation - definitions and boundaries, in K. Cooper (ed.) *Curriculum Evaluation Today: Trends and Implications*. London: Macmillan.

Harlen, W. & Elliott, J. (1982) A Checklist for Planning or Reviewing an Evaluation, in R. McCormick (ed.) *Calling Education to Account*. London: Heinemann and the Open University Press.

House, E.R. (1986) *New Directions in Educational Evaluation*. Lewes: Falmer.

Norris, N. (1990) *Understanding Evaluation*. London: Kogan Page.

Simons, H. (1987) *Getting to Know Schools in a Democracy*. Lewes: Falmer.

2 How Do I Plan an Evaluation?

It was suggested in chapter one that what distinguishes evaluation from the everyday judgements we make is the degree of formality, conscious planning, deliberate structure which we bring to evaluation. Chapter one provided an inroad into this by laying out the main elements of evaluation, the sorts of questions which evaluation planning needs to ask, and how this might actually be put into practice. The chapter closed with the suggestion that evaluations need to be tailored to a particular situation and context. The interpretation of these elements and questions often requires careful consideration of all the subtleties, sensitivities, nuances and different interpretations of those elements and questions. It was suggested that the complex interplay of personalities, politics and purposes involved in an evaluation was both inviting and risky. In this and subsequent chapters the 'risk' factor is addressed and indications are provided for reducing - or anticipating - risk. This chapter invites the reader to address planning issues and then moves to discussing methodologies and indicating how models of evaluation might be useful in organizing aspects of planning. It seeks to provide the reader with an introduction to evaluation design in order to clarify how to set up a particular evaluation.

WHY IS IT IMPORTANT TO PLAN AN EVALUATION?

As long as a set of key considerations is held in the mind (or on paper!) when planning an evaluation, the evaluator can be certain that major features will have been addressed. Whilst the range of considerations is not vast the fervent teacher-as-evaluator needs to ensure that they are addressed, resolved and agreed by all parties to an evaluation *before* that evaluation begins. This reduces the risk of evaluations 'going wrong'. To change the 'rules of the game' in midstream once the evaluation game has begun is a sure recipe for problems. The terms of the evaluation and the mechanism of its operation must be ironed out *in advance* if it is to be credible, legitimate and practicable. Once they have been agreed the evaluator is in a very positive position to undertake an evaluation which will be useful to all parties. What then are these considerations?

The setting up of an evaluation is an exciting balancing act, for it requires the harmonizing of *planned possibilities* with *workable, coherent practice* - i.e. the resolution of the difference between idealism and reality, between what could be done and what will actually work, for at the end of the day an evaluation only has utility value. In planning an evaluation there are two phases - a divergent phase and a convergent phase. The divergent phase will open up a range of possible options facing the evaluator, whilst the convergent phase will sift through these possibilities, see which ones are desirable, which ones are compatible with each other, which ones will actually work in the situation, and move towards an action plan which can really operate. How can this be approached?

WHAT ARE THE MAIN AREAS OF AN EVALUATION PLAN?

The planning of an evaluation can be set into four main areas:

- orienting decisions
- handling data
- managing the evaluation
- presenting the results

Orienting decisions are those decisions which will set the boundaries, parameters or constraints on the evaluation. For example, let us say that the over-riding feature of the evaluation is that it has to be completed within six months; this could exert an effect on the evaluation. On the one hand it will 'focus the mind', really requiring priorities to be settled and data to be provided in a relatively short time. On the other hand this may reduce the variety of possibilities available to the evaluator. Hence questions of time scale will affect:

- the evaluation questions which might be feasibly and fairly answered (for example, some evaluation questions might require a long data collection period);
- the number of data collection instruments used (for example, there might only be enough time for a few instruments to be used);
- the sources (people) to whom the evaluator might go (for example, there might only be time to interview a handful of people);
- the number of foci which can be covered in the time (for example, for some foci it will take a long time to gather relevant data);
- the size and nature of the reporting (there might only be time to produce one interim report and a final report).

By clarifying the time scale a valuable tone of realism is injected into an evaluation, which enables questions of practicability to be answered.

Let us take another example. Let us say that the over-riding feature of the evaluation is that the costs in terms of time, people and materials for carrying it out are to be negligible. This too could exert an effect on the evaluation. On the one hand again it will inject a sense of realism into proposals, identifying what is and is not manageable. On the other hand it might reduce, again, the variety of possibilities which are available to the evaluator. Questions of cost will affect:

- the evaluation questions which might be feasibly and fairly answered, (for example, some evaluation questions might require interviewing which is costly in time both to administer and transcribe, expensive commercially produced data collection instruments, e.g. tests, and costly computer services, e.g. purchasing software);
- the number of data collection instruments used (for example, some data collection instruments, e.g. postal questionnaires are costly in reprographics and postage);
- the sources, i.e. people, to whom the evaluator might go (for example, if teachers are to be released in order to be interviewed then cover for their teaching may have to be found);
- the number of foci which can be covered in the time (for example, some foci might take a lot of costly evaluator's time to uncover relevant data);
- the size and nature of the reporting (for example, the number of written reports produced, the costs of convening meetings, teaching cover for teachers who are released to go to reporting meetings).

Certain time scales permit certain types of evaluations, e.g. a short time scale permits answers to short-term issues, long-term or large questions might require a long-term data collection period to cover a range of foci. Costs in terms of time, resources and people might affect the choice of data collection instruments. Time and costs will require the evaluator to determine, for example, what is the minimum representative sample of the teachers or children in a school. For example, interviews are time-consuming and questionnaires are expensive to reproduce. These are only two examples of the real constraints upon the evaluation which must be addressed. Planning an evaluation will have to identify early on the boundaries within which the evaluation must operate and what the constraints are on the evaluation.

Within each of the four main areas of evaluation, (i.e. orienting decisions, handling data, managing the evaluation, presenting the results), are contained the several sub-questions which were highlighted in chapter one.

Orienting Decisions

1. Who has asked for the evaluation?
2. Who wants the evaluation?
3. Who will receive the evaluation?
4. What powers do the recipients of the evaluation have?
5. What are the purposes of the evaluation?
6. What are the evaluation questions?
7. What do I need to focus on in order to meet the evaluation questions?
8. What time scales do I have?
9. What costs are there - human, material, temporal?
10. Who owns the evaluation?
11. At what point does the ownership pass from the respondent to the evaluator and from the evaluator to the recipients?

Handling Data

12. How will I achieve validity?
13. How will I achieve reliability?
14. What kinds of data do I need?
15. To whom will I go for data?
16. To what will I go for data?
17. How will I gather data?
18. What will I do with the data when I have gathered it?
19. How do I know if my interpretation is correct?
20. Who owns the data?

Managing the Evaluation

21. Who will carry out the evaluation?
22. What are the powers of the evaluator?
23. What are the roles and tasks of the evaluator?
24. Who will lead the evaluation?

Presenting the Results

25. How do I present the results in written form?
26. How do I present the results in non-written form?
27. To whom do I need to report?
28. How often do I need to report?

Answers to these questions furnish the evaluator with an action plan for an evaluation.

Elements of Evaluation	Areas of Evaluation Design	Sub-questions of Evaluation Design	Key Terms in Evaluation Design
	ORIENTING DECISIONS		
(1) Answering specific given questions		Who commissions the evaluation?	Commissioners
		Who wants the evaluation?	Definite audiences
		Who will receive the evaluation?	Possible audiences
		What powers do the recipients of the	Powers
(2) Addressing the politics of the situation		evaluation have?	
		What are the purposes of the evaluation?	Purposes
		What are the evaluation questions?	Evaluation questions
		What do I need to focus on in order to	Foci
(4) Making judgements		meet the purposes of the evaluation?	
		What time scales do I have?	Timing and time scales
		What costs are there - human, material,	Costing
(5) Taking decisions		temporal?	
		Who owns the evaluation?	Ethics and ownership
		At what point does the ownership pass from the respondent to the evaluator and from the evaluator to the recipients?	Control of release
	HANDLING DATA		
(3) Gathering information		How will I achieve validity?	Validity
		How will I achieve reliability?	Reliability
		What kinds of data do I need?	Methodology
		To whom will I go for data?	Sampling
		To what will I go for data?	Sources
		How will I gather data?	Instruments
		What will I do with the data when I have gathered them?	Data processing
		How will I know if my interpretation is correct?	Data verification
		Who owns the data?	Ownership and ethics
	MANAGING THE EVALUATION		
(2) Addressing the politics of the situation		Who will carry out the evaluation?	Evaluator
		What are the powers of the evaluator?	Powers
		What are the roles and tasks of the evaluator?	Roles and tasks
(3) Gathering information		Who will lead the evaluation?	Leadership
(4) Making judgements			
	PRESENTING THE RESULTS		
(1) Answering specific given questions		How do I present results in written form?	Format and style
		How do I present results in non-written form?	Reporting
		To whom do I need to report?	Audiences
(4) Making judgements		How often do I need to report?	Formative/summative intermittent reporting

Figure 2.1 Key Elements of an Evaluation

HOW CAN I ADDRESS THE KEY ELEMENTS OF AN EVALUATION PLAN?

The whole field of evaluation design, its key elements (from chapter one), its key sub-questions (from chapter one) and its key terms can be summarized as in Figure 2.1 *opposite*. How does the embryonic evaluator use this matrix to move from being asked to evaluate X to actually coming up with a firm plan of an evaluation?

Let us see how this approach can be developed. Imagine that you have been asked to evaluate a recently introduced innovation in the school. Let us say that a new piece of the modern languages curriculum has been brought into the school in the last two years and, as head of the modern languages department, you have been asked to evaluate its progress to date, for example its content, management, resourcing, effects on teachers, effects on pupils, effects on the department generally. Further, you have not had the experience of actually planning an evaluation before. How can you proceed? Figure 2.2 is a matrix, in the left hand column of which are the questions which figure in the four main areas *above*. Questions 1 - 11 are the orienting decisions, questions 12 - 20 concern the data handling, questions 21 - 24 cover managing the evaluation and questions 25 - 28 deal with presenting the results.

Within each of these twenty-eight questions there are several sub-questions which you as planner would have to address. For example, within question 5 ('what are the purposes of the evaluation?') you would have to recognize major and minor purposes of the evaluation, explicit, declared, and implicit, unsaid purposes of the evaluation, whose purposes are being served by the evaluation, whose interests are being served by the evaluation, etc. An example of these sub-questions is contained in the second column headed 'sub-issues and problems' (i.e. moving towards question 6: 'what are the evaluation questions?').

At this point you are still at the divergent phase dealing with *planned possibilities*, opening up the evaluation to all facets and interpretations. If time allows, it might be advisable for everyone involved in the evaluation (the stake-holders) to complete this exercise, thus providing an agenda for discussion. This process continues in the column headed 'possible solutions'; for each of the sub-issues and problems already identified it is possible to suggest a range of solutions; an example of these is also given in Figure 2.2. Hence for each issue in the left hand column ('issues') you work *across* the row starting from the left and moving right.

It is not until you reach the column headed 'decisions' that you are moving into a *convergent* phase, where you are actually weighing up all the planned possibilities and seeing which are feasible within the terms and constraints available to you. To do this you will have to move *down* the column marked 'decisions' to see how well the decision which you take in regard to, say, issue 7 ('what do I need to focus on in order to answer my evaluation questions?') fits in with the decisions in regard to other questions, say question 8 ('what time scales do I have?'). For one decision to fit with another four factors must be present:

(1) all of the cells in the 'decisions' column must be coherent together - they must not contradict each other;

(2) all of the cells in the 'decisions' column must be mutually supporting;

(3) all of the cells in the 'decisions' column must be practicable when taken separately;

(4) all of the cells in the 'decisions' column must be practicable when taken together.

Not all of your planned possibilities will be practicable when these four criteria are applied. It would be of very little use if the methods of data collection listed in the 'decisions' column of question 17 ('how will I gather data?') offered little opportunity to fulfil the needs of acquiring information to answer question 7 ('what do I need to focus on in order to answer my evaluation questions?'), or if the methods of data collection were impracticable within the time scales available in question 8. Further, the completion of the 'decisions' column would have to be agreed with all parties involved in the evaluation *before* the evaluation was begun. An example of a completed matrix for the evaluation is given in Figure 2.2 pp. 21 - 28.

In this example the matrix has been deliberately completed in a content-free way, i.e. it does not deal with the specific, actual points which might emerge in a particular evaluation proposal. If the matrix were to be used for planning an actual evaluation, then, instead of couching the wording of each matrix cell in generalized terms, it would be more useful if *specific*, *concrete* responses were given which addressed particular issues and concerns in the proposal. The example here does not dwell on substantive issues; a 'real' proposal would have to indicate these.

ORIENTING DECISIONS			
ISSUE	SUB-ISSUES AND PROBLEMS	POSSIBLE SOLUTIONS	DECISIONS
(1) Who commissions the evaluation?	Who has asked the headteacher to ask me to undertake the evaluation? Why has a formal evaluation been requested? Can I refuse to participate in it?	Find out who are the commissioners and why they require the evaluation. Determine how obligatory the evaluation is and why.	The headteacher has commissioned the evaluation for departmental use only. Colleagues need not take part at any time.
(2) Who wants the evaluation?	Is the evaluation going to be useful? Who might wish to use this evaluation for or against us? Are the data going to be publicly available? What if different people want different things from the evaluation?	Find out the controls over the evaluation which can be exercised by the respondents. Find out what the commissioners of the evaluation perceive to be the scope and audiences of the evaluation. Determine the reporting mechanisms.	Control of the data and its release remains with the respondents. The senior staff and the department will receive the evaluation. A written summative report
(3) Who will receive the evaluation?	Will it go outside the department or school? Will we be able to veto the release of the evaluation or parts of it to specified audiences? Will we be able to give the evaluation to whomsoever we wish? Will we be told to whom the evaluation will go?	Determine the proposed internal and external audiences of the evaluation. Find out the controls over the evaluation which can be exercised by the respondents. Determine the rights of the respondents and the evaluators to control the release of the evaluation.	The department and senior staff will receive the report. Respondents are to plan and implement the evaluation.
(4) What powers do the recipients of the evaluation have?	What use will be made of the evaluation? How might the evaluation be used for or against us? What might happen if the data falls into the 'wrong' hands? Will we know in advance what use will and will not be made of the evaluation?	Find out what the recipients are allowed to do, are able to do, and are forbidden to do with the evaluation. Determine the respondents' rights to protection as a result of the evaluation. Determine the recipients' reasons and purposes for the evaluation.	Control of the planning and implementation of the evaluation resides with the respondents. The evaluation is for curriculum development, not for appraisal or promotion.

figure 2.2 continued→

(5)	What are the purposes of the evaluation?	What are the formal and hidden agenda here? Whose purposes are being served here? Who decides the purposes of the evaluation? How will different purposes be served in a single evaluation?	Find out all the possible uses of the evaluation. Determine the powers of the respondents to control the uses made of the evaluation. Decide on the form of reporting and the intended and possible audiences of the evaluation.	The evaluation is for curriculum development only. Respondents have control of the data and its uses. A written report will be presented to senior staff and respondents.
(6)	What are the evaluation questions?	Who decides what the questions will be? Do we have rights to refuse to answer or to take part? Can we add our own questions?	Determine the respondents' powers to participate in the planning, form and implementation of the evaluation. Agree on the balance of all interests in the evaluation.	Respondents will plan and implement the evaluation. Respondents may agree to disagree.
(7)	What do I need to focus on in order to meet the evaluation questions?	Do I have time to focus on all aspects of the innovation? How can priority foci be decided? Who decides on the foci?	Determine all the aspects of the innovation, prioritise them, and agree on the minimum areas of the evaluation. Determine the respondents' powers to decide the foci.	Respondents will decide the areas for evaluation. Respondents will decide the foci.
(8)	What time scales do I have?	Is there enough time to do all we might want to do? Who decides on the timing of the data collection? How will we decide what to do within the time scale?	Determine the time scales and timing of the evaluation. Determine whether the evaluation is formative and/or summative.	A final report to be made after one year, with two interim reports which are only for documentary purposes.
(9)	What costs are there - human, material, temporal?	Who will I need to go to for data? Will people be released from teaching in order to take part in the evaluation? What happens if we run out of money? What secretarial help will be available to me? What materials must I buy?	Cost out the evaluation in terms of the least expense, the greatest expense - i.e. prepare different types of evaluation for different costs and agree to one of them with the commissioners.	£500 to be made available to buy materials, supply teachers, computer software. Time to be made available on professional development days. School secretarial help available.

(10) Who owns the evaluation?	Who controls the release of the final report? What protection can be given to the participants? Will participants be identified and identifiable?	Determine who controls the release of the evaluation. Agree the rights of veto. Agree on how to protect those who will be identifiable in the evaluation.	Control resides with respondents. Individuals may veto those parts of the evaluation in which they are identifiable.
(11) At what point does the ownership pass from the respondent to the evaluator and from the evaluator to the recipient?	Who decides the ownership of the evaluation? Can participants refuse to answer certain parts if they wish, or, if they are given the option not to take part, must they opt into everything? Can I edit out certain responses if I wish?	Determine the ownership of the evaluation at all stages of its progress. Agree the options available to the respondents. Agree the rights of different parties, in the evaluation - respondents, evaluators, recipients.	Control resides with respondents.

HANDLING DATA

ISSUE	SUB-ISSUES AND PROBLEMS	POSSIBLE SOLUTIONS	DECISIONS
(12) How will I achieve validity?	How might having the head of department as the evaluator affect people's responses? Will there be the opportunity for cross-checking issues? Do I have time to explore each issue in sufficient depth and breadth? Who decides on what to focus on in order to answer the evaluation questions? How do I know that the questions are fair? How will I know if people are telling the truth?	Agree who will carry out the data collection, processing and reporting. Determine the process of respondent validation of the data and the data collection process. Agree on a necessary minimum of topics to be covered. Subject the plans for the evaluation to scrutiny by all the stake-holders. Pilot the evaluation. Build in cross-checks on data.	Whole department gathers and processes the data. Respondents will validate data and interpretation at the three stages of evaluation. Respondents to agree on topics to be covered, then decisions on these passed on to senior staff. Piloting unable to be carried out.

figure 2.2 continued→

(13) How will I achieve reliability?	Will I be able to take the evaluation back to the respondents for them to check that my interpretation is fair? How will I gather data consistently over time? How will I ensure that each respondent is given the same opportunity to respond?	Determine the process of respondent validation of data. Agree the list of questions to be asked and the methods used to ask them. Determine the balance of open and closed questions.	Data to be given to a 'critical friend' to cross-check the interpretation. Respondents to agree methods and formats.
(14) What kinds of data do I need?	Do I need words, numbers or both? Do I need opinions, facts or both? On what aspects of the innovation do I need to canvass opinion? Do I want to be able to compare responses and results or simply to illuminate an issue?	Determine the most appropriate types of data for the foci and the evaluation questions. Balance objective and subjective data. Determine the purposes of collecting different types of data and the ways in which it can be processed.	A combination of opinion and facts to be used, using words and numbers (the latter from test scores and rating scales). Open-ended data will be coded and frequencies and correlational data determined by statistical techniques.
(15) To who will I go for data?	Will I have time to go to all the interested parties? How will I achieve a representative sample of children? What if people see this as an opportunity to cause trouble?	Determine the minimum and maximum sample. Decide on the criteria for sampling. Agree on the degree of representativeness of the sample. Agree on how to follow up and not to follow up on data gathered.	All staff involved in the innovation will be asked to participate. It will be made clear which staff and children are represented. The evaluation will be used for curriculum development only.
(16) To what will I go for data?	What documents and other written data can I use? How will I access and use confidential material? What will be the positive or negative effects on individuals of using certain documents?	Determine the necessary and possible documentary sources of data. Agree access and publication rights and protection of sensitive data.	Test scores and exam results will be used. The control of the release of data resides with respondents.

(17) How will I gather data?	What methods of data gathering are available to me? How will I construct my interview schedules or questionnaires? Who decides what methods will be used to gather data? What will be the effects of observing teachers at work in classrooms? How many methods should I use? Will I be able to use more than one method to gather data on the same issue? Will I need many methods in order to gather fair data? Will some methods be unsuitable for some people or for some issues?	Determine the most appropriate data collection instruments to gather data to answer the evaluation questions validly. Pilot the instruments. Decide on the strengths and weakness of different data collection methods in the short and long term. Decide which methods are most suitable for which issues. Decide on which issues will require more than one data collection method. Decide whether the same data collection methods will be used with all the respondents.	Semi-structured interviews and structured and semi-structured questionnaires will be used, together with test scores and exam results. Data on each issue will be gathered where possible by more than one method. The same interview schedule and questionnaires will be used with each respondent.
(18) What will I do with the data when I have gathered it?	How will I process all the different responses to open ended questions? What statistical treatments will I need? Will I report results person by person, or issue by issue, or both? Do I want to be able to make generalizations? Who will process the data?	Clarify the legitimate and illegitimate methods of data processing of quantitative and qualitative data. Decide on the data processing methods which will be most suitable for answering the evaluation questions. Check that the data processing will serve the purposes of the evaluation. Determine the data protection issues if the data are to be processed by outsiders or particular insiders.	Coding of data from semi-structured interviews, correlations, frequencies, chi-square and t-tests used on structured questionnaire data and test scores and exam results. Respondents have control of the data. Outsider processors asked to respect any confidential data.

figure 2.2 continued→

(19)	How do I know if my interpretation is correct?	What opportunities will there be for respondents to check my interpretation? At what stages of the evaluation do I need to make such checks? What will happen if the respondents disagree with my interpretation?	Determine the process of respondent validation during the evaluation. Agree the reporting of multiple perspectives. Agree respondents' rights to have their views expressed or to veto reporting.	Respondent validation occurs at every stage. Multiple perspectives are to be reported as such. Respondents control data.
(20)	Who owns the data?	Do I have the ultimate decision on what data to include?	Agree the rights and powers of the evaluator.	Respondents own data.

MANAGING THE EVALUATION

	ISSUE	SUB-ISSUES AND PROBLEMS	POSSIBLE SOLUTIONS	DECISIONS
(21)	Who will carry out the evaluation?	Am I the only one to carry out the evaluation? Can I delegate the whole task to somebody else? Can different people plan and carry out different parts of the evaluation? How can I arrange for a collegial approach to the evaluation?	Determine who will carry out the evaluation in the best interests of all the stake-holders. Determine the divisibility of the tasks in the evaluation. Agree the allocation of tasks to different parties in the evaluation.	Tasks agreed and shared by the respondents. Data collection, processing and reporting to be shared.
(22)	What are the powers of the evaluator?	Do I simply gather information, or make judgements, or make recommendations? Will I be able to insist on action following any recommendations? What guarantees do I have that my powers will be respected?	Agree the powers, duties and responsibilities of the evaluator. Agree on the action which must and must not be taken by the commissioners and recipients of the evaluation. Determine the possible actions which could be taken by the commissioners and recipients of the evaluation.	The evaluator can only gather data, judge and recommend. Follow-up action to be agreed by respondents. Control of the follow-up action resides with the respondents.

(23) What are the roles and tasks of the evaluator?	What must I do and not do? What may I do and not do? Who decides what I must or must not do? What can I delegate? What should I or should I not delegate?	Determine the stake-holders' perceptions of the tasks and roles of the evaluator. Define what must, should and could be done by the evaluator and the long and short term effects of such actions. Prioritise the tasks of the evaluator and agree on a necessary minimum of tasks.	Respondents to consult with other interested parties in drawing up the plans for evaluation. Respondents to decide on follow-up action. Respondents to agree planning.
(24) Who will lead the evaluation?	What are the advantages and disadvantages of having the evaluation led by myself or by another named person?	Determine the leadership of the evaluation and the powers of the leader.	Head of department to take nominal responsibility for jointly owned evaluation.

PRESENTING THE RESULTS

ISSUE	SUB-ISSUE	POSSIBLE SOLUTIONS	DECISIONS
(25) How will I present the results in written form?	How will I ensure that everyone will understand the language or the statistics? Will different parties require different reports? How will I respect the confidentiality of respondents? How will I report multiple perspectives? Will I need to provide any interim reports?	Agree the most appropriate form of reporting. Agree to provide a glossary of terms if requested. Agree on the number and timing of the reports. Agree on the format(s) of the reports. Agree on the protection of the individuals' rights, balancing this with the stake-holders' rights to know.	A full report to be written which includes raw data; an executive summary to be written. Two interim reports (at four months and eight months). Final report at one year. Respondents control release of data.

figure 2.2 continued→

(26) How will I present the results in non-written form?	Will different parties require different reports? How will I report different perspectives? How will I respect the confidentiality of respondents? How will I know that an oral report will itself be reported faithfully in the future?	Agree on the most appropriate form of reporting. Agree on the number and timing of reports. Ensure that a written record will be kept of oral reports. Agree on the protection of individuals' rights, balancing this with the stake-holders' rights to know.	Oral reporting as agreed by the respondents. Written transcript kept of oral reporting. Respondents control release of data.
(27) To whom do I need to report?	Should I report to all the stake-holders, not just the commissioners of the evaluation? What will be the effects of not reporting to stake-holders?	Identify the stake-holders and commissioners. Determine the least and most material to be made available to the stake-holders and commissioners.	Headteacher is the commissioner, the stake-holders are the respondents and the pupils.
(28) How often do I need to report?	Do I need to provide interim reports? If I provide interim reports how might this effect the future reports or the course of the innovation, when do I need to make them available?	Decide on the timing and frequency of the reporting. Determine the formative or summative nature of the evaluation.	Reports written at three points in the year; reports available at the end of the period. Interim documents for record only.

Figure 2.2   A Matrix for Planning an Evaluation

HOW CAN I PLAN THE STAGES OF AN EVALUATION?

Clearly there is a certain threshold which must be crossed in planning an evaluation; the evaluator has to go in up to the waist of issues if they are all to be appropriately addressed rather than dipping a toe into the water! How can this be managed? A simple four stage model can be proposed:

Stage One: Identify the purposes of the evaluation.

Stage Two: Identify and give priority to the constraints under which the evaluation will take place.

Stage Three: Plan the possibilities for an evaluation within these constraints.

Stage Four: Agree an evaluation design.

Each stage contains several operations; Figure 2.3 clarifies this four stage model, drawing out the various operations contained in each stage.

HOW WILL THIS PLAN WORK IN PRACTICE?

Let us take an example of how this model might work in practice. Suppose that you as a primary headteacher have been asked to evaluate the *continuity* between the oldest year of the primary school and the first year of the secondary school to which most of the students proceed. The purposes of the evaluation, 'stage one', are clearly stated but highly ambiguous. These will have to be clarified in 'stage three' - planning the evaluation. In 'stage two' let us imagine there is a time constraint in that the final reporting must take place at the end of a year of evaluation activity, but that costs are not a problem as the evaluation is being paid for out of the two schools' in-service budget. The reporting will be solely to the staff of both the primary and the secondary schools and the governing bodies thereof. You complete the matrix activity (*as above*, Figure 2.2) and then attempt to draw up a proposal which meets 'stage three' requirements.

You decide that the best time to commence the evaluation is at the beginning of the final term of the school year; in that way you will be able to see how students are approaching the point of transfer and how they settle in after the transfer has occurred. Hence the evaluation will be completed by the end of the second term of the following school year. You have negotiated the co-operation of the relevant teachers in your own school, the teachers whom the students will meet in their new classes, the pastoral teams in the secondary school, and a selection of parents who have volunteered to take part in the project. You are assuming the full participation of the students in the project. Such a framework immediately has its strengths and weaknesses.

On the plus side you have secured a total representation of teachers for your sampling, so you will be able to place credence in teacher-derived data. On the other hand you do not know how representative your parent volunteers will be of the whole parent population of the students concerned - you may have a distorted view if you rely too much on data derived from this sample. Further, you have not sought the permission of the students to involve themselves in the project; you have simply assumed their compliance. Whilst this may be a safe assumption for many of them, you have violated an ethical principle in not affording the students the opportunity not to participate in the project - some nervous or anxious

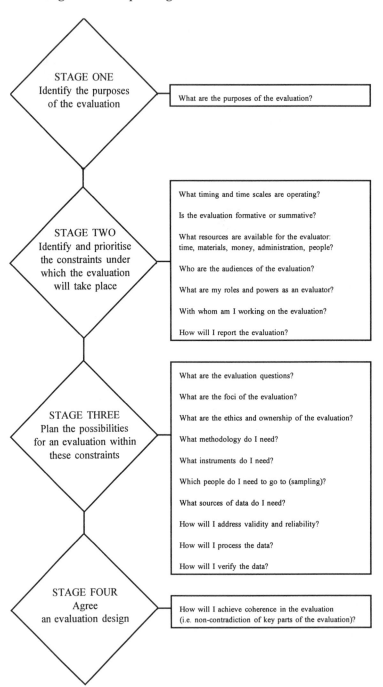

Figure 2.3 Stages in Planning an Evaluation

students perhaps may not wish to expose their fears and anxieties to another person, particularly if that person - you the headteacher - is in a position of power. These students may not be completely honest in an endeavour to save their own embarrassment. Hence there may be some doubts over the validity of the student-level data.

You decide that the purpose of the evaluation - 'to evaluate the continuity between the oldest year of the primary school and the first year of the secondary school'- needs clarification. Hence you break down the term 'continuity' into its component areas to determine the different elements of continuity (e.g. experiences, teaching and learning styles, skills, concepts, knowledge, attitudes, organizational arrangements, aims and objectives, management styles, ethos, assessment criteria, social experiences). You agree with colleagues at this stage that the field is too large to cover in the time available, hence you agree that continuity of pedagogy might be a useful area to investigate and evaluate. This field is then broken down into *its* component parts:

(a) level of continuity of pedagogy;
(b) nature of continuity of pedagogy;
(c) degree of success of planned continuity;
(d) extent of unplanned but occurring continuity;
(e) focus of continuity (through school, across curriculum areas, across the transition from one school to the next, across departments in the secondary school);
(f) responsibility for continuity;
(g) record keeping and documentation of continuity;
(h) resources available to support continuity;
(i) balance of uniformity and freedom in continuity and deliberate discontinuity;
(j) desirability of continuity.

You decide that a mixture of interviews and questionnaires would be useful to gather data - interviews with a representative group of teachers and questionnaires to all the teachers and pupils. Time prevents you from interviewing too many teachers or any students; also you feel that the guaranteed anonymity of a questionnaire to students might avert problems raised above which are caused by *requiring* students to be involved in the project. Because you will be targeting some twenty teachers and sixty students you decide that closed questions on the questionnaire will be most suitable, enabling you to aggregate responses to the same questions - thus enabling comparisons and correlations to be made.

You decide that the interviews will focus on the same issues as in the questionnaires, but, being more open, will enable respondents to give a fuller picture (in words rather than numbers) of how they feel about the nature, degree and level of success of the continuity. Here lie *three key criteria* of the evaluation - the *nature* of the continuity (i.e. the provision of information); the *degree* of continuity (i.e. a measure against a given criterion); the *level of success* of the continuity (i.e. a judgement). As a result of this you will be able to make recommendations for improving the continuity within and between the schools (i.e. taking actions and decisions).

You formulate your evaluation questions, then, as follows:

(1) How much continuity of pedagogy do you think is occurring across the transition stages in your curriculum area; how do you know; on what criteria will the level of continuity be decided; what kind of evidence do we need to be able to answer questions of the level of continuity?

(2) What pedagogical styles can you observe in your curriculum area; what are the most frequent or most preferred; what is the balance of pedagogical styles; how is pedagogy influenced by resources; how far is pedagogical continuity discussed, planned, recorded or evaluated; what kind of evidence do we need to be able to answer questions of the nature of the continuity of pedagogy?

(3) On what aspects of pedagogy does planning take place; on what criteria will the success of planned pedagogical continuity be judged; over how many students/teachers will the incidence of continuity have to occur for success to be said to be enjoyed; what kind of evidence do we need to be able to answer questions of the degree of success of planned continuity?

(4) How will we decide if observed continuity occurred by accident or design; how will we decide on the extent of unplanned continuity - what markers will we use to gauge degree; in whose eyes will continuity be judged (evaluators', teachers', students', parents', headteachers' etc.); what kind of evidence do we need to be able to answer questions of the extent of unplanned but occurring continuity?

(5) On what criteria will the focus of the continuity be decided; on whose criteria will the focus of continuity be decided; what kinds of evidence do we need to be able to answer questions of the focus of continuity?

(6) Who has responsibility for continuity in the school; what formal and informal responsibility is vested in different colleagues in the school?

(7) How are records kept on continuity in the school; who keeps these records; who has responsibility for such record keeping; in what

terms or areas are records kept on continuity (e.g. curricular, cross-curricular, teaching and learning styles, etc.); how often are these records updated; if no such records exist how can this be justified; do we need to keep such records; what format can be used for such records?

(8) How will we find out what resources there are for continuity; what kinds of evidence do we need to answer questions of the resourcing for continuity in the school; what kinds of resources are there for continuity - e.g. curricular, cross-curricular, material, human, financial, administrative etc?

(9) How is a balance achieved between too much uniformity brought about by continuity and too little continuity; in what terms and whose terms will uniformity be discussed; what kinds of evidence do we need to be able to answer questions of the *degree of uniformity* brought about by continuity; how will we decide whether there is too little or too much uniformity?

(10) How much continuity is desirable; in what and whose terms will the degree and desirability of continuity be discussed; how will we know if continuity is desired or desirable; what kinds of evidence do we need in order to able to answer questions of the *desirability* of continuity?

These questions have then 'operationalized' the evaluation purposes; the evaluation has moved from simply an expression of interest or concern into a series of issues in continuity which now lend themselves to being investigated. It is possible by this stage to envisage what specific, concrete questions might be asked in the evaluation or what areas and terms need to be clarified before the evaluation can proceed.

HOW LONG WILL IT TAKE ME TO PLAN AN EVALUATION?

It was argued at the beginning of this chapter that the planning and debate over the terms of the evaluation should be agreed by all participants - those who ask for the evaluation to be undertaken, evaluators, respondents - before the evaluation begins. It has been demonstrated in this chapter that this might take some time to complete. However this is not wasted time. For an evaluation to be successful, for all problems to be anticipated and resolved, for all parties to agree to the evaluation, for validity to be addressed and bias minimized the need for exactitude of the proposal cannot be over-stressed. It is of little value embarking on a game if one does not know its rules! Furthermore, the planning of an evaluation by members of a school staff can not only enable them to take a leadership role in the school and improve the collegial nature of the school but can also act as a team-building exercise, a form of staff development, and the promotion of a healthy organizational ethos.

WHAT ARE THE METHODOLOGIES OF AN EVALUATION?

A key factor in the planning of an evaluation is the methodology or style of evaluation that will be used. Let us be clear that we are not talking here about the particular data gathering instruments or methods but about the approaches which can be adopted. In this sense the decision on which methodology to adopt precedes the decision on which methods to adopt. The methods flow from the methodology. Just as the choice of methods is not arbitrary so the choice of methodology is not arbitrary. The methodology must be appropriate to the purposes and foci of the evaluation. What methodologies are there?

Imagine a continuum. At one end of the continuum are numbers, statistics, objective facts, quantitative data; at the other end are transcripts of conversations, interview comments, subjective accounts, essentially words which we could call qualitative data.

Imagine another continuum. At one end are closed questions, multiple choice questions where respondents have to select from a given, pre-determined range of responses that response which most accurately represents what they wish to have recorded for them. At the other end of the continuum are much more open-ended questions which do not require the selection from a given range of responses - respondents can answer the questions in their own way and in their own words, i.e. the evaluation is made responsive to their particular frames of response.

Imagine a third continuum. At one end is a desire to measure responses, to compare one set of responses with another, to correlate responses, to see how many people did or said this, how many scored such and such on a test. At the other end of the continuum is a desire to capture the uniqueness of a particular situation, person or programme - what makes it similar to and different from others, i.e. to record the quality of a situation, the value systems operating in the situation.

Imagine a fourth continuum. At one end is a desire for formality and the precision of numbers and prescribed categories of response where we already know in advance what it is we are looking at. At the other is a more responsive, informal intent where what we are looking for is far less pre-determined, we only know what we are looking for when we have found it! We have to go into a situation and respond to what we find the important issues to be rather than know in advance what the important issues are.

Imagine a fifth continuum. At one end we are trying to find regularities - say of behaviour, of scores, of opinions - in order to begin to make generalizations from our results, to describe what is happening. At the other end we are trying to portray uniqueness, the quality of a particular situation, the complexity of a situation - for example, where we are trying to understand why individuals behave in certain ways (which may all differ from each other), i.e. to reflect the complexity of a situation as revealed through the eyes of participants rather than through the pre-ordained categories of the outside evaluator. Here we are striving to explain rather than to describe.

Where do all these continua take us? We can cluster the sets of poles of the continua thus:

Quantitative Approaches	Qualitative Approaches
numbers	words
predetermined, given	open-ended, responsive
measuring	capturing uniqueness
short term, intermittent	long term, continuous
comparing	capturing particularity
correlating	valuing quality
frequencies	individuality
formality	informality
looking at	looking for
regularities	uniqueness
description	explanation
objective facts	subjective facts
describing	interpreting
looking in from the outside	looking from the inside
structured	unstructured
statistical	ethnographic, illuminative

The left hand column appears far more formal and pre-planned to a high level of detail, whilst the right hand column is far less formal and the fine detail only emerges once the evaluator is *in situ*.

Evaluations in the left hand column are front-loaded, that is, they require all the categories, multiple choice questions, tests, criteria of the evaluation to be worked out in advance. This usually involves running a pilot evaluation to try out material and refine it (*see* chapter three). Once the detailed planning of this type of evaluation is completed the analysis of the data is relatively straightforward, because the categories for analysing the data and the statistical tests and treatments will have been worked out in advance, at the preparation stage. It is quicker to carry out the later stages of the evaluation (i.e. the data analysis and presentation) than the earlier stages (planning the evaluation questions and instruments).

Evaluations in the right hand column are end-loaded, that is, it is much quicker to 'get going' in these evaluations because the important categories only emerge once initial data have been gathered and sifted. However, once data have begun to be gathered there then begins a process of coding (*see* chapter five) and perusing the data to see which issues seem to be emerging as significant and then enquiring further about them (progressive focussing - discussed later in this chapter and in chapter five) in order to ascertain their importance or to find other emerging issues of importance. Evaluations in this mould therefore tend to be time consuming in their later stages rather than their earlier stages.

The two columns differ because they derive from very different backgrounds. The left hand column has a clear affinity with the natural sciences and their appeal to measurement and statistical analysis in clinically controlled circumstances. The right hand column has a clear affinity with the anthropological sciences whose practitioners study social groups to determine the uniqueness of their specific situations and with the social scientists of the interactionist school whose practitioners start from the premise that people behave to each other on the basis of their own judgements or interpretations about each other or about situations. The intentions of the former are to observe as an outsider, the intentions of the latter are to present the situations as they are seen through the eyes of the participants.

The left hand column has given rise to two main types of evaluation study - the experimental model and the survey model (discussed in detail later in this chapter) - whilst the right hand column has given rise to the illuminative model (also discussed in detail later in this chapter).

Let us not pretend that there are no overlaps between the two columns. Polarizing these methodologies in a sense caricatures their nature and overlooks the fact that in reality many evaluations are an admixture of the two. For example:

- an evaluation might wish to draw on illuminative *and* qualitative approaches (the two are different, the first requiring progressive focussing and a lengthy stay in the institution, the latter requiring only word data);
- a qualitative approach might be used to identify the categories which are to be used in a large scale survey or in a structured interview, questionnaire or observation schedule;
- an evaluation might begin with a survey approach which then identifies respondents who are then interviewed in detail in a qualitative mode;
- a questionnaire or interview might contain both structured and

unstructured elements, closed and open questions;

● a survey, questionnaire or interview might ask for details which are factual, statistical, opinions, perceptions, reactions etc., i.e. a whole range of features which draw on both poles of the continua;

● some statistics are purely descriptive (*see* pp. 131-4), whilst others are inferential (*see* pp. 134 - 147); some qualitative data are able to be aggregated (*see* pp. 152-4), whilst other qualitative data remain context specific.

However, the importance of being clear on an evaluation methodology is twofold:

● It must be appropriate to the purposes of the evaluation (in the sense that it will enable the appropriate data to be gathered to answer the evaluation questions);

● It must suggest the appropriate instruments (methods) of data gathering to be devised and data from them to be processed fairly which then answer the evaluation questions.

HOW CAN I USE EVALUATION MODELS TO HELP MY PLANNING?

Given that evaluation serves many purposes, and given that the translation of purposes into an evaluation proposal will necessitate holding in the mind an array of factors, how can an evaluator's initial tasks be made easier? How can we gain some leverage into the potential complexity of evaluation? A straightforward way is to employ models of evaluation.

WHY SHOULD I USE A MODEL OF EVALUATION?

A model is an abstraction, a distillation from out of a whole world of factors of those key features which can be clustered together to constitute an approach to that world. It is a bundle of concepts and constructs which seem to hang together to form an identifiable approach to, or way of looking at, the world. A model has the tidiness of internal coherence; all its central features are in sympathy with one another. A model does not pretend to describe the world as it really is, rather it deliberately highlights key features which both bear sufficient likeness to the world that they are portraying for them to be valid and yet which pare away any details which might fog any clearness of the key features. It is simply an organizational device designed to be useful and to clarify approaches to evaluation.

Models of evaluation reduce the complexity of the world of evaluation to manageable proportions; they simplify the reality from which they are abstracted in the interest of clarity. As such they can be of great benefit to evaluators. For some writers this reductionism is a model's greatest strength, for it enables some purchase on a complex reality to be achieved; for other writers this reductionism is a model's greatest weakness, being a *reductio ad absurdum* of the complex social and educational reality it is trying to capture.

The test of a model's utility lies in the responses which are given to three questions:

- Is the model useful in organizing my thoughts and proposals?
- Does the model bear sufficient likeness to the world it is portraying for it to be honest?
- Does the model strike a fair balance between, on the one hand, such reductionism for it to be an over-simplification and, on the other hand, such complexity for it to lose sight of its purpose in promoting conceptual clarity?

Whilst an evaluation would be relatively straightforward if it were cast in one model alone, the reality of evaluation is that it is an eclectic and much more complex activity than the pristine clarity of a model would suggest. The use of models, then, is at the organizational and planning level. They outline the central elements of different *approaches* to evaluation and they can clarify that bundle of concepts and constructs which can serve different purposes of an evaluation. Hence in approaching evaluation planning one begins with an outline of the purposes of the evaluation and then one can ask 'which model of evaluation might assist me here in translating the purposes of the evaluation into an actual proposal?' I do not intend to present an exhaustive catalogue of evaluation models here, rather I intend to outline a selection of these which will be of use to those evaluators who might be meeting formal evaluation for the first time.

WHAT IS THE SURVEY MODEL OF EVALUATION?

This model has several characteristics, attempting to scan a wide field of issues, populations, programmes etc. in order to measure or describe any generalized features. It can be used both formatively and summatively though, in practice, it is used on a one-shot basis. It is useful in that it can:

- represent a wide target population (hence there is a need for

careful sampling - discussed in chapter four);
● generate numerical data;
● manipulate key factors and variables to derive frequencies (e.g. the numbers registering a particular opinion or test score);
● ascertain correlations (e.g. to find out if there is any relationship between gender and scores);
● present material which is uncluttered by specific contextual factors;
● capture data from multiple choice, closed questions, test scores or observation schedules;
● support or refute hypotheses about the target population;
● generate accurate instruments through their piloting and revision;
● make generalizations and law-like accounts of the objects of study;
● gather data which can be processed statistically;
● rely on large scale data gathering from a wide population in order to enable generalizations to be made about given factors or variables.

Examples of surveys are:

● opinion polls (which refute the notion that only qualitative data can capture opinions);
● test scores (e.g. the results of testing children in the United Kingdom by the Assessment of Performance Unit in the 1980s);
● students' preferences for particular courses (e.g. in the Technical and Vocational Education Initiative in the United Kingdom);
● reading surveys (e.g. Whitehead's example of reading preferences, 1977, and Southgate's *et al* example of teaching practices in 1981 in the United Kingdom).

Hence an evaluator when using this model will be seeking to gather large scale data from as representative a sample population as possible in order to say with a measure of statistical confidence that certain observed characteristics of a programme - its contexts, inputs, processes or outcomes - or its participants' perceptions and opinions occur with a degree of regularity, or that certain factors cluster together (factor analysis) or that they correlate with each other (correlation and covariance).

WHEN CAN I USE THE SURVEY MODEL OF EVALUATION?

The attractions of a survey lie in its appeal to generalizability or universality within given parameters, its ability to make statements which are supported by large data banks and its ability to establish the degree of confidence which can be placed in a set of findings.

On the other hand, if the evaluator is concerned to catch local, institutional or small scale factors and variables - to portray the specificity of a situation, the uniqueness of a situation and the complexity of the dynamics of a situation, the interpersonal aspects of a programme, the explanations of why a situation occurred or why a person behaved in a particular way or what a person's intentions were in a situation, or how a situation or programme changes and develops over time, then this approach is unsuitable. Its degree of explanatory potential or fine detail is limited, it is lost to broad brush generalizations which are free of temporal and spatial contexts. The individual instance is sacrificed to the aggregated response.

The survey model would be useful for a small scale evaluator if, for example, he or she wished to evaluate a whole school issue - maybe the effectiveness of parental involvement, a school-wide reading programme, the implementation of Records of Achievement, the links between the school and its local community, the nature and incidence of bullying. It could also be used if a cluster of schools is targeted. For example, several schools may be combining to organize their professional development days, involving, let us say, up to two hundred teachers in seven schools and the local authority may wish to know if this organization has been worth the considerable effort needed to prepare for it. A local authority wishing to evaluate the usefulness of, for example, its outdoor centres which cater for several thousand students over the period of an academic year would find the survey model useful here. These examples would probably use the questionnaire methods of data gathering and processing (*see* chapters three and five). The survey model is appropriate for gathering scores, for example, test scores, attendance rates, results of public examinations, all of which would enable comparisons to be made over time or between groups (discussed in chapters three and five).

WHAT IS THE OBJECTIVES MODEL OF EVALUATION?

If a piece of the curriculum or educational programme of the school has explicitly prescribed aims and objectives (which is often the case with new pieces of the curriculum and specific innovatory programmes), then one of the main tasks of an evaluation may be to see how far those objectives have been achieved - a *summative* style of evaluation. An objectives model of evaluation can be useful here. The key elements of this model of evaluation are the statement of objectives or goals, the means of achieving these (both in terms of content and what will be done with the content -

e.g. the teaching style), and the criteria for judging just how well those objectives have been realized in practice.

Whilst this accords with a traditional planning model of the curriculum (which embraces a statement of aims and objectives, a delineation of content and teaching style, and the provision for the assessment of achievement of these objectives), one has to guard against the assumption that the objectives can only be measured in terms of student-level outcomes. For example, the objectives might be 'outcome' objectives - detailing the expected outcomes of learning which students are to be able to demonstrate - or they may be 'process' objectives, the teaching and learning styles to be involved, the experiences which students are going to have. The objectives then might refer to the content or curriculum, the teachers, the task, the students, the inputs, the outcomes, indeed part of the negotiation of an objectives-based evaluation proposal will be the determination of exactly what the objectives are which will feature in the evaluation. For a piece of curriculum innovation this task may already have been carried out. However, for an established curriculum, the evaluator and stake-holders might have to carry out a pre-evaluation task of clarifying the goals of the curriculum or programme.

An evaluation in the objectives model is useful in identifying the extent to which prescribed objectives have been reached and the discrepancies between *intended* and *observed* achievement. A clear example of this can be seen in the example from the United Kingdom where children are formally assessed at four points in their school lives to see how far they have achieved the objectives (called attainment targets) of the centrally prescribed national curriculum, the evidence for such assessment being derived from formal testing at a national level and from observational evidence gathered by teachers.

WHAT ARE THE STRENGTHS AND WEAKNESSES OF THE OBJECTIVES MODEL?

Whilst the objectives model is very useful in detailing which objectives have been achieved and the level of their achievement, it does not address those types of evaluation which seek to explain why the objectives may or may not have been achieved. Hence its simplicity is bought at the price of explanatory potential. It is the model which is useful for describing rather than explaining.

Because it operates with *given* objectives this style of evaluation places no relevance on the evaluation of the *worth* of the objectives in the first place - it is a model which could be employed with great success in teaching children how to be pickpockets or thieves. As such it is blind to moral judgements, it operates within the terms set by the curriculum or programme planners and hence can be a very conservative, bounded model of evaluation. If the measurement of the achievement of objectives is desired, then this is a useful model; however, if an evaluation of the context, causes, worth or justifications of the objectives are desired, then this model will not serve the evaluator. It is a good example of a clear but selective model. Furthermore, the discussions so far have dwelt on the political nature of evaluation; in this model the politics of the evaluation is irrelevant or anodyne, thereby enabling it to be brought into the service of a variety of political purposes.

WHEN CAN I USE THE OBJECTIVES MODEL OF EVALUATION?

One attraction of the objectives model is that the objectives usually translate very easily into the *criteria* for evaluation, a significant element of evaluation. This might be very useful if an evaluator wishes to conduct an evaluation without having a control and experimental group in an experimental model (discussed later in this chapter). For example, if an innovation is being undertaken in a school and there are no *existing* criteria against which to judge its success, the evaluator can go to the objectives of the programme and use them to judge the success of the innovation. This might be the case if, for instance, a school or class is undertaking a piece of 'enterprise education' and the only criteria for judging its success are the objectives of enterprise education - published or 'home-grown'. Similarly a school or group of schools might wish to evaluate a piece of in-service education. Here the participants might wish to set their own objectives for the in-service development, or the local authority might set the objectives for the development; either way the setting of objectives enables clear criteria for success to be established.

Within a school an evaluator might wish to find out how successful is a new piece of equipment or a new way of organizing material resources. The objectives of the use of the new materials having been set out clearly in advance of their introduction, the evaluator has clear criteria against which to judge the success of the new materials. In this case criteria (objectives) might be tiered; for example, criteria for *highly* successful, *moderately* successful and *not significantly* successful use may be described in the objectives. Clearly this tiering of success has very strong parallels both with teacher appraisal, Records of Achievement and the awards of grades in criterion-referenced assessments (*see* chapters three and five) where different criteria are attached to different objectives.

In the United Kingdom the objectives model is particularly appropriate for staff - either individually or collectively - setting targets in their school development plans (short-term, medium-term and long-term) and reviewing the achievement of these (either on their own or with a local authority inspector) after an agreed period of time (Hargreaves and Hopkins, 1991).

HOW MIGHT A GOAL-FREE EVALUATION FIT WITH AN OBJECTIVES MODEL?

Whilst there might be a strong argument for the use of an objectives model, the stage of the evaluation at which the objectives of the programme are revealed to the evaluator is problematic. It might actually be useful for an evaluation if the objectives of a programme are not revealed too early, since, if they are revealed at the very outset of the evaluation, there is a risk that this might create in the evaluator a 'tunnel vision' such that he or she is only looking for evidence of the achievement of those objectives. It is human nature to use any information we have at our disposal which we think might be relevant for an evaluation. That surely is the essence of intelligent behaviour and is often done sub-consciously.

For example, a headteacher might have made it clear to the evaluator that 'what we are trying to do in our language programme is to encourage children to select reading books which are appropriate to their abilities without the assistance or direction of the teacher'. In this case the evaluator might well be looking for confirming evidence only of this in class, which might be slight but nevertheless would be recorded, thus ignoring the more frequent occasions on which the teacher had to direct students to particular reading books or comment to a student that a book was 'too easy' or 'too hard'. It might have been more appropriate if the headteacher had said nothing to the evaluator and simply seen if the evaluator had found any appreciable autonomous or directed book selection by the students taking place. In this latter case the evaluator's ignorance of the objectives of the programme would be an asset rather than an impediment; such ignorance serves validity.

There might be, then, a powerful case for the objectives of the programme *not* to be revealed to the evaluator in advance in order to avoid any bias which might be brought to the evaluation either consciously or subliminally. Hence a 'goal-free' model of evaluation (Stake, 1976) might be useful in serving the required disinterestedness of the evaluator. Here an evaluator might go into a situation deliberately unprepared for what to look for, i.e. simply to gather data on what is happening and what is being learnt - e.g. processes and outcomes or effects. Once data on these are acquired it is at *this* point that the objectives of the programme are revealed to the evaluator. The evaluator, without prior knowledge of the programme objectives, can then ascertain from the evidence how far the now-declared objectives of the programme are being achieved.

Of course this goal-free strategy runs the risk of the evaluator gathering irrelevant data (as in the illuminative model discussed later); however, where relevant data are acquired in this manner, it is strong on validity and authenticity. The degree of prior knowledge of the objectives, therefore, is an important issue in the objectives model. It has its own strengths and weaknesses. With too little prior knowledge the evaluator may or may not capture relevant data, with too much prior knowledge the evaluator may miss counter evidence, disconfirming examples, relevant data to refute the achievement of the objectives, in short may risk tunnel vision.

WHAT IS THE EXPERIMENTAL MODEL OF EVALUATION?

A very clear - and clean - model of evaluation is the experimental model. This model has been imported into the social sciences from the natural sciences and is essentially a summative style of evaluation. Imagine that we have been transported into a laboratory to investigate the properties of a new wonder-fertilizer which farmers could use on their cereal crops, let us say wheat. The scientist would take the bag of wheat seed and randomly split it into two equal parts. One part would be grown under normal existing conditions - controlled and measured amounts of soil, warmth, water and light and no other factors. This would be called the control group. The other part would be grown under the same conditions - the same controlled and measured amounts of soil, warmth, water and light as the control group *but*, additionally, the new wonder-fertilizer. Then, four months later the two groups are examined and their growth measured. The control group has grown half a metre and each ear of wheat is in place but the seeds are small. The experimental group, in contrast, has grown half a metre but has significantly more seeds on each ear, the seeds are larger, fuller and more robust.

The scientist concludes that because both groups came into contact with nothing other than measured amounts of soil, warmth, water and light then it could not have been anything else but the new wonder-fertilizer which caused the experimental group to flourish so well. The key factors in the experiment were:

- the identification of key variables (soil, warmth, water and light);
- the control of the key variables (the same amounts to each group);
- the exclusion of any other variables;

- the random allocation of the whole bag of wheat into two matched groups (the control and the experimental group), involving the initial measurement of the size of the wheat seed to ensure that it is the same for both groups (the pre-test);
- the giving of the special treatment to the experimental group whilst holding every other variable constant for both groups;
- the final measurement of yield and growth (the post-test);
- the comparison of one group with another;
- the stage of generalization - that this new wonder-fertilizer improves yield and growth under a given set of conditions.

As a model for evaluation this has considerable attraction. It is particularly useful if one wishes to determine whether programme X makes any difference to, let us say, a child's reading performance, or whether this innovation in mathematics teaching improves a student's computational skills in comparison to the existing programme of study.

For example, let us say that we wished to find out whether a new method of teaching history improved children's scores on a national test of history at the age of eleven. One would randomly allocate two groups of students drawn from a group of eleven year-olds into a control group and an experimental group (the children are the equivalent of the initial bag of seed!) and test their performance in history to ensure that it was well matched in each group. Then one would isolate and control any extraneous factors (variables) which might be exerting an effect on the children's abilities in history. The experimental group would receive the new method of teaching history whilst everything else was the same as for the control group. A final post-test of the two groups would enable the teacher to ascertain how the experimental group's performance in history on the national test compared to that of the control group's performance. If it is significantly better, then the teacher might assume that it must have been because of the new method of teaching history. The teacher would infer that the cause of the improvement is the new method.

WHAT ARE THE STRENGTHS AND WEAKNESSES OF THE EXPERIMENTAL MODEL?

This model seems straightforward and simple to use. It appears to offer us more than the objectives model in that it can *explain* why such and such an effect was observed - it can attribute cause. Furthermore, it simply involves sorting children into two groups, measuring and testing them before and after and seeing if improvements are significant (often defined statistically - as will be discussed in later chapters). Moreover, it is a model which not only has the prestige of the tag of 'science' but which can serve political situations wonderfully well, as, in its generation of comparisons and sets of figures to prove that such and such was more effective than something else, it is highly attractive to simplistic notions of accountability. It quickly identifies, with all the respectability which is accorded to the objectivity of numbers, criteria for success and failure. It therefore can hold people and curricula accountable for that success or failure.

But pause; there are massive assumptions and concerns in many fields which are raised by the importation of agricultural models into the social sciences. Do children, or should children, really behave like inanimate ears of wheat? Should they be treated as if they were totally controllable and manipulable? Is it actually possible - whether desirable or not - to render the dynamics of classrooms as identifiable, controllable and operable as a science laboratory? Is not that to create a totally artificial situation in the school or classroom? Furthermore, is it ever really possible to say with any certainty that it was this particular treatment that improved a child's performance? In the example of history teaching *above*, the children who were put into the experimental group might have felt 'I must be important to be in this group and to be given this new curriculum, therefore I must try harder' whilst the children in the control group might have felt 'it's not fair that we're not getting this new curriculum, I never did like history anyway so I'm not going to try at all in this'. Any changes in performance might have been to do with the children and not the new method of teaching history - their perceptions, their concerns, their feelings.

To suggest that any changes might have come from the new history method might be to miss the point; we must always be cautious about assuming that we can know the causes of changes in behaviour, particularly if we think monocausally. It may be folly to assume that behaviour Y results from treatment X. Humans are much more complex than that, there are a host of other variables which may be exerting just as strong an influence on behaviour as any specific treatment. The experimental model assumes a simplicity of isolating and controlling variables which probably does not exist in the real world of students and teachers. Hence the evaluator using this model to organize his or her plans would have to be as aware of what *could not* be said as a result of the evaluation as what *could* be said as a result of the evaluation.

This model is useful in that it is deliberately pragmatic, it concerns which method is better than another for achieving a particular objective rather than a consideration of whether the object itself is worth achieving. Like the objectives model the experimental model is silent on moral debate about the worth of the objective; indeed the worth of a particular programme is decided *instrumentally* - e.g. how much better it is than another programme at achieving a given end - rather than *ethically*. This is a case of the end justifying any means rather than a consideration of the value of the end or the morality of the means.

There are then many important moral and practical reservations which must be taken into consideration in employing this model.

WHEN CAN I USE THE EXPERIMENTAL MODEL OF EVALUATION?

The experimental model is particularly strong if one wishes to evaluate the comparative effects of a particular piece of curriculum innovation or practice in achieving a particular goal. If it is possible to isolate significant variables and hold them constant whilst exposing an experimental group to another independent variable (e.g. the discovery method of science), then this model is clearly useful.

WHAT IS THE DECISION-MAKING MODEL OF EVALUATION?

Part of the everyday behaviour of teachers and programme planners is the taking of decisions - shall I do X or Y, shall I continue with this teaching style or switch to another, does this child need to follow this course of action or that course of action, will this programme be more suitable than that programme in this context, etc.? A decision-making model of evaluation is useful in that it focusses squarely on the systematic informing of decisions at different stages of a programme or at different elements of a programme. It is therefore chiefly a formative model, though clearly a summative evaluation might also be produced.

With regard to the former - the different stages of a programme - we can identify three important stages: the development stage of a programme, the implementation stage of a programme and the outcome stage of the programme - the antecedent, transaction and outcomes respectively (Stake, 1976).

Set in the context of curriculum evaluation one could imagine the following example of the helpfulness of the decision-making model. At the antecedent stage the evaluator gathers data on which decisions are taken concerning the context of the programme, what salient features of the context the programme needs to address. For instance, data are collected on curriculum proposals, the students' backgrounds, the school context, the teachers, the existing curricular arrangements compared to the proposed curricular arrangements. At the implementation stage the evaluator gathers data on which decisions are taken concerning what content is being addressed and how, the teaching and learning styles, the organization and use of resources, what is actually happening, what teachers and children are doing, how the learning is being structured and organized, how the curriculum or tasks are introduced, continued, completed, followed up. At the outcome stage the evaluator gathers data on which decisions are taken about the actual outcomes in relation to the student, the teacher, the curriculum, the management etc. The intention at all stages is to chart the degree of accord between what was intended to occur and what actually occurred and reasons for the accord or discrepancy.

With regard to the elements of a programme, the evaluator would have to identify the key features of a programme and gather data on them; for instance in a curriculum programme this could cover the aims, objectives, content, resourcing, teaching styles, learning patterns and assessments contained in the programme, again to determine the level of accord between what was intended to be the case and what actually turned out to be the case, and the reasons for the accord or discrepancy.

WHAT ARE THE STRENGTHS AND WEAKNESSES OF THE DECISION-MAKING MODEL?

With increasing attention being given in the educational press to decision-making and management this model has taken on a renewed vigour since it was first mentioned in the late 1960s. The evaluator identifies the key decision times in a programme and then plans how to gather data which will better enable the participants to take informed decisions at those points.

However, the reality of much of the implementation of a programme is that decisions are neither taken at all at the planned key decision times nor is decision-making confined to the proposed key decision times - it may be that the decision-making is much more of an ongoing, even process than in a decision-making model which asks the evaluator to identify crucial and critical times. Hence whilst a carefully planned evaluation in the decision-making model enables useful and often timely information to be provided which, formatively, feeds into the cycle of development or renewal of a programme, a fully worked out decision-making model must also contain room for a review of why decisions did or did not occur as anticipated.

Hence, ironically perhaps, users of the decision-making model must also make a decision about what the boundaries of the model are, whether and how to involve participants, how to be sensitive to unanticipated occurrences, who will be taking the decisions (and the effects this will have on other participants) and whether to operate with prespecified or emerging criteria and the sources of relevant data for the evaluation.

This model, therefore, necessarily has to address the political aspects of the evaluation; this marks it out from the previous two models. In its wide sweep of concerns and stages it allows a wide interpretation of evaluation to be employed, taking in judgements of worth and value as well as more instrumental concerns of which is the best way to proceed once we have decided that the objectives of a programme are morally tenable. In its consideration of outcomes it also allows consideration to be given to whether a programme can be run again, whether it has to be modified or whether it has to terminate.

WHEN CAN I USE THE DECISION-MAKING MODEL OF EVALUATION?

This model is particularly useful if a piece of curriculum innovation is being monitored either as it unfolds over time or perhaps in the pilot stage of a programme. For example, let us say that a school was considering adopting an integrated day but did not wish to move to its wholesale adoption until it had been tried in one or two classes so that problems and issues might be exposed. In the pilot classes the evaluator gathers data on the *preparations* which are made before the trial period and the areas in which decisions can be foreseen (e.g. team teaching, time-tabling of shared spaces and shared resources, record keeping and forecasting, planning for groups and individuals).

At the *implementation* stage the evaluator gathers data not only on the extent to which the preparations are successful (or unsuccessful) but additional decisions which the initiators take and the reasons for these, why they could not have been foreseen. At this stage it would be important also to identify the areas in which decisions had to be taken, for example teaching styles, students' movements round the room and access to resources, organization of mixed ability groups, key lessons and follow-up lessons and their organization, induction of parents and ancillary helpers into the scheme, use of supply teachers to cover for absent colleagues. At this stage it would also be important to indicate the significance of the decisions taken, for example to indicate whether they are trivial, day-to-day matters which an individual teacher takes to ease organizational issues for the particular session or whether they are major decisions about the organization, rationale and operation of the scheme, for example a decision to limit the curriculum areas which are covered by an integrated day, a decision to limit the number of sessions each week in which the programme operates, a decision that it only appears to work if a team of teachers can operate together and agree with its rationale.

There will, of course, be several stages in the implementation process. The evaluator may be able to identify key decisions which are taken during the implementation which affect the future course of the programme. In the example of the trialling of the integrated day these may concern the staffing, resourcing, management and week-to-week operating of the programme. If the evaluator is able to classify the types of decision taken, then this may have significant formative potential for future adopters in the school. At the *outcome* stage the evaluator will gather data on the level of success of the pilot programme and judge according to previously agreed criteria - for example, children's ability to work autonomously, the development of a shared, collegial approach to task management and planning, the collective promotion of a positive approach to prevent disruptive behaviour, children's social, academic and emotional development, the utilization of space or material resources.

In identifying decisions which are taken (both planned and unplanned) this model is particularly useful if the fine-grain detail of day-to-day practices is sought. If the significance of decisions is also established, then this enables not only the fine grain to be recorded but it will also chart patterns of development, which might be useful if several sites - classrooms, schools - are being involved in the innovation.

WHAT IS THE ILLUMINATIVE MODEL OF EVALUATION?

The first two models deliberately attempted to build out any influences of the participants in a programme, either by confining the evaluation to a measure of the achievement of objectives or by isolating and controlling a range of variables. The decision-making model, by contrast, hinted at the need for an evaluator to take into account the perceptions and the perspectives of those involved in a programme. The illuminative model places this issue at the very heart of its rationale. Whereas the first two models were 'outside-in' models, that is, we shone our light onto the programme to see if we could find what we were told to look for, this model is an 'inside-out' model. We go inside a programme or a situation not certain what it is we shall see, we shine our light around and see what is taking place. The image is of the child's hallowe'en lantern from out of which a candle light shines eerily through the carved out eyes, nose and mouth! We illuminate the programme *in the terms of its participants* - children, teachers, headteachers, parents, indeed whoever are the stake-holders. It is less concerned with measurement than with the honest and accurate portrayal of what it is like to be an insider to the programme. It is a model which generates 'thick descriptions', it is 'strong on reality' and enables the evaluator really to enter the situation in a fully-fledged way and to capture the dynamics of a situation.

Illuminative evaluation attempts to describe, understand and explain what is happening in a programme, why it is happening in the way that it is, and with what effects on the participants, all of which, importantly, are described by the participants themselves. It is essentially a formative model. Hence evaluators will have an outline brief to which to work which contains areas of interest, but the interpretation of those areas, the specific evaluation questions and indeed other issues arising will all be generated from the wide data base which is acquired from the participants and judged in their terms. Data are acquired from observations, interviews, questionnaires, documentary sources, in short from as many instruments as possible which yield data. An attempt to reduce data overload is made by progressive focussing. This is a technique which is characterized by the evaluator beginning with very full and rich data and reading and re-reading them to pick out the key issues, and then focussing on these key issues at the next stage of evaluation.

The evaluation has strong internal validity in that the evaluator repeatedly takes back his or her interpretation to the respondents for their verification. Further, the richness of the data and the identification of the key features of a programme are reinforced by the fact that in illuminative evaluation the evaluator usually remains in a situation for a considerable length of time - weeks and months rather than hours and days. Thus important features emerge over time, gathering potency as the weeks go by, rather like a fine cheese!

WHAT ARE THE STRENGTHS AND WEAKNESSES OF THE ILLUMINATIVE MODEL?

The illuminative model is a very powerful approach to generating case studies which celebrate the particulars of a situation. The attraction of this approach lies in its ability to generate an evaluation which is rich in authenticity and honesty, being very close to the objects of the evaluation, rich in multiple perspectives, having high explanatory potential, and being capable of identifying key features of a programme as experienced by the participants. One understands from it exactly what is taking place and why. In this model people matter, their views matter, their agency matters. In this respect it captures the activity and dynamics of a situation very impressively.

On the other hand illuminative evaluation does not seek to make generalizations, it has to cope with a massive amount of data, it does not operate within any external criteria, in short, it is descriptive, time-consuming and introspective, blindly subjective, impressionistic, involving small samples, open to prejudice on the part of the respondents, and sometimes impossible to process or report multiple perspectives.

In approaching an illuminative evaluation an evaluator will have to address some important practical points:

(a) negotiating one's way into a situation - if the evaluator is going to stay in an institution for a lengthy period this might depend on the good will of others and, in the case of teachers, ensuring supply teacher cover; (how will the evaluator avoid being seen as a threat to other parties or regarding them as evaluation fodder?)

(b) finding a role for the evaluator to be accepted and yet maintain a distance; respondents will have various perceptions of the evaluator;

(c) timing the point of entry to be in at the beginning of a programme in order to see movements and changes over time;

(d) retaining some distance from those involved;

(e) gaining access to certain groups of informants (e.g. how will an evaluation of truancy be undertaken if the truants are never present?); gaining access to deeper, less superficial responses from certain groups;

(f) identifying key respondents and yet avoiding the danger of simply taking the view of somebody in a powerful position;

(g) recording multiple perspectives and multiple realities and still giving a representative view;

(h) agreeing the ownership of the data;

(i) writing the report in such a way that it avoids too much narrative and description and yet captures the flavour of a situation;

(j) identifying whose views should be included (all the stake-holders or simply some of them).

Hence if an evaluator wishes to capture the flavour of what it feels like to be involved in a programme, to provide a candid report in the terms of the participants themselves, and to explore fully a unique situation in order to discover what makes it unique, what are the dynamics of the situation, and what are the key features as expressed by the participants, then illuminative evaluation is a useful organizing model.

WHEN CAN I USE THE ILLUMINATIVE MODEL OF EVALUATION?

This model is often used for small scale evaluations or for teachers evaluating their own classes. It lends itself very well to this because it is concerned with the particular rather than the general. For example, let us imagine that a headteacher has recently appointed three teachers to incentive allowances and wishes to find out whether they are being used to optimum effect in the school. Such appointments are seldom completely free of problems, for example, other colleagues may feel disaffected as they thought they were better fitted to the appointment, there may be a lack of credibility in the persons appointed, an incentive allowance might have been given for an area of school life which is not deemed central to the school, etc., an incentive allowance might have been given to a 'bandwagon' innovation or a 'bandwaggoner' career teacher. The operation of the allowance holders will almost always be a sensitive issue.

To capture this sensitivity an evaluation of their effectiveness will require, inevitably perhaps, a close-grained reporting and analysis of sensitive factors which are capable of several interpretations; there are as many 'realities' being studied here as there are people involved. It would be necessary here to catch, for instance, the institutional, interpersonal, managerial, resourcing, staff development and curriculum development factors which make for the success or otherwise of the appointments. The task of the evaluator will be to portray these multiple realities and to tease out from them a range of significant issues which appear to be affecting the level of effectiveness of these appointments in this particular institution. It is not a cut-and-dried, generalizable evaluation, rather it is complex, convoluted and context-specific. Different *personae* in the institution will have different criteria for 'effectiveness'; even if the criteria for effectiveness are either given or agreed then different *personae* will use them to judge the incentive allowance holders differentially.

Moving away from a management example an evaluator might be asked to ascertain those factors which are making for the apparently successful implementation of a new piece of the curriculum in a particular department, let us say a languages department whose grades on national examinations have improved dramatically in a two year period. An illuminative evaluation may seek the views of all participants, asking them to suggest their reasons why the scores have improved and will then try to organize and arrange these several responses. For example, it might be a change in teaching styles, syllabus and examination styles; it might be the result of the appointment of two new colleagues who have made innovatory suggestions; it might be a new openness led by a newly appointed head of department; it might be because of increased resources in the department; it might be because of coincidental increased parental communication or pressure, it might be because of increased status given to the department by a 'new broom' headteacher. What an illuminative evaluation should capture is not only the incidence of an array of factors but, more sensitively, their complex interplay, indicating why a certain cluster of factors has combined to bring improved results.

A teacher evaluating his own classroom practices might find illuminative evaluation feasible because he has immediate access to all the necessary sources, he is able to gather rich data over time and he is always on hand to catch significant events. Whilst this clearly has several attractions - not the least of which is utility value to the teacher - it nevertheless contains a double problem. *Firstly*, all the data are filtered, as it were, by the teacher who is also a major participant in the situation, i.e. who may not be a neutral figure (*see* the discussions of reliability and validity in chapter six and the discussions of insider evaluation in chapter eight). *Secondly*, not only is the teacher researching his own institution but he is *primus inter pares* - i.e. he has greater power in the classroom than the children. Hence not only is the teacher a major contributor to class-room events but students may not be as open or honest to the teacher as they would be to an outsider.

In summary, if a teasing out of issues from the complexity of one or more case studies is required, then indeed an illuminative evaluation is a fascinating approach to this type of evaluation.

HOW CAN I SUMMARIZE THE DISCUSSION OF MODELS?

There are several other models of evaluation which can be employed to organize an evaluation. However, these five models - the survey model, the objectives model, the experimental model, the decision-making model and the illuminative model capture the very different flavours of evaluation. They vary in their purposes, their foci, their key descriptors or key terms, and their characteristics. This can be summarily presented in a matrix (Figure 2.4).

Whilst these models have a measure of conceptual clarity, a full evaluation would not necessarily conform to one model alone. In many cases an evaluation might have several purposes and foci and hence would draw on more than one model. Further, there is a certain 'cleanness' about these models which removes them from the actuality of the world of evaluation where negotiations between those who ask for the evaluation, evaluators and respondents often result in the real evaluation being a compromise of principles or a trade-off of types of evaluation between the parties involved. Some models are capable of addressing many tiers of the politics of evaluation (e.g. the decision-making model). Others take little account of the micro-politics or macro-politics of the institution or the uses of the evaluation (e.g. the objectives and experimental models), others deal only in micro-politics (e.g. the illuminative model), others are capable of addressing many tiers of the politics of evaluation (e.g. the decision-making model). The point here is that the model should not drive the evaluation unless that is appropriate. Models have no magical powers and an appeal to a model affords no extra status to an evaluation; they exist only as tools which can assist the planning of an evaluation.

Model	Purposes	Foci	Key Terms	Characteristics
Survey	Gathering large scale data in order to make generalizations Generating statistically manipulable data Gathering context-free data	Opinions scores outcomes conditions ratings	Measuring Testing Representativeness Generalizability	Describes not explains Represents wide population Gathers numerical data Much use of questionnaires
Objectives	Measuring the degree of success of the achievement of prespecified objectives Objective measurement of achievement	Outcomes Processes Teacher and student behaviour	Measurement Assessment Achievement Comparing intentions and actuality	Describes not explains Does not judge worth Operates within framework of planners Politically useful for accountability
Experimental	Comparing under controlled conditions Making generalizations about efficacy Objective measurement of treatments	Initial states, treatment and outcomes	Pre-test and post-test Identification, isolation and control of key variables Generalizations Comparing Suggesting cause	Control and experimental groups Treats situations like a laboratory Causes due to experimental treatments Does not judge worth Simplistic Politically useful for accountability

figure 2.4 continued→

Model	Purposes	Foci	Key Terms	Characteristics
Decision Making	Systematic informing of decisions at different elements of a programme Development, implementation and outcome stages	Contexts, inputs, processes, outcomes	Identification of key features and key decision times of a programme Comparing intentions and actuality	Assumes key features and key decision times are identifiable in advance Formative Addresses the politics of a situation Allows room for judgements of worth
Illuminative	Portrayal of programme in participants' terms Subjective and reporting of multiple views of stake-holders Description, understanding and explanation of a specific situation	Perceptions and views of participants Issues as they emerge over time	Subjectivity Honesty, authenticity Non-generalizable Multiple perspectives Exploration and rich reporting of a specific context Emergent issues	Context specific Formative Responsive to emerging features as well as to predetermined concerns Builds in the politics of a situation Allows room for judgements of worth Wide data base gathered over a long period of time Time consuming to process data

Figure 2.4   Using Models to Organize Evaluation Approaches

CONCLUSION

This chapter has suggested how an evaluator can 'operationalize' any evaluation questions, moving from general areas of interest and general questions to very specific questions which can be answered by appropriate data. It has been suggested that it is important that all the major questions of an evaluation are addressed and, importantly, resolved *before* the evaluation is undertaken. The following areas have been addressed in the planning stage:

- setting up an evaluation;
- key areas of an evaluation design;
- using a matrix to assist planning;
- 'operationalizing' evaluation questions;
- staging an evaluation;
- identifying an appropriate methodology;
- using models of evaluation.

An acceptable evaluation design, then, will bear several hallmarks; clarification and agreement amongst the stake-holders will have been reached on the following issues:

- the identification of the stake-holders;
- the constraints on the evaluation and a proposal agreed which takes these into account;
- the purposes of the evaluation;
- the nature of the evaluation (e.g. formative or summative);
- the specific evaluation questions and sub-questions;
- the comprehensiveness of the questions;
- the foci of the evaluation;
- foci will be comprehensive enough to answer the evaluation questions;
- methodologies will be appropriate to the task of the evaluation;
- the style and models of evaluation;
- the piloting of the evaluation;
- the kinds of information required for the evaluation;
- instruments will be appropriate to the tasks of the evaluation;
- the timing and time scales of the evaluation;
- the data processing and presenting of the data for the evaluation;
- the reporting of the evaluation;
- the audiences of the evaluation;
- the costing of the evaluation;
- the control of data and control of the evaluation;
- the management of the evaluation;
- the powers of the evaluation;
- what controls there are on the evaluator;
- the roles of the evaluator;
- the dissemination of the evaluation;
- the reliability and validity of the evaluation;
- the balance of objectivity and subjectivity of the evaluation;

- the ethics of verification of the evaluation data and their inter-pretation;
- levels of confidence in the data;
- the ownership of the evaluation.

Though the list appears long, it ensures that all aspects of the planning and implementation of the evaluation are covered. Teachers and other evaluators have here a useful checklist of items to assist them in designing an evaluation. Having agreed an evaluation design, the next task is to undertake the examination of the particular methods of gathering data. This is the substance of the next chapter.

RECOMMENDED READING

Brinkerhoff, R., Brethower, D.O., Hluchyi, T., Nowakowski, J.R. (1983) *Program Evaluation*. Boston: Kluwer-Nijhoff.

Guba, E.G. & Lincoln, Y.S. (1991) What is the Constructivist Paradigm?, in D.S. Anderson & B.J. Biddle (eds.) *Knowledge for Policy: Improving Education Through Research*. London: Falmer.

Morrison, K.R.B. & Ridley, K. (1988) *Curriculum Planning and the Primary School*. London: Paul Chapman Publishing.

Moser, C.A. & Kalton, G. (1977) *Survey Methods in Social Investigation*. London: Heinemann.

Parlett, M. & Hamilton, D. (1976) Evaluation as Illumination, in D. Tawney (ed.) *Curriculum Evaluation Today: Trends and Implications*. London: Macmillan.

Stufflebeam, D.L. (1976) Educational evaluation and decision-making, cited in D. Jenkins Six Alternative Models of Educational Evaluation, Unit 20, E203, *Curriculum Design and Development*. Milton Keynes: Open University Press.

Stufflebeam, D. & Shuckfield, A. (1985) *Systematic Evaluation*. Boston: Kluwer-Nijhoff.

University of Newcastle upon Tyne (1990) *Evaluating INSET* . Newcastle upon Tyne: School of Education, University of Newcastle upon Tyne.

Weiss, C. (1986) The Stake-holder Approach to Evaluation: origins and promises, in E.R. House (ed.) *New Directions in Educational Evaluation*. Lewes: Falmer.

Weiss, C. (1986) Toward the Future of the Stake-holder Approach, in E.R. House (ed.) *New Directions in Educational Evaluation*. Lewes: Falmer.

3 Instruments for Collecting Data

The previous chapter suggested that a variety of *approaches* to evaluation were available to an evaluator and that these approaches could be *modelled* in order to gain some purchase on deciding how to go about an evaluation. Quantitative approaches served one set of purposes (e.g. to compare, to derive generalizations, to measure) whilst qualitative approaches were able to serve a different set of purposes (e.g. to portray a unique situation, to generate 'thick descriptions' of particular practices and perceptions of those involved). The importance of avoiding an arbitrary decision on which methodology or model to select was considered to be fundamental if validity were to be served. So it is with instrumentation - the design and selection of particular *methods* of gathering data. Whilst there is a battery of data-gathering instruments available to the evaluator, the choice of which ones to use is not arbitrary but determined by the appropriacy of the instrument to the purposes, style and methodology of the evaluation.

For example, it might be wholly inappropriate to use a uniform, closed-question format of a questionnaire if one wanted to capture the unique features of a situation - an approach to evaluation which necessarily requires the instruments used to be capable of gathering a diversity of perspectives responsively and, hence, requiring open-ended questionnaires or semi-structured interviews. On the other hand it might be equally inappropriate to try to carry out a large-scale survey through a series of open-ended interviews, using an instrument which builds in the opportunity for massive differences of interpretation and response which are, by definition, more suited to a small scale piece of evaluation. This case might be better served by a closed-question questionnaire. Further, it might be just as inappropriate to use an observational instrument for gathering data if one were really interested in gathering opinions and perceptions; in this case some sort of interview schedule or questionnaire might be more appropriate. The golden rule for selecting, devising and constructing a data gathering instrument is *fitness for purpose*. Different purposes require different instruments.

WHAT METHODS OF DATA GATHERING ARE AVAILABLE?

The evaluator can select from an embarrassment of riches of data-gathering techniques. These can be organized into *written forms* and *interpersonal forms*, though clearly there will be occasions when the written forms and the live, interpersonal forms will both tap the same issues. For example, if one were wishing to address the degree of parental participation in a school, it might be useful to administer a questionnaire to all parents and also to conduct interviews with a selection of parents of students in the school. The former instrument might capture patterns and trends, the latter might capture specific insights, critical moments, a richness of data denied to a closed-question questionnaire. It is not that one instrument is better than another, it is simply that one instrument is more fitted to one set of purposes than another. The two forms of instrumentation are written and face-to-face, interpersonal methods.

WHAT ARE THE WRITTEN FORMS OF DATA COLLECTION?

There are several ways of eliciting written data:

- Delphi techniques
- diaries, journals and logs which record both facts (events) and opinions/reflections/attitudes/comments/observations;
- personal constructs;
- questionnaires using closed response items (e.g. dichotomous yes/no questions, multiple-choice questions, rating scales - attitude ratings, Likert scales, Guttman scales, semantic differential scales);
- questionnaires using open responses items;
- documents (e.g. reports, records, minutes);
- survey data;
- test results (e.g. norm-referenced, criterion-referenced, essays, course work);
- content analysis;
- resource analysis;
- sociometry.

The list is long but certainly not exhaustive, the principal methods of gathering data through questionnaires, using documentary evidence, using Delphi techniques and using published tests or tests which have been constructed by the evaluator will be discussed *below*.

WHAT ARE THE STRENGTHS AND WEAKNESSES OF WRITTEN FORMS OF DATA COLLECTION?

Written forms of data collection do not require the face-to-face contact of live, interpersonal forms. This can have several advantages - the attraction of anonymity, the facility for enabling perusal of materials over time. Further, these forms do not require the evaluator to be present whilst the respondents complete their writing. This is an important issue for teachers and evaluators whose time is limited. On the other hand, these same attractions can be disadvantages, for example, anonymity might promote bias in that respondents might be far freer with comments than they really feel, or indeed respondents may tell lies - wittingly or unwittingly.

Similarly, perusing materials over a long period of time which were essentially gathered on a one-shot basis might overlook significant changes to the situation which had taken place since the data were gathered. In these circumstances it might be preferable for the evaluator to have face-to-face contact with respondents, using live, interpersonal forms of data collection.

WHAT ARE THE LIVE INTERPERSONAL FORMS OF DATA COLLECTION?

Just as there are several forms of written data so there are several ways of acquiring data from live, face-to-face situations:

- evaluation meetings;
- interviews - structured to unstructured, group or individual;
- nominal group techniques (the live, interpersonal form of the Delphi technique cited *above*);
- observation - structured to unstructured;
- snowball techniques.

This book will deal particularly with the most popular forms of 'live' data gathering - interviews, observation and nominal group technique.

WHAT ARE THE STRENGTHS AND WEAKNESSES OF LIVE FORMS OF DATA COLLECTION?

Face-to-face interviews are not only fascinating and dynamic but are often the heart of evaluations which teachers and other educationists undertake in their own institutions, with colleagues, students, parents etc. They capture what for many is the excitement of evaluation - meeting and discussing issues in unrehearsed and rehearsed ways in a live and evolving situation with 'real' people rather than the faceless recipients of questionnaires or candidates undertaking tests. They catch the richness and complexity of evaluative activity which was suggested at the start of the book to be not only a central feature of everyday life but one of its principal delights. There are several advantages and disadvantages of face-to-face forms of data collection. For example, they offer the opportunity for the evaluator to gather data in detail and in depth, they build in the attraction of the respondents putting a human face on to what might otherwise be an impersonal activity. On the other hand when we talk to each other, we give out non-verbal clues to what we are thinking or valuing, we can unwittingly censure some responses or support others. Our body posture, our tone of voice, the nature of our responses, the arrangement of chairs in an interview situation, our control of questions, prompts and probes, the way we record data, all give signals which may be both supportive or censorious (i.e. may convey judgemental messages). These may affect the situation and hence the validity of the data; as humans most of us quickly 'read' the non-verbal messages which we receive and we respond accordingly.

An interview is not simply a fact-gathering exercise, it is a form of interpersonal behaviour wherein subliminal messages are exchanged in code. Factors concerning social distance between evaluator and respondent, differentials of power in the evaluation interview (particularly between adults and children), gender differences (where a woman might be interviewed alone with a man), racial differences, degrees of mutual trust, all play their part in the context of the interview. Evaluators may have to ensure that respondents:

- understand the questions;
- actually have the knowledge appropriate to answer the question (a concern particularly important when interviewing children);
- are sufficiently articulate to be able to give a response;
- are given the opportunity to remain silent (some respondents will say anything rather than say nothing!);
- are enabled to give a considered response rather than saying the first thing that comes into their mind;
- are not compelled to divulge what they might not wish to divulge;
- do not say just what they think the evaluator wants to hear;
- have the opportunity to veto parts of their comments which are to be reported;
- who are shy are treated sensitively (an issue which is particularly relevant when interviewing children);
- are put at their ease or else they may repeat the headteacher's view or the 'institutional' response or, in the case of children, give the opinion that they think will avoid recriminations.

The evaluator will not only have to be aware of these issues at the time of devising face-to-face methods of gathering data but also be watchful during their administration for verbal and non-verbal signs, e.g. the nervous shuffle of the young child, the reticence of adults to commit themselves. A very useful way for the evaluator to become sensitive to verbal and non-verbal behaviour is to observe and comment on video material of interviews. For example, there is a growing amount of video material available on job interviews, talking with students in negotiating programmes of study and Records of Achievement (in the United Kingdom), discussing performance and future planning in appraisal interviews. Alternatively it is sometimes a useful exercise to stand back in a classroom situation or staff meeting and observe the non-verbal behaviour of participants. I am reminded of an autocratic headteacher who was extolling the virtues of collegial and democratic decision-making whilst shaking her head vigorously from side to side and pressing the flat of her hand in a downwards motion away from her as if to silence discussion! Morris's (1977) book on *Manwatching* and Neill and Caswell's (1993) book on *Body Language for Competent Teachers* provide fascinating introductions to this field and indicate some positive steps which evaluators can take to maximize the benefits of face-to-face interviews.

WHEN SHOULD I USE DIFFERENT METHODS?

Though the lists of data collection instruments are lengthy, there is a useful rule of thumb: the larger the scale of the evaluation or the sample, the more structured, closed and numerical the methods may have to be; the smaller the scale, the less structured, open and word-based the data may have to be. For example, if large quantities of data are required (e.g. in a survey), then highly structured, closed questions are useful, enabling frequencies of response to be calculated and statistical analysis to be employed. Indeed it would be almost impossible (and maybe unnecessary) to process vast quantities of open-ended interview data within a short time. If a site-specific case study is required, then qualitative, less structured, word-based and open-ended data may be more appropriate as they can capture the specificity of a particular situation. Where measurement is sought a quantitative approach is needed; where rich and personal descriptions are sought, then a word-based qualitative approach might be more suitable.

If a closed and structured approach is sought, enabling patterns to be observed and comparisons to be drawn, then the instruments to be used for gathering such data will need to be piloted and refined so that their final versions contain as full a range of possible responses as can be reasonably foreseen. Such methods are heavy on time early on in the evaluation in devising and refining instruments. However, once one has set up the instrument, the mode of analysis will be 'built-in' and hence quick to operate. For example, it may take two or three months to devise a survey questionnaire, pilot it, refine it and set it out in a format which will enable the data to be processed and statistics to be calculated. However, the trade-off from this is that data analysis can be undertaken fairly rapidly - we already know the categories of response, the nature of the data and the statistics to be used; it is simply a matter of processing the data - often through a computer analysis.

If it is more fitting that a rich description be presented in the respondents' own terms, then devising the instruments will consist of *outlining* areas of interest to the evaluator and a series of points noted - a schedule of open-ended questions or observations. As the evaluator may have little prior knowledge of the situation, this approach is essentially *responsive*, noting down a wealth of observations or responses to semi-structured interviews and then sifting through them to glean out those areas and issues which yield answers to the evaluation questions. Data analysis in this approach is more time-consuming, as possible responses could not have been anticipated.

These two continua - closed to open, structured to unstructured - feature in all the types of data collecting instruments which will be discussed below.

WHAT KINDS OF INTERVIEW CAN I USE?

An evaluator can choose from several types of interviews which lie on the continuum from highly structured to unstructured. A *highly structured* interview will have every question worked out in advance, the wording and sequence of the questions being the same for all respondents. There will be multiple-choice closed questions where the respondents choose from a list of responses that response which most closely resembles that which they would wish to have recorded as their own. There is little or no freedom for the evaluator to vary the sequence of questions or indeed to tailor them to the individual respondent. Hence the need to pilot this form of interview is paramount, as categories of response have to be exhaustive and discrete.

In using this form of interview the evaluator has to ensure that the categories which are used represent what the respondent feels or wishes to say in response to the question. When constructing the interview schedule it must actually be possible for the respondent to give an honest response. Not to do so would be to court bias by the limiting of the categories of response. Further, this method could easily become mechanistic, going for a superficial rather than an in-depth response.

Because the same wording and the same sequence of questions are used for each respondent, the responses will be capable of being aggregated and frequencies of response calculated. This is obviously true, but the evaluator has to address the *validity* of those frequencies and what is done with them. For example, suppose that an evaluation asked respondents to give their rating of the potential of a new science scheme in the school to generate understanding of science processes, and that the ratings were as follows, from a rating of one to a rating of five:

1 = none at all
2 = very poor
3 = adequate
4 = very good
5 = excellent

Supposing that this rating scale were to be given to each of twenty teachers in three schools and that five teachers rated the science scheme as 'adequate', thirteen as 'very good' and two as 'excellent', would it be fair to infer from these results that the scheme was very good? The evaluator would have to exercise extreme caution in making this claim for this reason: *the same words mean different things to different people.* Herein lies the greatest problem of word-based data. What teacher one means when she says that the scheme is 'adequate' might be the same as that for which teacher two calls the scheme 'very good'. In a structured interview we have no way of checking this. Hence an evaluation which used this form of rating scale would have to declare the parameters of the data - their utility, reliability and validity (discussed in chapter six).

To steer round the problems inherent in such a tightly structured interview one can move to a form of interview where such constrictions are relaxed. A semi-structured interview is a widely used and useful way of combining a concern for structure and a concern for freedom and individuality. In a semi-structured interview it may be that the wording and sequence of questions is the same for all respondents - thereby enabling some standardization to take place - but questions are open-ended, enabling the respondent to give an answer to the question in his or her own words. This has greater potential for an honest response whilst still preserving a measure of comparability across respondents. That honesty is bought at the price of the extra time taken to analyse what might be a vast range of disparate responses which may not in the end pattern themselves across respondents. Similarly respondents may interpret the verbal and non-verbal messages of the interview in different ways, thereby questioning the reliability and validity of the data.

Alternatively, a semi-structured interview may be more open than this, wherein the evaluator has a checklist schedule of points or topics to be covered, but does not adhere to the exact, same wording or sequence for each respondent but tailors the questions and their order to individual respondents who can answer in their own words and follow up their own comments in their own ways. The evaluator also has a list of *prompts* and *probes* for the evaluation interview; prompts enable the evaluator to clarify topics or questions as the respondents' needs dictate whilst probes enable the evaluator to ask for elaboration on the topics in question, thereby looking for that richness, depth, fullness, comprehensiveness and honesty of response given from an involved respondent which is denied to the highly structured interview respondent. An example of an interview schedule is provided in Appendix B; it is taken from an evaluation which examined the views of participants involved in a piece of curriculum innovation in history over a two year period and which took place at the end of the first year of the innovation.

This is a very popular and commonly used form of interviewing as it is able to follow trains of thought set up by both the evaluator and the respondent. Its popularity is well deserved, for it is both focussed and flexible, really taking into account the personalities, feelings and opinions of people and treating them as *people* rather than simply *data fodder*.

The interview schedule establishes a framework for the interview but does not constrict its scope - it is a ladder rather than a cage. Further, the interview situation becomes less formal and more 'humane' as it moves towards a more conversational style. However, one must note that the advantages of this style of interview exact their price. On this occasion the very fact that the sequence and wording of the interview is open to ongoing negotiation raises the question of the degree to which one can then infer patterns or comparability of responses, for as soon as one asks a question which is worded differently for each respondent one is in effect asking a different question. Questions concerning attitudes and opinions are particularly susceptible to this problem as they are particularly sensitive to changes in wording (Oppenheim, 1966). In order to avoid this it is perhaps necessary to ask several questions about the same topic, attitude or opinion. Moreover, in this style of interview (as in the following conversation style interview) there is an increased risk of the evaluator intruding his or her own opinion into the interview, thereby reducing the disinterestedness which should accompany an evaluation.

Too easily this style of evaluation can enable leading questions to be asked - e.g. 'when did you last stop complaining to the headteacher?', or 'how satisfied are you with the new mathematics scheme?', instead of 'how frequently do you have conversations with the headteacher?', and 'what is your opinion of the new mathematics scheme?'

The further one moves away from the rigidly structured interview the more one moves towards the conversation style of interview. The end point of this movement is an interview which is completely informal, where the agenda of items for the interview are not fixed and where there is the minimum of control or direction from the evaluator. This is a high risk style of interview, for though the rewards are high in that honest, subjective, context-specific and negotiated data may emerge, equally there is the risk that nothing may emerge which the evaluator may use. The interview may fail to generate useful data. Furthermore, this style of interview is prone to bias caused by the interpersonal relationships between respondent and evaluator, just as in any conversation there is a restricted code of meanings and attitudes in which the conversation is embedded. The loss of an agenda for the interview may be a powerful force for naturalness and the handing over of the responsibility for the interview to the respondent but it raises the potential of the interview being largely useless.

HOW DO I KNOW WHICH TYPE OF INTERVIEW TO USE?

Which type of interview one selects is judged by the criterion of appropriacy to the style and methodology of the evaluation. If an evaluator wishes to make comparisons, to find patterns, to make generalizations, to generate frequencies of response, to collate data and to systematize the interview, then a more heavily structured and closed type of interview is appropriate. If, however, an evaluator wishes to capture the particular and detailed flavour of a context which derives from the individually expressed opinions of the respondents in *their* terms, where patterning of response and aggregation of data are not sought, in short where diversity rather than uniformity of response are sought, then a semi-structured approach might be more suitable. The semi-structured and conversational style interview are particularly suited to case studies whereas the more structured approach is more suited to a small scale survey.

SHOULD I GATHER REPRESENTATIVE OR SELECTIVE DATA FROM INTERVIEWS?

Choosing the subject matter of interviews, whilst usually straightforward in that the evaluation questions will have been agreed before the evaluation proceeds, sometimes can merit greater attention. For example, the evaluator will have to decide whether to ask respondents about *everyday* incidents (i.e. to gather data on routine practices and responses in order to establish data which fairly represent the situations being evaluated) or whether to ask respondents about *critical* incidents, those out-of-the-ordinary incidents which can often illuminate most sharply the factors involved in the situation or phenomenon being evaluated. It may be, for instance, that one teacher's reaction to a particular innovation might contain more gems for an evaluator than the rest of the school's staff put together.

Let us take an example. A school has brought in a new reading scheme in an attempt to raise the standards of reading in the middle years of schooling; the reading co-ordinator wishes to evaluate its effectiveness so she interviews the teachers of the middle years children in the school. The teachers all comment on the utility of the scheme in planning a coherent progression of decoding skills from simple to complex. However, one teacher comments on a critical incident which occurred during a period of what was supposed to be 'uninterrupted sustained silent reading' (USSR); one group of children was obviously not doing the reading and was holding whispered conversations during the lesson. When asked about this, the children all said that the books were boring, even though they could read them perfectly well. This critical incident showed the evaluator that coherence of progression in the programme was inadequate in explaining the supposed benefits of the programme, that motivational factors also exerted an important influence on the children's reading. Critical incidents can not only provide confirmatory evidence, but, as in the natural sciences, can provide evidence to refute the claims made by a programme, in the case here the claim that a coherent progression necessarily improved reading. The inability of structured interviews to capture this type of critical incident must be weighed against the time taken to undertake open-ended interviews, for open-ended interviews are time-consuming both to administer and to analyse. Structured, closed interviews, on the other hand, are quick to administer and quick to process. This is a distinct advantage where time is a major constraint on evaluation.

WHAT ISSUES FEATURE IN DESIGNING QUESTIONNAIRES?

Many of the features of interview design can apply equally well to the construction, administration and processing of questionnaires - indeed one might regard a questionnaire as an interview which has been written down. One can construct a questionnaire with closed questions or open questions, with factual and attitudinal questions, and also with a structured or less structured format.

WHAT IS A STRUCTURED QUESTIONNAIRE?

Highly structured questionnaires ask closed questions. These can take various forms. *Dichotomous* questions require a 'yes'/'no' response, e.g. 'have you ever broken rules at school?', 'do you sometimes feel like teasing animals?'. Though it is possible to code responses quickly, there being only two categories of response, the evaluator must ask, for instance, whether a 'yes'/'no' response actually provides any useful information. Requiring respondents to make a 'yes'/'no' decision may be inappropriate; it might be more appropriate to have a range of responses, say in a rating scale. There are very few evaluations questions which can be answered with a 'yes' or a 'no'; because evaluations are often concerned with subtle and complex issues the crudity of responses encapsulated in a 'yes' or a 'no' belies that complexity and subtlety. It is quite simply inappropriate to a situation whose complexity is better served by a series of questions which reflect that complexity.

In addition to dichotomous questions ('yes'/'no' questions) an evaluator can ask for information about *dichotomous variables*. For example, the evaluator may be seeking information about gender (male or female), type of school (elementary or secondary), type of course (vocational or non-vocational). In these cases one of only two responses must be selected. This enables *nominal data* to be gathered (*see* pp. 131 - 134) and processed using the chi-square statistic, cross-tabulations and the Mann-Whitney statistic (*see* pp. 134 - 142).

To try to gain purchase on that complexity one can move towards *multiple-choice* questions where the range of choices is designed to capture the range of likely responses to given statements. For example, the evaluator could ask a series of questions about a new mathematics scheme in the school; a statement precedes a set of responses thus:

The Great Educational Mathematics Scheme (GEMS) is:
(a) a waste of time;
(b) an extra burden on teachers;
(c) not appropriate to our school;
(d) a useful complementary scheme;
(e) a useful core scheme throughout the school;
(f) well presented and practicable.

The categories would have to be discrete (i.e. having no overlap and being mutually exclusive) and would have to exhaust the possible range of responses. Guidance would have to be given on the completion of the multiple-choice, clarifying, for example, whether the respondents would be able to tick only one response or several from the list. Like dichotomous questions multiple-choice questions can be quickly coded and quickly aggregated to give frequencies of response. If that is what is appropriate to the evaluation, then this might be a valuable instrument.

Just as dichotomous questions had their parallel in dichotomous variables, so multiple-choice questions have their parallel in *multiple elements of a variable*. For example, the evaluator may be asking to which form a student belongs - there being maybe up to forty forms in a large school, or the evaluator may be asking which post-16 course a student is following (e.g. a vocational, academic, professional, manual, non-manual course). In these cases only one response may be selected. As for the dichotomous variable the listing of several categories or elements of a variable (e.g. form membership or course followed) enables *nominal data* to be gathered (*see* pp. 131 - 134) and processed using the chi-square statistic, cross-tabulations and the Kruskall-Wallis statistic (*see* pp. 134 - 142).

HOW CAN I ENSURE CLARITY IN QUESTIONNAIRES?

The multiple-choice questionnaire, like the semi-structured interview above, seldom give more than a crude statistic, for words are inherently ambiguous. In the example *above* the notion of 'useful' is unclear, as are 'appropriate', 'practicable' and 'burden'. Respondents could interpret these words differently in their own contexts, thereby rendering the data ambiguous. One respondent might see the utility of the mathematics scheme in one area and thereby say that it is useful - ticking (d). Another respondent might see the same utility in that same one area but, because it is only useful in that *one* area, may see this as a flaw and therefore not tick category (d). With an anonymous questionnaire this difference would be impossible to detect.

This is the heart of the problem of questionnaires - that different respondents interpret the same words differently. 'Anchor statements' can be provided to allow a measure of discrimination in response (e.g. 'strongly agree', 'agree' etc.), but there is no guarantee that respondents will always interpret them in the way that was intended. In the example above this might not be a problem as the evaluator was only after an indication of utility - without wishing to know the areas of utility or the reasons for that utility. The evaluator might only be wishing for a crude statistic (which might be very useful statistically in making a decisive judgement about a programme) in which case this crude statistic might be quite acceptable.

What we see in the example above is not only ambiguity in the wording but a very incomplete set of response categories which is hardly capable of representing all aspects of the mathematics scheme. That this might be politically expedient cannot be overlooked, for if the choice of responses is limited, then those responses might enable bias to be built into the evaluation. For example, if the responses were limited to statements about the *utility* of the mathematics scheme, then the evaluator would have little difficulty in establishing that the scheme was useful. By avoiding the inclusion of negative statements or the opportunity to record a negative response the evaluation will surely be biased.

The problem of ambiguity in words is intractable, at best we can *minimize* it rather than *eliminate* it altogether. The most innocent of questions is replete with ambiguity. Take the following examples:

● Does your child regularly do homework?

(What does 'regularly' mean - once a day; once a year; once a term, etc.?)

● How many children are there in your school?

(What does this mean: on roll; on roll but absent; marked as present but out on a field trip; at this precise moment or this week (there being a difference in attendance between a Monday and a Friday, or between the first term of the academic year and the last term of the academic year for secondary school students as some of them will have left school to go into employment or further education)?

● How many television sets do you have in school?

(What does this mean: present but broken; including those out of school because they are being repaired; do you mean the property of the school or of identified members of the staff or students; on average or exactly in school today?)

● Have you had a French lesson this week?

(What constitutes a 'week': the start of the school week (i.e. from Monday to a Friday), since last Sunday (or Saturday depending on your religion) or, if the question were put on a Wednesday, since last Wednesday; how representative of all weeks is this week -

what if there is an 'environmental' week or an 'arts' week taking place so that the time-table has been altered?)

● How far do you agree with the view that without a Parent/ Teacher Association you cannot talk about the progress of your children?

(The double negative ('without' and 'cannot') makes this question a difficult one to answer. If I wanted to say that I believe that Parent/Teacher Associations are necessary for adequate consultation between parents and teachers, do I answer with a 'yes' or a 'no'?)

● How old are you?   15 - 20
                            20 - 30
                            30 - 40
                            40 - 50
                            50 - 60

(The categories are not discrete; will an old-looking forty year-old flatter himself and put himself into the 30 - 40 category, or will an immature twenty year-old seek the maturity of being put into the 20 - 30 category?)

● Vocational education is only available to the lower ability students but it should be open to every student.

(This is, in fact, a double question. What does the respondent do who agrees with the first part of the sentence - 'vocational education is only available to the lower ability students' - but disagrees with the latter part of the sentence, or *vice versa*? The rule in questionnaire design is to ask only one question at a time.)

Though it is impossible to legislate for the interpretation of wording, the evaluator, of course, has to adopt a commonsense approach to this - recognizing the inherent ambiguity but nevertheless still feeling that it is possible to live with ambiguity. After all, it is part of the richness of human behaviour which was celebrated in chapters one and two!

WHAT IS A RATING SCALE?

One way in which degrees of response, intensity of response, and the move away from dichotomous questions have been managed can be seen in the notion of *rating scales* - Likert scales and semantic differential scales. These are very useful to the evaluator as they build in a degree of sensitivity and differentiation of response. A Likert scale provides a range of responses to a given statement, for example:

Curriculum evaluation is the highest possible form of human endeavour.

1 = strongly disagree
2 = disagree
3 = neither agree or disagree
4 = agree
5 = strongly agree

In this the categories need to be discrete and to exhaust the range of possible responses which respondents may wish to give. Notwithstanding the problems of interpretation which arise as in the previous example - one respondent's 'agree' might be another's 'strongly agree', one respondent's 'disagree' might be another's 'strongly disagree' - the greater subtlety of response which is built into a rating scale renders it a very attractive instrument for evaluators.

A semantic differential is a variation of a rating scale which operates by putting an adjective at one end of a scale and its opposite at the other, for example:

How useful do you consider the new set of geography text books to be?

	1	2	3	4	5	6	7	
useful	__	__	__	__	__	__	__	useless

The respondent indicates on the scale by circling or putting a mark on that position which most represents what he or she feels.

Osgood *et al* (1957), the pioneers of this technique, suggest that semantic differential scales are useful in three contexts: *evaluative* (e.g. valuable-valueless, useful-useless, good-bad); *potency* (e.g. small-large, weak-strong, light-heavy); *activity* (e.g. quick-slow, active-passive, dynamic-lethargic).

Rating scales are widely used in evaluations and rightly so, because they combine the opportunity for a flexible response with the ability to determine frequencies, correlations and other forms of quantitative analysis (*see* chapter five). They afford the evaluator an opportunity to fuse measurement and opinion, quantity and quality.

HOW CAN RATING SCALES BE USED TO GREATEST ADVANTAGE?

Though rating scales are powerful and useful instruments for an evaluator, nevertheless one needs to know their limits. For example, the evaluator would be well advised to avoid trying to infer a degree of sensitivity and subtlety from the data that it really cannot bear. There are other cautionary notes which one must sound about rating scales, be they Likert scales or semantic differential scales:

(a) There is no assumption of equal intervals between the categories, hence a rating of 4 indicates neither that it is twice as powerful as 2 nor that it is twice as strongly felt; one cannot infer that the intensity of feeling in the Likert scale between 'strongly disagree' and 'disagree' somehow matches the intensity of feeling between 'strongly agree' and 'agree'. These are illegitimate inferences.

(b) We have no check on whether the respondents are telling the truth. Given the message of this book - that evaluation is inescapably political - one has to concede that some respondents may falsify their response.

(c) We have no way of knowing if the respondent might have wished to add any other comments about the issues under investigation. It might have been the case that there was something far more pressing about the issue than the rating scale included but which was condemned to silence for want of a category. A straight-forward way to circumvent this issue is to include a category entitled 'other (please state)'.

(d) Most of us would not wish to be called extremists, we often prefer to appear like each other in many respects. For rating scales this means that we might wish to avoid the two extreme poles at each end of the continuum of the rating scales, reducing the number of positions on the rating scales to a choice of three (on a five point scale). That means *in fact* that there could be very little choice for us. The way round this is to create a larger scale than a five point scale - say a seven point scale. To go beyond a seven point scale is to invite a degree of detail and precision which might be inappropriate for the factor in question, particularly if the argument is accepted from above that one respondent's scale point three might be another's scale point four.

(e) On the scales so far there have been mid-points; on the five point scale it is the category three, on the seven point scale it is the category four. The use of an odd number of points for a scaling enables this to occur. However, let us not be innocent in evaluation; if we were to create a six point scale, then there would be no mid point, thus *requiring* a decision on rating to be indicated.

That this is intensely political can be seen from the following extended example: suppose I had brought in a new staffing structure into the school and I wished to have some guidance on its effectiveness. I could ask respondents to rate their response to the statement below:

The staffing structure of the school has enabled teamwork to be managed within a clear model of line management.

(Circle one number)

		1	2	3	4	5	6		
strongly agree		—	—	—	—	—	—		strongly disagree

Let us say that one member of staff circled 1, eight staff circled 2, twelve staff circled 3, nine staff circled 4, two staff circled 5, and seven staff circled 6. There being no mid point on this continuum, I could perhaps infer that those respondents who circled 1, 2 or 3 were in some measure of agreement, whilst those who circled 4, 5, 6 were in some measure of disagreement. That would be very useful for me, say as a headteacher, in publicly displaying agreement - there being twenty-one staff $(1 + 8 + 12)$ agreeing with the statement and eighteen $(9 + 2 + 7)$ displaying a measure of disagreement. However, we would have to point out that the measure of 'strongly disagree' attracted seven staff - a very strong feeling, which was not true for the 'strongly agree' category which only attracted one member of staff. The extremity of the voting has been lost in a crude aggregation.

Further, if we were to aggregate the scoring around the two mid-point categories 3 and 4 we would have twenty-one members of staff represented, leaving nine $(1 + 8)$ from categories 1 and 2 and nine $(2 + 7)$ from categories 5 and 6; adding together categories (1, 2, 5 and 6) a total of 18 is reached, which is less than the twenty-one total of the two categories (3 and 4). It seems on this scenario that it is far from clear that there was agreement with the statement from the staff, indeed taking the high incidence of 'strongly disagree', it could be argued that those staff who were perhaps ambivalent (categories 3 and 4), coupled with those who registered a 'strongly disagree' indicate not agreement with the statement but rather disagreement.

The interpretation of the data has to be handled very carefully, ordering them to suit one's own purposes can be very easy to arrange! The golden rule is that crude data can only generate crude interpretations, subtle statistics require subtle data. The interpretation of data must not distort the data unfairly.

It has been suggested that the attraction of rating scales is that they provide more opportunity than dichotomous questions for rendering data more sensitive and responsive to the respondents who complete questionnaires. This makes rating scales particularly useful for tapping

For the following questions please tick the box which most closely describes your views. The numbers for each box are interpreted thus:

1 = not at all
2 = very little
3 = a little
4 = a lot
5 = a very great deal

2. To what extent would your choices for last year have altered if taught modules had run at a time of the day other than that at which they did run?

3. To what extent would your choices for last year have altered if taught modules had run at a time of the week other than that at which they did run?

4. To what extent would you prefer to attend a module in the evenings only?

5. To what extent would you prefer to attend a module in the daytime only?

6. To what extent would you prefer to attend a module which ran on a mixture of daytimes and evenings?

7. To what extent would you like to have more modules on specific areas of the curriculum, e.g. maths, science etc?

8. To what extent would you like to have more modules on non-curriculum-specific issues, e.g. classroom organisation, teacher appraisal, cross curricular planning, SEN, school development plans?

9. To what extent would you like to have more modules which are phase specific?

Figure 3.1 A Sample Extract from a Questionnaire

attitudes and perceptions of respondents. The need for a pilot to devise and refine categories, making them exhaustive and discrete, has been suggested as a necessary part of this type of data collection.

An example of a rating scale can be seen in Figure 3.1. It is taken from a questionnaire which was devised to gather the views of students attending a modular higher degree programme in order to see which times of day they would prefer to attend modules and their choice of modules on offer.

Because the questionnaire is going to a large sample of students (say 300) a series of fixed, closed questions has been devised with instructions given to the students on how to complete the questionnaire. Notice also that there is a right hand column into which has been put a series of numbers (2 to 9). These numbers are the coding of the questionnaire items for computer analysis purposes, one number for each variable. Each number in the right hand column indicates the column number for that piece of data to be entered on a data file which will be opened on a mainframe computer in order to process the data using the computer package SPSS (the Statistical Package for the Social Sciences). Data from the questionnaire will be entered in the appropriate column for each respondent. Hence if I were to receive all 300 questionnaires returned and completed, then there would be 300 cases in the data file.

I would then write a short command so that the data from all 300 respondents could be analysed, commanding the computer, for example, to draw a bar chart of all the responses to question one. If an evaluator is going to process large quantities of numerical data using computing facilities, then it is essential that the correct coding system is built into the questionnaire before it is circulated to respondents. The novice evaluator will have to seek advice on the numbering of the right hand column for easy data entry into the computer, a simple technique which can be learned in a matter of minutes.

WHAT IS AN OPEN-ENDED QUESTIONNAIRE?

Rating scales have been shown to be more sensitive instruments than dichotomous scales, nevertheless these two types of question are inextricably rooted in the agenda of the evaluator, with a certain fixity of response caused by the need to select from a given choice. A questionnaire might be tailored even more to respondents by having the evaluator ask genuinely *open-ended* questions to which respondents can reply in their own terms and own opinions. This is a very attractive device for smaller scale evaluations or for those sections of a questionnaire which invite an honest, personal comment from the respondent in addition to ticking numbers and boxes. It is in the open-ended responses that the jewels of an evaluation might lie. This puts the responsibility for the data much more firmly into the respondents' hands. It also carries the problem that open-ended data can be tricky to handle.

For example, if one tries to convert opinions into numbers (e.g. so many people indicated some degree of satisfaction with the new deputy head's management plan), then one charge can be levelled that the evaluator should have opted for rating scales in the first place. A second charge could be that the evaluator is violating the principles of word data which suggest that they are not validly susceptible to aggregation, i.e. that it is trying to bring to word data the principles of numerical data, borrowing from one paradigm (quantitative methodology) to inform another paradigm (qualitative methodology). Furthermore, if a genuinely open-ended question is being asked, it is perhaps unlikely that responses will bear such a degree of similarity to each other to enable them to be aggregated too tightly. Open-ended questions make it difficult for the evaluator to make comparisons between respondents, as there may be little in common to compare. Moreover, to complete an open-ended questionnaire takes much longer than placing a tick in a rating scale; not only will time be a constraint here but there is an assumption that respondents will be sufficiently or equally capable of articulating their thoughts and committing them to paper.

Despite these cautions the space provided for an open-ended response is a window of opportunity for the respondent to shed light on an issue or course. Thus an open-ended questionnaire has much to recommend it.

HOW CAN I CONSTRUCT A QUESTIONNAIRE?

Taking the issues discussed so far in questionnaire design we can address fifteen principles for designing a questionnaire:

(1) Decide on the most appropriate *type* of question - dichotomous, multiple-choice, rating scales, closed, open.
(2) Ensure that every issue has been explored thoroughly - exhaustively and comprehensively - decide on the content and explore it in depth and breadth.
(3) Ask, for ease of analysis (particularly of a large sample), more closed than open questions.
(4) Balance comprehensiveness and exhaustive coverage of issues with the demotivating factor of having respondents complete several pages of a questionnaire.
(5) Ask only one thing at a time in a question.

(6) Strive to be unambiguous and clear in the wording.

(7) Be simple and brief wherever possible.

(8) Ensure a balance of questions which ask for facts and opinions, (this is especially true if statistical correlations and cross-tabulations (*see* chapter five) are required).

(9) Avoid leading questions.

(10) Put sensitive questions later in the questionnaire in order to avoid creating a mental set in the mind of the respondents.

(11) Be very clear on the layout of the questionnaire so that it is clear and attractive (this is especially true if statistics are to be derived using computing facilities).

(12) Ensure that the respondent knows how to enter a response to each question - e.g. by underlining, circling, ticking, writing; provide the instructions for introducing, completing and returning the questionnaire (provide a stamped, addressed envelope if it is to be a postal questionnaire.

(13) Pilot the questionnaire - on a group of respondents who will not receive the finished, refined version.

(14) Decide how to avoid falsification of responses (e.g. introduce a checking mechanism into the questionnaire responses to another question on the same topic).

(15) Be grateful if you receive a 50% response to the questionnaire; decide what you will do with missing data and what is the significance of the missing data.

A covering explanation, giving thanks for anticipated co-operation, should be enclosed with the questionnaire. It should indicate the purpose of the enterprise, how anonymity and confidentiality will be addressed, who you are and what position you hold, who will be party to the final report.

HOW CAN I DESIGN THE GATHERING OF OBSERVATIONAL DATA?

Observational data are very attractive as they afford the evaluator the chance to gather 'live' data from 'live' situations. The evaluator is given the opportunity to look at what is taking place *in situ* rather than at second hand. It has all the attractions of face-to-face interviews in that it concerns *people*, their behaviour, feelings and interactions; it concerns dynamic situations and a richer tapestry of circumstances than that usually tapped by questionnaires. Because observed incidents are less predictable there is a certain freshness to this form of data gathering that is often denied in a questionnaire or test. Just as the nature of interviews and questionnaires can be plotted on a continuum from structured to unstructured, pre-ordinate to responsive, so the setting up of observational data gathering can be said to lie on the same continuum.

WHAT KINDS OF OBSERVATIONS CAN I USE?

A *highly structured* observation will know in advance what it is looking for (i.e. pre-ordinate observation) and will have its observation categories worked out in advance. A *semi-structured* observation will have an agenda of issues but will gather data to illuminate these issues in a far less determined or systematic manner. An *unstructured* observation will be far less clear on what it is looking for and will therefore have to go into a situation and observe what is taking place before deciding on its significance for an evaluation. In a nutshell, a structured observation will already have its hypotheses decided and will use the observational data to confirm or refute these hypotheses. On the other hand a semi-structured and, more particularly, an unstructured observation, will be hypothesis-generating rather than hypothesis-testing. The semi-structured and un-structured observations will review observational data before suggesting an hypothesis to explain what is taking place. Observations will enable the evaluator to gather data on:

(1) the *physical setting* of schools and classrooms (e.g. layout of the school and classrooms, resource organization, groupings of children and teachers);
(2) the *human setting* of schools and classrooms (e.g. gender, racial, ability factors);
(3) the *interactional setting* of schools and classrooms (e.g. the interactions - formal, unplanned and non-verbal - of children, teachers, support services, headteachers);
(4) the *programme setting* of schools and classrooms (e.g. resources available, teaching and learning styles and their uses, curriculum content and organization).

If we know in advance what we wish to observe - i.e. if the observation is concerned to chart *incidence, presence* and *frequency* of elements of the four settings outlined above and maybe wishes to compare one situation with another, then it may be more efficient in terms of time to go into a situation with an already designed observation schedule. If, on the other hand, we want to go into a situation and *let the elements of the situation speak for themselves*, perhaps with no concern with how one situation compares with another, then it may be more appropriate to opt for an unstructured observation.

The former, structured approach, takes much time to prepare but the data analysis is fairly rapid - the categories of the observation having already been established - whilst the latter, unstructured approach is necessarily quick to prepare but the data take much longer to analyse. The former approach operates within the agenda of the evaluator and hence tends to neglect aspects of the four settings outlined *above* if they do not appear on the observation schedule, i.e. it looks selectively at situations. On the other hand, the latter operates within the agenda of the participants, i.e. it is responsive to what it finds and therefore by definition is honest to the situation which it finds. Selectivity derives from the *situation* rather than from the *evaluator* in the sense that key issues emerge from, follow from the observation rather than the evaluator knowing in advance what those key issues will be.

The first decision for an evaluator who wishes to use observational data is whether it is more fitting for an observation to be structured or unstructured.

HOW WILL I SET UP A STRUCTURED OBSERVATION?

A structured observation is very systematic and enables the evaluator to generate numerical data from the observation. Numerical data facilitate the making of comparisons between settings and situations and frequencies, patterns and trends to be noted or calculated. The observer-as-evaluator adopts a passive, non-intrusive role, merely noting down the incidence of the factors which are under observation - the factors of one or more of the four settings shown *opposite*. Observations are entered onto an observational schedule. An example of this appears in Figure 3.2. This is taken from a schedule which was used to observe student and teacher conversations over a fifteen minute period. The upper seven categories indicate who is speaking to whom, whilst the lower four categories indicate the nature of the talk. Looking at the example of the observation schedule several points must be made:

(1) The categories for the observation are discrete - i.e. there is no overlap between any of the categories. For this to be the case it is necessary to pilot the schedule in order to iron out any problems of overlapping of cells.
(2) Each column represents a thirty second time interval, the evaluator has to enter data in the appropriate cell of the matrix every thirty seconds (instantaneous sampling - *see below*).
(3) Because there are so many categories which have to be scanned

every thirty seconds the evaluator will need to practise completing the schedule until he or she becomes proficient and consistent in the entering of data (i.e. that the observed behaviours, settings etc. are consistently entered into the same categories). This can be done either through practising with video material or through practising in a 'real' classroom with students who eventually will not be part of the actual observation. If there is to be a team of evaluators using the observation schedule (e.g. a group of teachers evaluating the events in classrooms) then it is necessary to provide training sessions so that the team proficiently and consistently enters data in the same categories, i.e. that there is a high degree of reliability in entering the data.

(4) The evaluator will have to decide what entry is to be made in the appropriate category, will it be a (✓), a mark (|), a forward slash (/), a backward slash (\), a figure (1, 2, 3, etc.), a circle (o)? Whatever set of codes is used, it must be understood by all the evaluators (if there is a team) and must be simple to use. Bearing in mind that every thirty seconds one or more entries must be made in each column, the evaluator will need to become proficient in fast data entry of the appropriate codes. It might well be the case (as in the example of Figure 3.2) that more than one entry is made in each column.

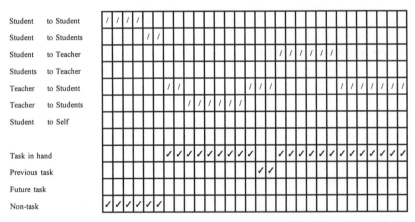

/ = participants in the conversation
✓ = nature of the conversation

Figure 3.2 A Structured Observation Schedule

The need to *pilot* a structured observation schedule, as in the example given, cannot be over-emphasized. Categories must be mutually exclusive and they must be able to yield the data which the evaluator seeks in order to be able to answer the evaluation questions. The categories must capture all aspects of the settings which are being evaluated - to neglect this is to risk bias in the evaluation, as selectivity threatens validity. The evaluator will need to decide:

(a) the foci of the schedule (e.g. a group of students, the teacher and the whole class, the teacher with two groups of children);

(b) the frequency of the observations (e.g. whether it is appropriate to enter data every thirty seconds, every ten seconds, every minute);

(c) the length of the observation period (e.g. thirty minutes, one hour, a morning, etc.);

(d) the nature of the entry (the coding system to be used).

Hence, structured observation will take much time in preparation but the evaluator will be able to analyse the data rapidly, as the categories for analysis will have to be built into the observation schedule itself. With respect to (a) the decision on foci is not arbitrary but is governed by the criterion of appropriacy to yield data which will answer evaluation questions. This is a matter of sampling (i.e. choosing the appropriate person or people to study) and of context (e.g. the history lesson, the mathematics session, the staff meeting, the school break).

With respect to (b), again the decision of how frequently to enter is governed by the criterion of appropriacy - if the evaluation questions demand very close and detailed study, then very short time intervals may be needed (e.g. in observing non-verbal behaviour); if less detail is required, then a longer time interval may be appropriate. The observation may need to be able to capture not only the *incidence* of a particular event, but also its *duration* (Adams, 1970).

With respect to (c) not only will the observation period need to be governed by the criterion of appropriacy, but the events/lessons/settings (the four settings as described *above*)/physical and temporal contexts will need to be appropriate to yield evaluation data. Is it appropriate to study the group of children in the history session, or playing together in the home corner, or working collaboratively in the physics session? Will a half hour's observation period be adequate or will it be necessary to have a full day's observation?

HOW CAN I ENTER DATA ON A STRUCTURED OBSERVATION?

With respect to (d) there are several ways in which entering data can be done. Three principal methods are: event sampling, instantaneous sampling, and interval recording.

Event Sampling

Sometimes known as a sign system this method requires a tally mark to be entered against each statement *each time* it is observed, for example:

teacher shouts at the child	/ / / / /
child shouts at the teacher	/ / /
parent shouts at the teacher	/ /
teacher shouts at the parent	/ /

The evaluator will have to devise the statements which will be necessary to yield data to answer the evaluation questions and then the entries can be made against the behaviours observed. This method is useful for finding out the frequencies or incidence of observed situations and statements so that comparisons can be made; we can tell that the teacher does the most shouting and that the parent shouts the least of all. That might be useful to know. However, whilst these data enable us to chart the incidence of observed situations, the problem with these data is that we are unable to determine the *chronological order* in which the statements were observed. It might be important to know the sequence of behaviour. For example, two different stories could be told from these data if the sequence of events were known. If the data were presented in a chronology, one story could be seen as follows, where the numbers 1 - 7 are the different periods over time (e.g. every thirty seconds):

	1 2 3 4 5 6 7
teacher shouts at the child	/ / / / /
child shouts at the teacher	/ / /
parent shouts at the teacher	/ /
teacher shouts at the parent	/ /

Imagine the scene: a parent and his child arrive late for school one morning and the child slips into the classroom; an event quickly occurs which prompts the child to shout at the teacher, the exasperated teacher is very cross when thus provoked by the child; the teacher shouts at the child who then brings in the parent (who has not yet left the premises), the parent shouts at the teacher for unreasonable behaviour and the teacher shouts back at the child. It seems in this version that the teacher only shouts when provoked by the child or parent.

If the same number and distribution of tally marks occurred in a different order, a very different story might emerge, thus:

	1	2	3	4	5	6	7
teacher shouts at the child	/	/	/	/		/	
child shouts at the teacher					/	/	/
parent shouts at the teacher						/	/
teacher shouts at the parent				/	/		

In this scene it is the teacher who is the instigator of the shouting, shouting at the child and then at the parent; the child and the parent only shout back when they have been provoked!

Instantaneous Sampling

If the evaluator needs to chart the chronology or sequence of events, then it might be more helpful to use instantaneous sampling, sometimes called time sampling. Here the evaluator enters what she observes at standard intervals of time, for example, every ten seconds, or every thirty seconds, or every minute etc. On the stroke of that interval she notes what is happening *at that precise moment* and enters it into the appropriate category. For example, imagine that the sampling will take place every thirty seconds; numbers 1 - 7 represent each 30 second interval thus:

	1	2	3	4	5	6	7
teacher smiles at the child	/	/	/	/			
child smiles at the teacher			/	/	/	/	
teacher smiles at the parent	/	/	/	/			
parent smiles at the teacher			/	/	/	/	

In this scene the evaluator notes down what is happening on the 30 second point and notices from these precise moments that the teacher initiates the smiling but that all parties seem to be doing quite a lot of smiling, with the parent and the child doing the same amount of smiling each! Instantaneous sampling involves recording what is happening *on the instant* and entering it on the appropriate category. Chronology of events is preserved.

Interval Recording

This method charts the chronology of events to some extent and, like instantaneous sampling, requires the data to be entered in the appropriate category at fixed intervals. However, instead of charting what is happening *on the instant*, it charts *what has happened* during the preceding interval. So, for example, if recording were to take place every thirty seconds, then the evaluator would note down in the appropriate category what *had* happened *during* the preceding thirty seconds. Whilst this enables frequencies to be calculated, simple patterns to be observed and an approximate sequence of events to be noted, because it charts what has taken place in the preceding interval of time some elements of the chronology might be lost. For example, if three events took place in the preceding thirty seconds of the example, then the order of the three events would be lost; we would know simply that they had occurred.

WHAT ISSUES ARE THERE IN USING STRUCTURED OBSERVATION?

Whilst structured observation can provide very useful numerical data for the evaluator (e.g. Bennett *et al*, 1984; Galton *et al*, 1980), there are several concerns which must be addressed in this form of observation. For example, the method is behaviourist, excluding any mention of the intentions or motivations of the people being observed; the individual's subjectivity is lost to an aggregated score; there is an assumption that the observed behaviour provides evidence of underlying feelings - i.e. that concepts can be crudely measured in observed occurrences. This latter point is of serious concern, for it strikes at the very heart of the notion of validity since it requires evaluators to satisfy themselves that it is valid to say that a particular behaviour indicates a particular state of mind or particular intention or motivation. The thirst to 'operationalize' concepts can too easily lead evaluators to provide simple indicators of complex concepts.

Further, structured observation neglects the significance of contexts - temporal and spatial - thereby overlooking the fact that behaviours may be context-specific. In their concern for the overt and the observable, evaluators may overlook unintended outcomes which may have significance; they are not able to show how significant are the behaviours of the participants being observed *in their own terms*. If we accept that behaviour is developmental, that interactions evolve over time and therefore are by definition fluid, then the three methods of structured observation outlined *above* appear to take a series of 'freeze-frame' snapshots of behaviour, thereby violating the principle of fluidity of action. Captured for an instant in time it is dangerous to infer a particular meaning to one or more events (Stubbs and Delmont, 1976) just as it is impossible to say with any certainty what is taking place when we study a single or a set of photographs of a particular event. Put simply, if structured observation is to hold water, then the evaluator may need to gather additional evidence from other sources to inform the interpretation of observational data.

WHAT ARE SEMI-STRUCTURED AND UNSTRUCTURED OBSERVATIONS?

An evaluator may wish to present a case study which fully portrays a unique situation rather than that which presents comparisons, frequencies and distributions of incidence over a given set of categories. In the former it may be more appropriate to opt for unstructured or semi-structured observation. Let us clarify the difference. In the discussions earlier of structured, semi-structured and unstructured interviews, the differences between them were seen to lie in two fields - the openness of the questions and the control of the agenda. A semi-structured interview asked open-ended questions with the interviewer having a clear agenda translated into a schedule of points to be covered (in any order, as the interview progressed) and questions which might be raised. An unstructured interview, on the other hand, worked to a negotiated agenda or even to an agenda dictated by the respondents, thereby avoiding the compulsion to work to a set of open-ended questions.

Similar points can be observed between semi-structured and unstructured observations. A semi-structured observation will know the kinds or sorts of issues and data which it seeks but will have a very open approach to the collection of such data and compilation of field notes, hence it may take a long period of time to gather important data as the evaluator would not wish to force any data by requiring certain behaviours to be demonstrated. What characterizes semi-structured but, more particularly, unstructured observation is the need for the evaluator to be responsive to the situation observed. We should avoid deciding in advance exactly what we should be observing, rather we should let the significance of the events under observation speak for themselves.

These two forms of observation are very powerful ways of generating rich, complex, valuable and close-grained data on specific situations, settings, students etc. Like semi-structured interviews and open-ended questionnaires they are a useful blend of focus and responsiveness and flexibility within a loosely defined framework. The evaluator will find these types of observations to be an ideal vehicle for capturing the vividness and significance of the singular incident, the one instance of a behaviour, the evolution of a relationship.

HOW DO UNSTRUCTURED OBSERVATIONS WORK?

Typically responsive, open-ended observations (both visual and aural) require the observer to go into a situation for some considerable time in order to absorb the particular context, dynamics, personalities, teaching situations, resource management, organization and organizational health. By being immersed in a particular context over time not only will the salient features of the situation emerge and present themselves but a more holistic view will be gathered of the interrelationships of factors. It is only when one has become fully aware of the specific and unique context that it is possible to hypothesize about or explain what is occurring. Further, it may not even turn out to be appropriate to operate in this *hypothetico-deductive* paradigm - a paradigm borrowed from the natural sciences. Rather, it might be all that the evaluator needs to do is to provide 'thick descriptions' of particular situations and to suggest reasons, causes or explanations for the situations, in the knowledge that they are not generalizable because they do not abide by the strict rules of verification, confirmation, refutation or falsification which characterize the natural sciences (and their paradigm of hypothesis generation and testing). In an unstructured observation one can only *induce* meaning after gathering the full flavour of a particular situation. That is both its glory and its frustration!

As the intention in this style of evaluation is to portray the insiders' points of view, often an evaluator will adopt the role of a participant observer, negotiating a role in the institution and carrying out tasks additional to the collection of data. For example, in a school a participant observer might undertake some supervision, join in with school activities and help to run certain events. In this way the evaluator is seen not only to have an identity in the institution but comes to be accepted in the institution.

WHAT ISSUES ARE THERE IN USING UNSTRUCTURED OBSERVATIONS?

In some observational data gathering exercises the very presence of the observer can cause participants to behave differently from normal, differently from how they would naturally behave if the observer were not there. For example, if I were in a class of students, some of them might show off, others might deliberately misbehave to test out the observer or the teacher, others might work much harder than usual - believing the presence of the observer to be somehow important. Simply by coming into a classroom an observer has an effect on the classroom processes, even if that observer sits on the sidelines and does nothing. This is known as the Hawthorne effect or *reactivity*. To try to minimize the Hawthorne effect the observer stays in the situation for some considerable time so that all participants become used to his or her presence and their behaviour slips back to normality.

Not only does this presuppose that evaluators have a considerable amount of time (weeks and months) to stay in a situation but it poses a moral problem for them. Do they declare their reasons and motives for the observation - i.e. become an overt evaluator - or might richer data be yielded if the evaluators either were deliberately silent on their motives or deliberately put participants 'off the scent' - i.e. become a covert researcher? It is impossible here to answer that question, but that does not sideline its importance; rather each evaluation which draws on qualitative observational data (semi-structured and unstructured observations) will require the evaluator to have resolved the moral dilemma that this poses for the particular situation being evaluated. This will be more of a problem for *outsider* rather than *insider* evaluators. Indeed the insider evaluator - let us say a teacher - has perhaps the greatest opportunity of all to use un-structured observations as he or she is with groups of students usually for several months. This would be the envy of outsider evaluators. It offers the teacher-as-evaluator an almost unrivalled source of rich, sensitive, evolutionary and subtle data. There is a huge seam of classroom life which is susceptible to the critical insights which are generated only by those participants who are able to stay in a situation for months at a time. Teachers are in a unique position to tap the insides of situations, persons or curricula which only reveal themselves over time, over a range of contexts and over a range of personalities.

HOW CAN I HANDLE DATA FROM AN UNSTRUCTURED OBSERVATION?

In an unstructured and semi-structured style of observation the evaluator will very quickly amass vast quantities of observational data in the form of diaries, documents, field notes, journals - all sorts of accounts of what was taking place in a particular situation and participants' interpretations and opinions on it and attitudes to it (either written up at the time the events occurred or soon after the event so as not to fall prey to a selective memory!) Behaviour is context-specific and it is the task of the evaluator in this mould to capture that context very fully in order to give meaning to data, events and perspectives.

To try to 'manage' the problem of data overload, the evaluator is involved in progressive focussing, discussed in chapter two. Here the evaluator reads through all the forms of the assembled notes, reads them again, reads them yet again, and goes on re-reading them until a clear picture of salient features emerges. These features may then be checked with the participants (in overt research) to see if they agree that the evaluator's interpretation is correct (a process known as respondent validation). In this situation, of course, the reactivity effect might rear its head, as the evaluator might be sowing seeds about a whole range of matters in the minds of participants which might not otherwise have been there.

If the data and their interpretation are agreed or if an agreement to differ on interpretation is reached, then the evaluator may discard some less important data and take only the key issues which have been identified and use them to set the agenda for further observations. Hence data will be gathered which relate to the emergent key issues. Having enquired further about these issues and thereby gathered more data about them, the evaluator takes the first tentative steps in seeking to *explain* what is happening in the situation and why it is unfolding in the way that it has been observed. This form of analysis is both 'strong in reality' - being grounded in the *in situ* observations of a particular situation or set of situations - and faithful to those situations by working on emerging explanations rather than on pre-ordinate hypotheses.

These three stages - observation, further enquiry and explanation - are the processes which at a stroke minimize the problem of data overload and enable key factors of a situation to be identified. The evaluator will then use these key factors and supplementary data to answer the evaluation questions.

WHAT IS TRIANGULATION?

To try to avoid the charges frequently levelled at this type of evaluation data (e.g. that they are impressionistic, subjective and therefore biased, non-generalizable, unable to be verified in the way that a science should be, lacking precision and being 'soft' data rather than the 'hard' data of numbers), evaluators in this field have striven to give validity to their work. The question of validity is treated in more detail in chapter six. Here it is perhaps useful to introduce the concept of triangulation. Recognizing that behaviours are specific to spatial, temporal and interpersonal contexts the evaluator has to ensure that this diversity of contexts is fully addressed in the data gathering process. Hence not only will observations be made over time and in different spatial and interpersonal contexts but to do justice to this will require a multi-method approach to data gathering, including all written forms, interviews and conversations, maybe even test scores. The important factor here is to gather data from as many sources and from as many perspectives as possible.

Further, in order to build out the problem of the subjectivity of the evaluator, it may be necessary - or even desirable - to have more than one evaluator involved, working either independently of the first evaluator so that any contamination or collusion is avoided or together to gain a shared perspective. Hence triangulation of contexts (spatial, temporal and interpersonal), sources (people), perceptions, methods and evaluators can singly and severally add to the credence which can be put in the evaluation data.

It must be added that whilst triangulation and a long stay in an institution might be desirable, this may be a luxury for evaluators who are working within severe time constraints or who do not have easy access to the institution. In this case a semi-structured observation might be practicable - where an agenda of items to be observed has already been drawn up by the evaluator. Alternatively, the evaluator may have to drop plans to undertake a long-term evaluation and opt for a series of short-term data gathering instruments. The message of the first chapter - that evaluation is a series of compromises and trade-offs - is rehearsed here whenever such decisions have to be taken.

WHAT TECHNOLOGY CAN I USE IN GATHERING OBSERVATIONAL DATA?

One cannot leave the question of observation without a footnote about the use of video technology, audio recording and photographic evidence. There is no doubt that these have their part to play in acquiring evaluation data. Photographic evidence has long been used for storing the memory of children's work - indeed in the United Kingdom, with the escalation of necessary documentary evidence of children's work, this medium has taken on a new lease of life, particularly to record the work of children whose English language is undeveloped or who are experiencing difficulty in writing.

Many interviews are recorded for future playback analysis; a flat microphone placed on a child's desk will pick up the conversations of a group of children in its immediate vicinity. The use of a video camera in schools is becoming more of an everyday occurrence so its general use to acquire observational data might have freed itself from the surrogate Hawthorne effect - the 'eye in the classroom'. However, photographs, video cameras and audio cassettes have a highly selective memory - photographs will only record the recordable; video cameras have a limited focus (the focus often being unconsciously determined by the camera operator); audio cassettes cannot pick up non-verbal communication and the transcription of material on an audio cassette loses valuable signals of tone of voice and the significance of different kinds of silence is lost. Hence unless these have been deliberately set up to catch evaluation data, it may be difficult to regard them as useful in providing evidence other than secondary back-up data for the evaluator.

HOW CAN I USE DOCUMENTARY EVIDENCE IN AN EVALUATION?

In the United Kingdom nurseries, infant schools, primary schools, middle schools, secondary schools, colleges, universities, sixth form centres all are straining under the weight of having to document nearly every aspect of their work as never before - the students, the management, the examinations, the assessments, the action planning, the school development planning, the curriculum development planning. Whilst this bears witness to the rampant and unchecked 'bureaucratization' of education, by a perverse stroke of fortune it provides rich pickings for the evaluator who looks to documentary evidence to use as evaluation data.

It is now possible for the evaluator to compute a vast range of parametric and non-parametric statistics (discussed later in this chapter and in chapter five) from data acquired from formal, legally required and documented assessments and examinations. Furthermore, it is now also possible for the evaluator to turn to a plethora of documentation issuing from government departments, local education authorities, advisory councils, curriculum development agencies, the educational institutions themselves, all of which can be found within the educational institutions and all of which can be used to set a full *context* of an institution for the evaluator.

Not only is there this vast store of formal documentation but educationists keep informal and internal documents - planning forecasts, records, reports, minutes of meetings, notes and diaries, logs and journals which supplement the commercially produced and disseminated documents which are finding their way into educational institutions.

In addition to keeping their own field notes for evaluation data, evaluators very often need go no further than the institution itself to find sufficient documentary data to enable them to understand the context of a particular institution or set of practices within it. People keep reports and records; during an evaluation they might be asked to keep a diary which records particular experiences, critical incidents, specific reflections, particular observations, personal feelings, descriptions of events or people, retrospective comments or plans for the future. Formal and informal documents, documents which would be kept in the institution even without the request of the evaluator and documents which are specifically kept for the evaluation, can be rich in data - 'strong on reality'.

The rise of documentation can be seen as the evaluator's dream as documents are often to hand and plentiful; this is a largely untapped field which is ripe for sampling.

WHAT ISSUES ARE THERE IN USING DOCUMENTARY MATERIAL?

The evaluator has to overcome several hurdles if documentary data are to be used in an evaluation:

(1) The ethics of using the data have to be addressed - permissions need to be sought to use the data and control of the data and their release need to be agreed.

(2) The evaluator must be aware that information in different forms probably will have been gathered for purposes other than an evaluation, i.e. documents may be selective in their inclusion of details or coverage of topics; what they are representing and how representative or selective they are need to be clarified.

(3) Verification and permissions may be difficult to obtain if the person or persons have left the institution.

(4) The process of sifting through a collection of documents which were not originally intended to be used for evaluation purposes might be time-consuming and laborious.

(5) The evaluator will need to know whether sources are primary or secondary sources - primary sources are the initial records of events, secondary sources are an interpretation of those events. Both primary and secondary sources are prone to the subjective selection of the writers. In the case of primary sources this might be less of a problem as the data can be verified by others, whereas the whole point about a secondary source is that it is an *interpretation*, perhaps a *selective interpretation* rather than a full and rounded verbatim report.

(6) The evaluator may need to know *why* a document was produced (in terms of causes and purposes), *what kind* of document it is (e.g. a position paper, a policy document, a mission statement, a proposal, a record of a meeting, an internal memorandum, a formal evaluation), *who owns* the document, what was the *intended circulation* of the document, *who issued* the document, (cf Bell, 1987), whether it is one of a series or a single issue.

(7) To ask a participant in an evaluation to keep a diary, log or journal might well be to introduce the Hawthorne effect into the evaluation, the keeping of a diary might alter the behaviour of the participant.

(8) If diaries, logs and journals are to be kept expressly for the recording of evaluation data by participants - *evaluands* - then directions for the completion of these diaries must be provided - to cover:

(a) the contents of the diary and the proposed length and coverage of each entry;

(b) its frequency of entry (for example, whether it will be a daily diary of events and reflections or a record of significant or critical events);

(c) its format and method of entry;

(d) required comment on the representativeness of the data (and what the criteria for that representativeness are - e.g. what is being represented);

(e) the obligatory or voluntary nature of the keeping of the diary.

The task of analysing documentary evidence is difficult as the evaluator not only needs to be aware of the context in which the documents were produced (it may be unsuitable for being taken out of one context and put into another context of evaluation) but to be aware that any particular document may only be telling part of the story of the event, experiences, reflections, etc. that it mentions. This holds true even if the evaluator goes to the documents with an agenda of issues upon which he or she wishes to find comments, for that agenda may only be partially or selectively addressed in the documents. The evaluator may wish to look at the frequency with which particular issues are mentioned or patterning of comments across different documents or respondents, or groups of issues, or silences on some issues in some key documents, or similarities and differences between respondents, or emerging themes and issues (Cohen and Manion, 1985), the life - duration - of a particular issue in an institution.

To use documentary evidence as anything other than a secondary, backup source, the evaluator would be advised only to use that documentary evidence which had been expressly kept for evaluation purposes or to use documentary evidence which had been verified not only as accurate but as representative of the situation, events etc. that it records. To do otherwise is to risk introducing bias into the evaluation through the selective use of data.

HOW CAN I USE NOMINAL GROUP TECHNIQUES AND DELPHI TECHNIQUES IN AN EVALUATION?

These two techniques for gathering evaluation data are an admixture of written and live, interpersonal forms of data collection. They are particularly useful for gathering information in a single instance (e.g. a staff meeting) from a group of respondents (e.g. a school staff, a cluster of teachers from the same department in several schools, a group of teachers on an in-service programme). Their administration is straight-forward, although the Delphi technique involves the evaluator in a lot of rapid work, gathering written data and presenting it back to the group. Though they are used principally with adults, it is possible also to use the techniques with students.

What is the Nominal Group Technique?

In this approach the evaluator provides the group with a series of questions and statements which will serve the evaluation questions. The process of data collection here can be put into four stages:

Stage 1: A short time is provided for individuals to write down without interruption or discussion with anybody else their own answers, views, reflections and opinions in response to questions or statements provided by the evaluator.

Stage 2: Their responses are entered onto a sheet of paper or a series of cards which are then displayed for others to view. The evaluator invites *individual* comments on the displayed responses to the questions and statements, but no group discussion, i.e. the data collection is still at an individual level, and then notes these comments on the display board on which the responses have been collected. The process of inviting individual comments which are then displayed for everyone to see is repeated until no more comments are received.

Stage 3: At this point the evaluator asks the respondents to identify *clusters* of displayed comments and responses, i.e. to put some structure, order and priority into the displayed items. It is here that control of proceedings moves from the evaluator to the participants. A group discussion takes place since a process of clarification of meanings and organizing issues and responses into coherent and cohesive bundles is required which then moves to the identification of priorities.

Stage 4: Finally the evaluator invites any further group discussion about the material and its organization.

A variant of this technique can be seen in the snowball technique. Here, instead of the individual responses being fed into the whole group discussion directly, the individual responses are shared initially with a single other, and a paired response is prepared; then this paired response is shared with another pair and the responses ordered by this new group of four. This process is repeated until the whole group has come together. At every stage the process involves discussion, clarification, agreement (or an agreement to disagree) and the identification of a set of issues or responses, i.e. there is a clearly identifiable outcome to the sequence of activities and discussions.

The process of the nominal group technique and its partner snowball technique enables individual responses to be included within a group response, i.e. the individual's contribution to the group delineation of significant issues is maintained. This technique is very helpful for an evaluator who wishes to gather data from individuals and to put them into some order which is shared by the group, e.g. of priority, of similarity and difference, of generality and specificity. It also allows individual disagreements to be registered and to be built into the group responses and identification of significant issues. Further, it gives equal status to all respondents in the situation, for example, the voice of the new entrant to the teaching profession is given equal consideration to the voice of the headteacher of several years' experience. The attraction of this process is that it balances writing with discussion, a divergent phase with a convergent phase, space for individual comments and contributions and group interaction. It is also a useful devise for developing collegiality in a school.

What is the Delphi Technique?

This is very similar to the nominal group technique, but its advantage is that it does not *require* participants to meet together as a whole group. This is particularly useful in institutions where time is precious and where it is very difficult to arrange a whole staff meeting. The process of data collection resembles that of the nominal group technique in many respects; it can be set out in a three stage process:

> **Stage 1:** The evaluator asks participants to respond to a series of questions and statements in writing. This may be done on an individual basis or on a small group basis - which enables it to be used flexibly, e.g. within a department, within an age phase.

> **Stage 2:** The evaluator collects the written responses and collates them into clusters of issues and responses (maybe providing some numerical data on frequency of response). This analysis is then passed back to the respondents for comment, further discussion and identification of issues, responses and priorities. At this stage the respondents are presented with a *group response* (which may reflect similarities or record differences) and the respondents are asked to

react to this *group response*. By adopting this procedure the individual has the opportunity to agree with the group response (i.e. to move from a possibly small private individual disagreement to a general group agreement) or to indicate a more substantial disagreement with the group response.

Stage 3: This process is repeated as many times as it is necessary. In saying this, however, the evaluator will need to identify the most appropriate place to stop the re-circulation of responses. This might be done at a group or staff meeting which, it is envisaged, will be the plenary session for the participants, i.e. an endpoint of data collection will be in a whole staff forum. There is a danger that, unless the evaluator is prepared to call a halt to the circulation of responses, the process will be repeated endlessly!

The attractions of this approach are similar to those of the nominal group technique. However, additionally, the Delphi technique need not take place at a single instance with everybody present. Further, by presenting the group response back to the respondents, there is a general progression in this technique towards a polarizing of responses, i.e. a clear identification of areas of consensus and areas of dissensus, echoing, perhaps the lines of Yeats (1962) in his poem *News for the Delphic Oracle*:

Down the mountain walls
From where Pan's cavern is
Intolerable music falls.

The Delphi technique brings advantages of clarity, privacy, voice and collegiality. In doing so it also engages the issues of confidentiality, anonymity and the disclosure of relevant information whilst protecting participants' rights to privacy (discussed in chapter eight). It is a very useful means of undertaking the behind-the-scenes data collection process which can then be brought to a whole group meeting; the price that this exacts is that the evaluator has much more work to do in collecting, synthesizing, collating, summarizing, 'prioritising' and re-circulating data than in the nominal group technique.

The nominal group technique and the Delphi technique are both very valuable tools for data collection which build in the involvement of participants. Hence they are useful instruments for use with a whole school staff who are reviewing the curriculum, pedagogy, aims, resources, developments, management, etc. in their institution. They are powerful tools for self-evaluation as well as for other types of evaluation.

HOW CAN I USE TESTS IN AN EVALUATION?

This final method of gathering data assumes that the evaluation will require numerical data rather than word data. The field of testing is massive; the comments *below* are only introductory and the reader wishing to gain further understanding of the issues will need to pursue studies of testing elsewhere. The *context* of the test scores must be clear; for example, are they parametric or non-parametric tests? Are they achievement, potential or aptitude tests? Are they to be norm-referenced or criterion-referenced? Are they commercially available for evaluators to use or will the evaluator have to develop a home-produced test? Do the test scores derive from a pre-test and post-test in the experimental method? Are they group or individual tests? Let us unpack some of these issues.

WILL THE TESTS BE PARAMETRIC OR NON-PARAMETRIC?

Parametric tests are designed to represent the wide population - e.g. of a country or age group. They make assumptions about the wider population and the characteristics of that wider population, i.e. the parameters of abilities are known. They assume:

(a) that there is a normal curve of distribution of scores in the population (the bell-shaped symmetry of the Gaussian curve of distribution seen, for example, in standardized scores of IQ or the measurement of people's height or the distribution of achievement on reading tests in the population as a whole),

(b) that there are continuous and equal intervals between the test scores (so that, for example, a score of 80% could be said to be double that of 40%; this differs from the ordinal scaling (*see* pp. 134-6) of rating scales discussed earlier in connection with questionnaire design where equal intervals between each score could not be assumed.

Parametric tests will usually be published standardized tests which are commercially available and which have been piloted on a large and representative sample of the whole population. They usually arrive complete with the backup data on sampling, reliability and validity statistics which have been computed in the devising of the tests. Working with these tests enables the evaluator to use statistics from interval and ratio levels of data (*see* p. 142).

On the other hand, non-parametric tests make few or no assumptions about the distribution of the population (the parameters of the scores) or the characteristics of that population, the tests do not assume a regular ball-shaped curve of distribution in the wider population; indeed the wider population is perhaps irrelevant as these tests are designed for a given specific population - a class in school, a chemistry group, a primary school year group. Because they make no assumptions about the wider population, the evaluator is confined to working with non-parametric statistics to be found in nominal and ordinal levels of data (*see* pp. 131 - 142).

The attraction of non-parametric statistics is their utility for small samples because they do not make any assumptions about how normal, even and regular the distributions of scores will be. Furthermore, computation of statistics for non-parametric tests is less complicated than that for parametric tests (*see* chapter five). It is perhaps safe to assume that a home-devised test (like a home-devised questionnaire) will probably be non-parametric unless it deliberately contains interval and ratio data (discussed on pages 142 - 147). Non-parametric tests are the stock-in-trade of classroom teachers - the spelling test, the mathematics test, the end-of-year examination, the mock-examination. They have the advantage of being tailored to particular institutional, departmental and individual circumstances. They offer teachers a valuable opportunity for quick, relevant and focussed feedback on student performance.

Parametric tests are more powerful than non-parametric tests because they not only derive from standardized scores but enable the evaluator to compare sub-populations with a whole population (e.g. to compare the results of one school or local authority with the whole country - e.g. in comparing students' performance in norm-referenced or criterion-referenced tests against a national average score in that same test). They enable the evaluator to use powerful statistics in data processing (e.g. means, standard deviations, t-tests, Pearson product moment correlations, factor analysis, analysis of variance), and to make *inferences* about the results. Because non-parametric tests make no assumptions about the wider population a different set of statistics is available to the evaluator (e.g. modal scores, rankings, the chi-square statistic, Spearman correlations). These can be used in very specific situations - one class of students, one year group, one style of teaching, one curriculum area - and hence are valuable to teachers.

WILL THE TESTS BE NORM- OR CRITERION-REFERENCED?

A norm-referenced test compares students' achievements relative to other students' achievements (e.g. a national test of mathematical performance or a test of intelligence which has been standardized on a large and representative sample of students between the ages of six and sixteen). A criterion-referenced test does not compare student with student but, rather, requires the student to fulfil a given set of criteria. For example, the driving test is criterion-referenced since to pass it requires the ability to meet certain test items - reversing round a corner, undertaking an emergency stop, avoiding a crash, etc. *regardless* of how many others have or have not passed the driving test. Similarly many tests of playing a musical instrument require specified performances - e.g. the ability to play a particular scale or *arpeggio*, the ability to play a Bach Fugue without hesitation or technical error. If the student meets the criteria, then he or she passes the examination.

Clearly criterion-referenced tests will have to declare their lowest boundary - a cut-off point - below which the student has been deemed to fail to meet the criteria. A compromise can be seen in those criterion-referenced tests which award different grades for different levels of performance of the same task, necessitating the clarification of different cut-off points in the examination. A common example of this can be seen in the GCSE examinations for secondary school pupils in the United Kingdom, where students can achieve a grade between A and F for a criterion-related examination.

The question of the politics in the use of data from criterion-referenced examination results arises when such data are used in a norm-referenced way to compare student with student, school with school, local authority with local authority, region with region (as has been done in the United Kingdom with the publication of 'league tables' of local authorities' successes in the achievement of their students when tested at the age of seven - a process which is envisaged to develop into the publication of achievements at several ages and school by school).

SHOULD I USE A COMMERCIALLY PRODUCED TEST OR DEVISE MY OWN TEST?

There is a battery of tests in the public domain which cover a vast range of topics and which can be used for evaluative purposes. Most schools will have used published tests at one time or another - diagnostic tests, aptitude tests (which attempt to predict a person's aptitude in a named area), achievement tests, norm-referenced tests, criterion-referenced tests, reading tests, verbal reasoning tests, non-verbal reasoning tests, tests of social adjustment, tests of intelligence, tests of critical thinking, the list is colossal.

There are several attractions to using published tests:

- They are objective;
- They have been piloted and refined;
- They have been standardized across a named population (e.g. a region of the country, the whole country, a particular age group or various age groups) so that they represent a wide population;
- They declare how reliable and valid they are (mentioned in the statistical details which are usually contained in the manual of instructions for administering the test);
- They tend to be parametric tests, hence enabling sophisticated statistics to be calculated;
- They come complete with instructions for administration;
- They are often straightforward and quick to administer and to mark;
- Guides to the interpretation of the data are usually included in the manual;
- Evaluators are spared the task of having to devise, pilot and refine their own test.

Several commercially produced tests have restricted release or availability, hence the evaluator might have to register with a particular association before being given clearance to use the test or before being given copies of the test. For example, in the United Kingdom the Psychological Corporation Ltd. not only holds the rights to a world-wide battery of tests of all kinds but requires registration with the Corporation before releasing tests. In this example the Corporation also has different levels of clearance, so that certain parties or evaluators may not be eligible to have a test released to them because they do not fulfil particular criteria for eligibility.

Published tests by definition are not tailored to institutional or local contexts or needs, indeed their claim to objectivity is made on the grounds that they are deliberately supra-institutional. The evaluator wishing to use published tests must be certain that the purposes, objectives and content of the published tests match the purposes, objectives and content of the evaluation. For example, a published diagnostic test might not fit the needs of the evaluation to have an achievement test; a test of achievement might not have the predictive quality which the evaluator seeks in an aptitude test, a published reading test might not address the areas of reading that the evaluator is wishing to cover, a verbal reading test written in English might contain language which is difficult for a student whose first language is not English. These are important considerations.

The golden rule for deciding to use a published test is that it must demonstrate *fitness for purpose*. If it fails to demonstrate this, then tests will have to be devised by the evaluator. The attraction of this latter point is that such a 'home-grown' test will be tailored to the local and institutional context very tightly, i.e. that the purposes, objectives and content of the test will be deliberately fitted to the *specific* needs of the evaluator in a specific, given context.

Against these advantages of course there are several important considerations in devising a 'home-grown' test. Not only might it be time-consuming to devise, pilot, refine and then administer the test but, because much of it will probably be non-parametric, there will be a more limited range of statistics which may be applied to the data than in the case of parametric tests.

WHAT MUST I CONSIDER IF I AM MAKING UP MY OWN TEST?

The opportunity to devise a test is exciting and challenging. In devising a test the evaluator will have to consider:

- the purposes of the test (for answering evaluation questions and ensuring that it tests what it is supposed to be testing, e.g. the achievement of the objectives of a piece of the curriculum);
- the *type* of test (e.g. diagnostic, achievement, aptitude, criterion-referenced, norm-referenced);
- the *objectives* of the test (cast in very specific terms so that the content of the test items can be seen to relate to specific objectives of a programme or curriculum);
- the *content* of the test;
- the *construction* of the test, involving *item analysis* in order to clarify the *item discriminability* and *item difficulty* of the test (*see below*);
- the *format* of the test - its layout, instructions, method of working and of completion (e.g. oral instructions to clarify what students will need to write, or a written set of instructions to introduce a practical piece of work);
- the nature of the *piloting* of the test;
- the *validity* and *reliability* of the test (these two terms are discussed fully in chapter six);
- the provision of a *manual of instructions* for the administration, marking and data treatment of the test (this is particularly important if the test is not to be administered by the evaluator or if the test will be administered by several different people - so that reliability is ensured by having a standard procedure).

In constructing a test the evaluator will need to undertake an item analysis to clarify the item discriminability and item difficulty of each item of the test. 'Item discriminability' refers to the potential of the item in question to be answered correctly by those students who have a lot of the particular quality that the item is designed to measure and to be answered incorrectly by those students who have less of the particular quality that the same item is designed to measure. In other words, how effective is the test item in showing up differences among a group of students? Does the item enable us to discriminate between students' abilities in a given field? An item with high discriminability will enable the evaluator to see a potentially wide variety of scores on that item, an item with low discriminability will see scores on that item poorly differentiated. Clearly a high measure of discriminability is desirable.

'Item difficulty', as its name suggests, refers to the level of difficulty of each item. If every student answers the question correctly, then presumably the item is too easy, just as, if every student answers the question incorrectly, then that item is too difficult.

HOW CAN I ENSURE ITEM DISCRIMINABILITY?

Suppose the evaluator wishes to construct a test of mathematics for eventual use with thirty students in a particular school (or with class A in a particular school). The evaluator devises a test and *pilots* it in a different school or class B respectively, administering the test to thirty students of the same age (i.e. she matches the sample of the pilot school or class to the sample in the school which eventually will be used). The scores of the thirty pilot children are then split into three groups of ten students each - high, medium and low scores. It would be reasonable to assume that there will be more correct answers to a particular item amongst the high scorers than amongst the low scorers. For each item compute the following:

$$\frac{A - B}{\frac{1}{2}(N)}$$

where
A = the number of *correct* scores from the high scoring group;
B = the number of *correct* scores from the low scoring group;
N = the *total* number of students in the two groups.

Suppose all ten students from the high scoring group answered the item correctly and two students from the low scoring groups answered the item correctly. The formula would work out thus:

$$\frac{8}{\frac{1}{2}(10+10)} = 0.80 \quad (\text{index of item discriminability}).$$

The maximum index of discriminability is 1.00. Any item whose index of discriminability is less than 0.67, i.e. is too undiscriminating, should be reviewed firstly to find out whether this is due to ambiguity in the wording or possible clues in the wording. If this is not the case, then whether the evaluator uses an item with an index lower than 0.67 is a matter of judgement. It would appear, then, that the item in the example would be appropriate to use in a test.

HOW DO I CALCULATE ITEM DIFFICULTY?

If we wished to calculate the *item difficulty* of a test, we could use the following formula:

$$\frac{A}{N} \times 100$$

where
A = the number of students who answered the item correctly;
N = the *total* number of students who attempted the item.

Hence if twelve students out of a class of twenty answered the item correctly, then the formula would work out thus:

$$\frac{12}{20} \times 100 = 60\%$$

The maximum index of difficulty is 100%. Items falling below 33% and above 67% are likely to be too easy and too difficult respectively. It would appear, then, that this item would be appropriate to use in a test. Here, again, whether the evaluator used an item with an index of difficulty below or above the cut-off points is a matter of judgement. In a norm-referenced test the item difficulty should be around 50% (Frisbie, 1981).

Given that the evaluator can only know the degree of item discriminability and difficulty once the test has been undertaken, there is an unavoidable need to pilot home-grown tests. Items with limited discriminability and limited difficulty must be weeded out and replaced, those items with the greatest discriminability and the most appropriate degrees of difficulty can be retained; this can only be undertaken once data from a pilot have been analysed.

WHAT DO I NEED TO CONSIDER IN DEVISING A PRE-TEST AND POST-TEST?

The construction and administration of tests is an essential part of the experimental model of evaluation, where a pre-test and a post-test have to be devised for the control and experimental groups. The pre-test and post-test must adhere to several guidelines:

(1) The pre-test may have questions which differ in form or wording from the post-test, though the two tests must test the same content, i.e. they will be alternate forms of a test for the same groups.
(2) The pre-test must be the same for the control and experimental groups.
(3) The post-test must be the same for both groups.
(4) Care must be taken in the construction of a post-test to avoid making the test easier to complete by one group than another.
(5) The level of difficulty must be the same in both tests.

Test data feature centrally in the experimental model of evaluation; additionally they may feature as part of a questionnaire, interview and documentary material. The evaluator will have to judge the place and significance of test data, not forgetting the problem of the Hawthorne effect operating negatively or positively on students who have to undertake the tests. There is a range of issues which might affect the reliability of the test - for example, the time of day, the time of the school year, the temperature in the test room, the perceived importance of the test, the degree of formality of the test situation, 'examination nerves', the amount of guessing of answers by the students (the calculation of *standard error* which the tests demonstrate feature here), the way that the test was administered, the way that the test was marked, the degree of closure or openness of test items and many more (*see* chapter six). Hence the evaluator who is considering using testing as a way of acquiring evaluation data must ensure that it is appropriate, valid and reliable.

DO I NEED TO PILOT MY DATA GATHERING INSTRUMENTS?

As a general rule evaluators would be well advised to pilot their evaluation instruments as much as possible. Most structured and semi-structured instruments will benefit from being piloted and some instruments will actually *require* a pilot - a pilot is as essential as the actual data gathering. For example, it was argued above that a 'home-grown' test risks major errors of omission, format, item discriminability and item difficulty if it has not been piloted. A pilot test is also necessary to establish certain forms of reliability (*see* chapter six), for example, the test-re-test method. Further, as was discussed earlier, a structured questionnaire, a structured interview and a structured observation schedule will need to be piloted to ensure that the categories of response are exhaustive, comprehensive, mutually exclusive, representative and comprehensible. In the case of a structured observation schedule, what might be a small matter of the layout of the schedule might turn out to be problematic: if the layout impedes a rapid data entry, it may be impossible to enter data at the required moments.

Semi-structured questionnaires, semi-structured interviews and semi-structured observation schedules will need to ensure that open-ended questions or areas for observation cover the range of topics which the evaluator needs in order to be able to answer the evaluation questions. In all of these cases the evaluator will need to follow up questionnaires, interviews and observations, be they structured or semi-structured, with a feedback session or an invitation to write comments about the instruments. A pilot questionnaire will need to make it clear to respondents that it is only a pilot and therefore may need to be refined in light of comments received.

In the case of unstructured interviews and observations, it is probably neither practicable nor desirable to try to undertake a pilot sample as every case will be different. This does not negate the value to the evaluator of trying out the *process* of unstructured interviews and observations in pilot situations; it must be borne in mind, however, that this process is very costly in time.

Piloting then is an inescapable feature of many evaluation instruments; the allowance of time for the development, piloting and consequent refining of instruments will have to be included in the planning of an evaluation. If this is not possible, then a fall-back position might be to show the instruments to a 'critical friend' for comment, though it must be said that this might be problematic if the 'critical friend' has little knowledge of the substantive areas under evaluation or of the issues involved in instrumentation.

An important issue which must be borne in mind when undertaking a pilot sample is that it should not involve any of the population or sample who will be involved in the actual, final data gathering. Piloting should be carried out on a *parallel* sample of respondents or participants (i.e. on a sample which is *matched* in important factors to the actual sample which will be used). This will avoid influencing the actual sample with resultant effects on the data. The pilot sample of respondents and participants need not be as large as the target sample but it must be *representative* of the key factors of the target sample. If possible, pilot the instruments with those who have no connection - e.g. locational, institutional, interpersonal - with the actual sample who will be targeted.

HOW CAN I USE MATRIX PLANNING TO HELP MY EVALUATION?

To clarify the planning of the instrumentation of an evaluation, the evaluator may find it useful to set the instrumentation into a planning matrix. Though there are several matrices which can be constructed, this chapter presents three. The three matrices here all deal with the planning of the same evaluation, hence the data from the three matrices are all interrelated in order to let the reader see how planning data might be presented. Matrix one (Figure 3.3) enables the evaluator to clarify which methods (instruments) will be used at which time stages of the evaluation.

Method \ Time	Stage 1 (start)	Stage 2 (2 months)	Stage 3 (4 months)	Stage 4 (6 months)	Stage 5 (9 months)
Documents	✓		✓		✓
Questionnaire no. 1	✓				
Questionnaire no. 2			✓		
Questionnaire no. 3					✓
Interview	✓	✓		✓	✓

Figure 3.3 A Matrix for Timing the Data Gathering Process

Study of this matrix might expose glaring omissions or might prompt questioning of why certain methods are to be used at certain times. In the matrix here one could ask why a complete recording is undertaken only at the start and finish of the evaluation period. It might be that in-depth study (e.g. using interviews) is time-consuming and therefore only undertaken at the start and the finish of the evaluation period. It might be that in-depth study (e.g. using interviews) is time-consuming and therefore only undertaken at the start and the finish; documentation does not alter frequently, so it is looked at less frequently; questionnaires are the mainstay of the methods. Such a matrix might also prompt questions of balance, timing, methods, asking, for example, why these timings are used, what makes each stage separate, why there is no observation or no testing, why questionnaires are seen to be the main data gathering instrument, why no teachers are interviewed.

Matrix two (Figure 3.4) enables the evaluator to clarify which methods will be used with which elements of the sample population (sampling is discussed more fully in chapter four).

Method / Sample	Documents	Questionnaire no.1	Questionnaire no.2	Questionnaire no.3	Interview
Headteacher	✓	✓	✓	✓	✓
Teacher 1		✓	✓	✓	
Teacher 2		✓	✓	✓	
Teacher 3		✓	✓	✓	
Pupils					✓
Parents		✓	✓	✓	
LEA officers	✓				✓

Figure 3.4   A Matrix for Planning the Data Gathering

Here too a study of the matrix might expose glaring omissions or might prompt questioning of why certain methods were used with some respondents and not others. For example, in matrix two only the headteacher and Local Education Authority (LEA) officers might hold the necessary documents; teachers and LEA officers might not have the time to be interviewed; pupils might not be able to read the questionnaires. Such a matrix might also prompt questions of balance, asking, for example, how many pupils and parents will be involved, why there are no school governors involved in the evaluation, why only three teachers are involved, how current validity is to be addressed (*see* chapter six), why pupils are approached on only one occasion, why teachers are not to be interviewed.

Matrix three (Figure 3.5) is a conflation of the previous two matrices, enabling the evaluator to clarify which methods will be used with which parts of the sample and when those methods will be used.

The same questions as with the other two matrices can be raised here to include coverage and omission of methods, sampling and timing, for example, to ask why the evaluation concentrates so heavily on the headteacher to the neglect of pupils and LEA officers (i.e. is there an 'institutional line' being traced here - a mechanism used in audit trails),

Time Sample	Stage 1 (start)	Stage 2 (2 months)	Stage 3 (4 months)	Stage 4 (6 months)	Stage 5 (9 months)
Headteacher	Documents Interview Questionnaire 1	Interview	Documents Questionnaire 2	Interview	Documents Interview Questionnaire 3
Teacher 1	Questionnaire 1		Questionnaire 2		Questionnaire 3
Teacher 2	Questionnaire 1		Questionnaire 2		Questionnaire 3
Teacher 3	Questionnaire 1		Questionnaire 2		Questionnaire 3
Pupils			Questionnaire 2		Interview
Parents	Questionnaire 1		Questionnaire 2		Questionnaire 3
LEA officers	Interview Documents				Interview Documents

Figure 3.5 A Summary Matrix for Planning the Data Gathering

or why so little seems to be occurring at stages two and four.

This matrix is slightly more complex than the previous two; hence, though the first two matrices might be used in the planning of the evaluation (i.e. have a formative function), it might be more appropriate to regard this as a summary matrix, maybe to be included in a formal evaluation plan or a formal report. Hence evaluation planners might work through the first two matrices and then present their final version on matrix three.

Matrix planning is useful for exposing key features of the planning of an evaluation. Whilst the three matrices have been concerned with timing, sampling and instrumentation, these are only three examples of how matrix planning might be used. Further uses might be found for matrix planning to cover:

● timing of the identification of the sample population;
● timing of the release of interim reports if it is to be a formative evaluation;
● timing the release of the final report if it is to be a summative evaluation;

- timing of pre-tests and post-tests if it is to be an experimental type of evaluation;
- timing of intensive necessary resource support (e.g. reprographics) to meet deadlines for circulation of questionnaires or test material;
- timing of evaluation team meetings.

These examples only cover *timings*; other matrices might be devised to cover other combinations (e.g. reporting by audiences, team meetings by reporting, instrumentation by team meetings etc.). Matrix planning has a certain tidiness which planners might find useful.

CONCLUSION

This chapter quite deliberately has focussed on the principal methods of data collection: interviews, questionnaires, observations, documentary evidence, nominal group technique, the Delphi technique and testing. These are likely to be the main methods of data collection in an evaluation. Whichever instrument is used to gather data, the decision to adopt it must be driven by the criterion of appropriacy. Hence other forms of data gathering (listed at the beginning of this chapter) might be necessary and appropriate. The instruments - selected or devised - must be able to gather data which will answer the evaluation questions. The timing of the administration of the instruments must be appropriate - *too soon* and the data may provide an incomplete picture of the object of the evaluation, *too late* and (a) the data may have become irrelevant - the context having changed since the data were gathered, (b) a selective memory may threaten the validity of interview, questionnaire and documentary data and (c) in some types of evaluation, e.g. the experimental model, extraneous variables might skew the results of a pre- or post-test.

This chapter has argued that the instrumentation and the administration of the data collection should not be arbitrary if useful, valid and reliable data are to be assembled and processed. The choice of instrumentation must flow from the objectives of the evaluation, the time scales and resource constraints under which the evaluation operates and the appropriate selection of methodology. In an attempt to address the necessity of careful planning the notion of matrix planning has been introduced. This review of instrumentation will provide useful material for the conduct of evaluations of all scales - from the single teacher or outsider evaluator to a team of teachers or evaluators undertaking large scale evaluations. Regardless of scale the golden rule of *appropriacy* still applies; it is in the interpretation of the term 'appropriacy' that the richness and diversity of evaluative activity resides.

RECOMMENDED READING

Bell, J., Bush, T. *et al.* (1984) *Conducting Small Scale Investigations in Educational Management*. London: Harper & Row.

Cohen, L. and Manion, L. (1985) *Research methods in Education* (2nd. ed.). London: Croom Helm.

Gronland, N.E. (1981) *Measurement and Evaluation in Teaching* (4th. ed.). New York: Collier Macmillan.

Harris, D. and Bell, C. (1986) *Evaluating and Assessing for Learning*. London: Kogan Page.

Hitcock, G. and Hughes, D. (1989) *Research and the Teacher*. London: Routledge.

Hopkins, D. (1985) *A Teacher's Guide to Classroom Research*. Milton Keynes: Open University Press.

McCormick, R. and James, M. (1988) *Curriculum Evaluation in Schools* (2nd. ed.). London: Croom Helm.

Moser, C.A. and Kalton, G. (1977) *Survey Methods in Social Investigation*. London: Heinemann.

Oppenheim, A.N. (1966) *Questionnaire Design and Attitude Measurement*. London: Heinemann.

Patton, M.Q. (1980) *Qualitative Evaluation Methods*. Beverly Hills: Sage Publications.

Simon, H. (1982) Conversation Piece: the practice of interviewing in case study research, in R. McCormick (ed.) *Calling Education to Account*. London: Heinemann.

Spradley, J.P. (1979) *The Ethnographic Interview*. New York: Holt, Rinehart and Winston.

Walker, R. (1987) Techniques for Research, in R. Murphy and H. Torrance (eds.) *Evaluating Education: Issues and Methods*. London: Paul Chapman Publishing Ltd.

Wilcox, B. (1992) *Time-Constrained Evaluation*. London: Routledge.

4 Sampling

The quality of an evaluation not only stands or falls on the appropriacy of methodology and instrumentation but also on the appropriacy of the *sampling strategy* which has been used.

Suppose I, as a class teacher, have been released from my teaching commitments in order to evaluate the abilities of thirteen-year-old students to carry out a set of science experiments and that the evaluation was to draw on three secondary schools which contained 300 such students each, a total of 900 students, and that the method I had been asked to employ for gathering data was through a semi-structured interview. Because of the time available to me it would be impossible for me to interview all 900 students (the total population being *all the cases*). Therefore I have to be selective and interview less than the full 900 students. How do I decide that selection; how will I select which students to interview?

If I were to interview 600 of the students, would that be too many? If I were to interview just twenty of the students, would that be too few? If I were to interview just the males or just the females, would that give me a fair picture? If I were to interview just those students whom the class teachers had decided were 'good at science', would that yield a true picture of the total population of 900 students? Perhaps I decide that it might be better if I went to those students who experienced difficulty in science and did not enjoy science as well as those who were 'good at science', so I turn up on the days of the interviews only to find that those students who did not enjoy science had decided to absent themselves from the science lesson. How will I be able to reach those students? Decisions and problems such as these face evaluators from the very start of planning an evaluation.

Decisions have to be taken about three key factors in sampling:

(1) the sample size;
(2) the representativeness and parameters of the sample;
(3) access to the sample.

HOW DO I DECIDE THE SAMPLE SIZE?

In small scale evaluations the evaluator may have the opportunity (e.g. if it is a teacher who is the evaluator who may have little choice about sampling), of simply going to all possible cases - the whole population. However, in a larger scale evaluation - e.g. using survey methods within or between institutions - the evaluator will need to consider carefully the sampling strategy to be used.

With respect to size, will a large size guarantee representativeness? Surely not! In the example *above* I could have interviewed a total sample of 450 females and still not have represented the male population. Will a small size guarantee representativeness? Again, surely not. The latter falls into the trap of saying that 50% of those who expressed an opinion said that they enjoyed science when the 50% was only one student, my having interviewed only two students in all. Furthermore, my former decision to interview 450 females might have been unworkable in practice. Too large a sample becomes unwieldy and might still be unrepresentative of the population of 900; similarly, too small a sample may be unrepresentative of the 900 students.

Sample size is also determined by the style of the evaluation. For example, if the evaluator were undertaking a *survey*, then necessarily the sample would have to be fairly large (e.g. several institutions, several classes, several students) in order to be faithful to this style of evaluation and if useful statistics were to be calculated (*see* pp. 131 - 142).

If the evaluator were undertaking an experimental style of evaluation, then the size of the sample might be small as long as it represented those characteristics of the wider population which were to feature in the isolation and control of variables in the experiment. If a decision-making or objectives-based evaluation were being undertaken, then the evaluator would have to decide whether to seek a large or a small sample, depending on whether or not he or she wished to make generalizations. If an illuminative evaluation were to be undertaken, then almost of necessity a small sample would have to be chosen in order not only to *manage* a very quickly amassed mountain of word data but also to do justice to the level of detail required. This latter may not always be true, as Miles and Huberman (1984) suggest that rich site-specific data can be patterned *across sites* - a claim that has been criticized for constituting an attempt to inject a positivistic note into essentially idiographic - unique - data.

Finally, sample size might be constrained by cost - in terms of time, money, stress, administrative support, and resources; a full sampling might be highly desirable but unworkable if costs become prohibitive.

HOW DO I DECIDE ON THE REPRESENTATIVENESS OF THE SAMPLE?

With respect to *representativeness* the evaluator will have to ensure that the sample in fact represents the whole population in question (the 900 students), if it is to be a valid sample. The evaluator will have to be clear on what has to be represented, i.e. to set the *parameters* of the wider population - the 'sampling frame'- clearly and correctly. There is a popular example of how poor sampling may be unrepresentative: a national newspaper reports that one person in every two suffers from backache; this headline stirs alarm in every doctor's surgery throughout the land. However, the newspaper fails to make clear the parameters of the study which gave rise to the headline. It turns out that the research took place (a) in a damp part of the country where the incidence of backache might be expected to be higher than elsewhere, (b) in a part of the country which contained a disproportionate number of elderly people, again who might be expected to have more backaches than a younger population, (c) in an area of heavy industry where the working population might be expected to have more backache than in an area of lighter industry or service industries, (d) by using two doctors' records only, overlooking the fact that many backache sufferers did not go to those doctors' surgeries because the two doctors concerned regarded backache sufferers with suspicion.

These four variables - climate, age, occupation and reported incidence - were seen to exert a disproportionate effect on the study , i.e. if the study were to be carried out in an area where the climate, age, occupation and reporting were to be different, then the results might be different. The newspaper report sensationally generalized beyond the parameters of the data, thereby overlooking the limited representativeness of the study.

HOW DO I DECIDE THE ACCESS TO THE SAMPLE?

With regard to *access* to the sample the evaluator will have to ensure that access is not only permitted but in fact practicable. For example, if one were asked to undertake an evaluation of truancy in a group of schools and decided to interview a sample of truants, the evaluation might never commence as the truants were never there! Similarly access to sensitive areas might not only be difficult but problematic both legally and administratively - for example, access to child abuse victims, child abusers, disaffected students, drug addicts, school refusers, bullies, victims of bullying etc.

The corollary of these points is to suggest that a sample size must not be so low that it becomes unrepresentative (a rule of thumb might be not to go below thirty cases) and not so large that it is impossible to manage, that a sample must be representative of the wider population about which it is making comment or declare that it does not seek to represent the wider population, and that access to the sample must be possible. The *sampling frame* - the identification of the characteristics of the wider population which must appear in the sample - must be clear on the nature of the wider population that it seeks to address. How can the evaluator proceed?

WHAT ARE PROBABILITY AND NON-PROBABILITY SAMPLES?

The evaluator must decide whether to opt for a probability sample (also known as a random sample) or a non-probability sample (also known as a purposive sample). The difference between them is this: in a probability sample the chances of members of the wider population being selected for the sample are known, whereas in a non-probability sample the chances of members of the wider population being selected for the sample are unknown. In the former (probability sample) every member of the wider population has an equal chance of being included in the sample; inclusion or exclusion from the sample is a matter of chance and nothing else. In the latter (non-probability sample) some members of the wider population definitely will be excluded and others definitely included (i.e. every member of the wider population does not have an equal chance to be in the sample). In this latter type the evaluator has *deliberately* - purposely - selected a particular section of the wider population to include in or exclude from the sample.

A probability sample, because it draws randomly from the wider population, will be useful if the evaluator wishes to make generalizations because it seeks representativeness of the wider population. It also permits two-tailed tests to be administered in statistical analysis of quantitative data (*see* p. 141). On the other hand a non-probability sample deliberately avoids representing the wider population, it seeks only to represent a particular group, a particular named section of the wider population, e.g. a class of students, a cohort of students sitting a particular examination, a group of mathematics teachers. A probability sample will have less risk of bias than a non-probability sample, whereas, by contrast, a non-probability sample, being unrepresentative of the whole population, may demonstrate skewness or bias. For this type of sample a one-tailed test will be used in processing statistical data (*see* chapter five). This is not to say that the former is bias-free - there is still likely to be a sampling error in a probability sample (for example, opinion polls always declare their error factors, usually ±3%).

The selectivity which is built into a non-probability sample derives from the evaluator targeting a particular group in the full knowledge that it does not represent the wider population, it simply represents itself. This is very frequently the case in small scale evaluations of, for example, particular instances - one or two schools, two or three groups of children, a particular group of teachers etc. - where no attempt to generalize is desired; this is the heart of the case study style of evaluation or of illuminative evaluation. It is also the style of sampling used when evaluators wish to contact significant members of a population, whether they represent the whole population or not. The non-probability sample will usually be selected deliberately or as a matter of convenience or access; it is useful for testing substantive but non-generalizable hypotheses.

N	S	N	S	N	S
10	10	220	140	1200	291
15	14	230	144	1300	297
20	19	240	148	1400	302
25	24	250	152	1500	306
30	28	260	155	1600	310
35	32	270	159	1700	313
40	36	280	162	1800	317
45	40	290	165	1900	320
50	44	300	169	2000	322
55	48	320	175	2200	327
60	52	340	181	2400	331
65	56	360	186	2600	335
70	59	380	191	2800	338
75	63	400	196	3000	341
80	66	420	201	3500	346
85	70	440	205	4000	351
90	73	460	210	4500	354
95	76	480	214	5000	357
100	80	500	217	6000	361
110	86	550	226	7000	364
120	92	600	234	8000	367
130	97	650	242	9000	368
140	103	700	248	10000	370
150	108	750	254	15000	375
160	113	800	260	20000	377
170	118	850	265	30000	379
180	123	900	269	40000	380
190	127	950	274	50000	381
200	132	1000	278	75000	382
210	136	1100	285	1000000	384

Note.- *N* is population size.

S is sample size.

Figure 4.1 Determining the Size of a Random Sample

DETERMINING SAMPLE SIZE FOR A PROBABILITY SAMPLE

The size of a probability (random) sample can be determined in two ways, either by the evaluator exercising prudence and ensuring that the sample represents the wider features of the population with the minimum number of cases or by using a table which, from a mathematical formula, suggests the appropriate size of a random sample for a given number of the wider population. One such example is provided by Krejcie and Morgan (1970) in Figure 4.1. This suggests that if the evaluator were devising a sample from a wider population of thirty or less (e.g. a class of students or a young group of children in a class) then he or she would be well advised to include the whole of the wider population as the sample.

The key point to note about sample size is that the smaller the number of cases there are in the wider, whole population the larger the proportion of that population must be which appears in the sample; the converse of this is true: the larger the number of cases there are in the wider, whole population, the smaller the proportion of that population must be which appears in the sample. Krecjie and Morgan (1970) note that 'as the population increases the sample size increases at a diminishing rate and remains constant at slightly more than 380 cases' (*ibid.*, p. 610). Hence, for example, an evaluation involving all the children in a small primary school or elementary school might require between 80% and 100% of the school to be included in the sample, whilst a large comprehensive secondary school of 1,200 students might require a sample of 25% of the school in order to achieve randomness. In a random sample the rough rule is that the larger the sample is the greater is its chance of being representative.

WHAT KINDS OF PROBABILITY SAMPLE ARE THERE?

There are several types of probability samples: simple random samples; systematic samples; stratified samples; cluster samples; stage samples and multi-phase samples. They all have a measure of randomness built into them and therefore have a degree of generalizability. A simple random sample of the population can be established by drawing names out of a hat until the required number for the random sample is reached (*see* Figure 4.1 above). A second way is by using a table of random numbers set out in matrix form (these are reproduced in most books on quantitative research methods and statistics) and allocating these random numbers to participants or cases.

A second type of probability sample is a systematic sample. Here the evaluator selects from a list of cases on a systematic basis, e.g. every fourth name, or every twentieth name on the list, until the desired sample size has been reached. One can decide on how frequently to make this systematic sampling by a simple statistic - the total number of the wider population being represented divided by the sample size required:

$$f = \frac{N}{sn}$$

where
f = frequency interval;
N = the total number of the wider population;
sn = the required number in the sample.

Let us say that the evaluator was working in a school of 1,400 students; by looking at the table of sample size (Figure 4.1) required for a random sample of these 1,400 students we see that 302 students are required to be in the sample. Hence the frequency interval is:

$$\frac{1,400}{302} = 4.635 \quad \text{(which rounds up to 5.0)}.$$

Hence the evaluator would pick out every fifth name on the list of cases.
    Such a process, of course, assumes that the names on the list themselves have been listed in a random order. A list of females and males might list all the females first before listing all the males; if there were 200 females on the list, the evaluator might have reached the desired sample size before reaching that stage of the list which contained males, thereby distorting (skewing) the sample. Another example might be where the evaluator decided to select every thirtieth person identified from a listing of school students, but it happened that:

(a) the school had approximately thirty students in each class;
(b) each class was listed from high ability to low ability students;
(c) the school listing listed the students by class.

In this case, although the sample would draw on each class, it would not fairly represent the whole school population since it would be drawing almost exclusively on the higher ability students. This is the issue of *periodicity*. Not only is there the question of the order in which names are listed in systematic sampling, but there is also the issue that this process may violate one of the fundamental premises of probability sampling, namely that every person has an equal chance of being included in the sample. In the example given *above* where every fifth name was selected, this guaranteed that names (1 - 4), (6 - 9) etc. would *not* be selected, i.e. that everybody did not have an equal chance to be chosen. The ways to minimize this problem are to ensure that the initial listing is selected randomly and that the *starting point* for systematic sampling is similarly selected randomly.

A third type of probability sample, and one which is widely used, is a stratified random sample. In this type of sample the evaluator will have to identify those characteristics of the wider population which must be included in the sample. In the example shown *above* of the students undertaking science experiments, the evaluator might consider that it is important to include students (a) of all abilities, (b) of both sexes, (c) with different motivations towards science, (d) with differing years' experience of undertaking science experiments, (e) with experience of several science teachers, (f) with experience of a very limited number of science teachers, (g) who have been in classes which contained (i) less than ten students, (ii) between eleven and twenty students, (iii) twenty-one students and above. What has been done here is to establish those characteristics (variables) of the wider population, that is, to identify the parameters of the wider population. This is the essence of establishing the *sampling frame.*

To organize a stratified random sample is a simple two-stage process. Firstly, identify those characteristics which appear in the wider population which must also appear in the sample, i.e., divide the wider population into homogenous and, if possible, discrete groups (strata) - for example, males and females, students aged sixteen and below and those aged seventeen and above (if that is appropriate for the purposes of the evaluation). Secondly, randomly sample within these groups the size of each group being determined either by the judgement of the evaluator or by reference to Figure 4.1.

The planning of the stratified random sampling can be undertaken in matrix form as in Figure 4.2 where the evaluator is setting up a stratified sample in order to examine the relationship between a set of *achieved characteristics* (independent variables) - computer ownership, computer use, enjoyment of computing and access to a computer - and a set of *ascribed characteristics* (dependent variables) - gender, age and ethnicity.

The decision on which characteristics to include should strive for simplicity as far as possible, as the more factors there are, not only the more complicated the matrix becomes, but often the larger the sample will have to be in order to include representatives of every cell in the matrix. In the example of the matrix in Figure 4.2 then it appears that the minimum number required if each cell contained only one case would be 120 - i.e. 20 rows × 6 columns (which then would not lend itself to very powerful statistical treatment, as this requires a minimum of five cases in at least 80% of the cells). For a stratified random sample to be effective, then clearly the characteristics of the wider population must be such as to enable homogenous groups to be established. Of course the evaluator may not wish to sample every cell of the matrix in Figure 4.2, choosing rather to sample those cells which she believes might contain data of particular importance; in this case the construction of a sampling matrix exposes clearly the various permutations of the sample categories so that the evaluator can make an appropriate selection.

Characteristics	Computer owner	Daily use of computer	Enjoyment of computer	Dislike of computer	Ambivalent about computer	Computer at home
White boys aged 5-11						
White girls aged 5-11						
White boys aged 12+						
White girls aged 12+						
Afro-Caribbean boys aged 5-11						
Afro-Caribbean girls aged 5-11						
Afro-Caribbean boys aged 12+						
Afro-Caribbean girls aged 12+						
Asian boys aged 5-11						
Asian girls aged 5-11						
Asian boys aged 12+						
Asian girls aged 12+						
African boys aged 5-11						
African girls aged 5-11						
African boys aged 12+						
African girls aged 12+						
Chinese boys aged 5-11						
Chinese girls aged 5-11						
Chinese boys aged 12+						
Chinese girls aged 12+						

Figure 4.2 A Matrix for a Random Stratified Sample

A stratified random sample is, therefore, a useful blending of randomization and categorization, thereby enabling both a quantitative and qualitative evaluation to be undertaken. A quantitative evaluation here will be able to use some powerful analytical and inferential statistical tools (e.g.

cross-tabulations, Mann-Whitney and Kruskal-Wallis statistics - discussed in chapter five) whilst a qualitative evaluation will be able to target those groups in the institution or clusters of participants who will be able to be approached to participate in the evaluation.

A fourth type of probability sample and one which is widely used in small scale evaluations and evaluations undertaken by teachers is a cluster sample, where a geographically close cluster is sampled (e.g. a school, a town, a village, a region). Here the parameters of the wider population are drawn perhaps more sharply; an evaluator here would have to comment on the generalizability of the findings (this resonates with the issues drawn in the sample of reported backache earlier in this chapter). The evaluator may also need to stratify within this cluster sample if useful data - i.e. those which are focussed and which demonstrate discriminability - are to be acquired.

A fifth type of probability sample is the staged sample (sometimes called a multi-stage sample). There is more than one stage to the selection of the sample (cf Cohen and Holliday, 1979). A staged sample is a useful way of deriving a large sample manageably.

For example, let us say that a geography teacher wanted to administer a questionnaire to all sixteen-year-olds in each of eleven secondary schools in one region. By contacting the eleven schools she finds that there are 2,000 sixteen year-olds on roll. Because of questions of confidentiality (*see* chapter eight) she is unable to find out the names of all of the students so it is impossible to draw their names out of a hat (and even if she had the names, it would be a mind-numbing activity writing out 2,000 names to draw out of the hat!). From looking at Figure 4.1 she finds that for a random sample of the 2,000 students the sample size is 322 students. How can she proceed?

The first stage is to list the eleven schools on a piece of paper and then to put the names of the eleven schools each onto a small card and place each card in a hat. She draws out the name of the first school, puts a tally mark by the appropriate school on her list and returns the card to the hat. The process is repeated 321 times, bringing the total to 322. The final totals might appear thus:

School	1	2	3	4	5	6	7	8	9	10	11	Total
Required number of students	25	21	13	62	33	22	38	47	46	22	23	322

For the second stage she then approaches each of the eleven schools and asks them to select randomly the required number of students for each school. Randomness has been maintained in two stages and a large number (2,000) has been rendered manageable.

The process at work here is to go from the general to the specific, the wide to the focussed, the large to the small. This type of evaluation is often applicable to larger scale evaluations in which teachers might be involved.

The staged or multi-stage sample should not be confused with the final type of probability sample - the multi-phase sample. In the multi-stage sample there was a single unifying purpose throughout the sampling. In the example of the previous paragraph the purpose was eventually to reach a group of students from a group of schools from a particular region. In a multi-phase sample the purposes change at each phase, for example, at phase one the selection of the sample might be based on a geographical criterion (e.g. to sample specific catchment areas), phase two might be based on an economic criterion (e.g. schools whose budgets are administered in markedly different ways), phase three might be based on a political criterion (e.g. schools whose catchment areas are drawn from areas with a tradition of support for a particular political party) and so on.

Another example might be this: for a teacher-as-evaluator the first phase might be to select classes which operate on a subject or a topic-based approach to teaching (i.e. an organizational criterion). The second phase might be to select a series of mathematics lessons to evaluate (i.e. on a curricular criterion). The third phase might be to select a team-teaching situation to evaluate (i.e. a pedagogical criterion). Clearly within each *phase* the evaluator might wish to operate a *multi-stage* sampling technique in order to reach individual respondents.

WHAT KINDS OF NON-PROBABILITY SAMPLES ARE THERE?

Just as there are several types of probability sample so there are several types of non-probability sample: convenience sampling, quota sampling, dimensional sampling, purposive sampling and snowball sampling. Each type of sample seeks only to represent itself or instances of itself in a similar population rather than attempting to represent the whole, undifferentiated population. A teacher-evaluator or an evaluator with access to a small section of a school or community will probably be using one or more types of non-probability sample.

A convenience sample (sometimes called an opportunity sample), as its name suggests, is simply that sample of the population to which the evaluator has easy access - a particular school, the teacher's own class, a cluster group of schools who have met together for an in-service day. As it does not represent any group other than itself, it does not seek to generalize about the wider population; to a convenience sample that is an irrelevance. The evaluator, of course, must take pains to report this point - that the parameters of generalizability in this type of sample are negligible. A convenience sample will often be the sampling strategy selected for a case study or series of case studies.

A quota sample (also known as a proportionate sample) bears many of the same characteristics as a stratified sample discussed earlier. Like a stratified sample it strives to represent significant characteristics (strata) of the wider population; unlike a stratified sample it strives to represent these characteristics in the *proportions* in which they can be found in that wider population. For example, suppose the wider population (however defined) were composed of 55% females and 45% males, then the sample must contain 55% females and 45% males; if the population of a school contained 80% of students below the age of sixteen and 20% of students aged seventeen years or above, then the sample would have to contain 80% of students below the age of sixteen and 20% of students aged seventeen years or above. A quota sample then seeks to give proportional weighting to selected factors (strata) which reflects the weighting in which they can be found in the wider population. The evaluator wishing to devise a quota sample can proceed in a three stage process:

Stage 1: Identify those characteristics (factors) which appear in the wider population which must also appear in the sample, i.e. divide the wider population into homogenous and, if possible, discrete groups (strata) - for example, males and females, Asian, Chinese and Afro-Caribbean.

Stage 2: Identify the proportions in which the selected characteristics appear in the wider population, expressed as a percentage.

Stage 3: Ensure that the percentaged proportions of the characteristics selected from the wider population appear in the sample.

One can use a matrix approach to planning a quota sample (as in the partner process of devising a random stratified sample), *see* Figure 4.3.

This figure takes the matrix from Figure 4.2 and puts into it the proportions of the wider population (entered as percentages). If quota sampling were being sought here, then it would be necessary to ensure that, as far as possible, the proportions in the representative sample maintained the proportions in the target community.

Ensuring correct proportions in the sample may be difficult to achieve if the proportions in the wider community are unknown (this draws on issues of *sampling error*); sometimes a pilot survey to the pilot community might be necessary in order to establish those proportions (with all the drawbacks of the survey method discussed in the previous chapter - e.g. low, unrepresentative return). It might be worthwhile for the evaluator to investigate to see if published statistics are available on the community in question. However, this does depend on what the evaluator takes the wider population to be; for example, if the evaluator wished to evaluate, let us say, the perceptions of students of the value of tutorial support throughout

Characteristics	Computer owner	Daily use of computer	Enjoyment of computer	Dislike of computer	Ambivalent about computer	Computer at home
White boys aged 5-11	50%	50%	50%	20%	30%	60%
White girls aged 5-11	30%	30%	30%	60%	40%	70%
White boys aged 12+	10%	10%	10%	10%	10%	80%
White girls aged 12+	20%	20%	20%	10%	10%	20%
Afro-Caribbean boys aged 5-11	50%	50%	50%	20%	20%	50%
Afro-Caribbean girls aged 5-11	20%	20%	20%	30%	20%	20%
Afro-Caribbean boys aged 12+	50%	40%	50%	10%	10%	50%
Afro-Caribbean girls aged 12+	30%	30%	30%	20%	20%	30%
Asian boys aged 5-11	50%	50%	50%	10%	10%	50%
Asian girls aged 5-11	40%	20%	40%	10%	10%	40%
Asian boys aged 12+	60%	40%	30%	40%	40%	60%
Asian girls aged 12+	20%	20%	20%	20%	20%	20%
African boys aged 5-11	30%	30%	20%	20%	30%	40%
African girls aged 5-11	40%	30%	30%	20%	20%	30%
African boys aged 12+	40%	40%	30%	40%	30%	40%
African girls aged 12+	30%	30%	30%	20%	20%	30%
Chinese boys aged 5-11	50%	50%	40%	40%	30%	50%
Chinese girls aged 5-11	50%	50%	40%	30%	20%	50%
Chinese boys aged 12+	30%	30%	30%	20%	20%	30%
Chinese girls aged 12+	30%	30%	30%	20%	20%	30%

Figure 4.3 A Sampling Matrix which Indicates Proportions of the Population

the various faculties of an institution, then the wider population would be known - i.e. the total numbers of students in each faculty. In this case the numbers might be thus:

Performing arts	300 students
Natural sciences	300 students
Humanities	600 students
Business and Social sciences	500 students

The proportions being 3:3:6:5 a minimum of seventeen students might be required (3 + 3 + 6 + 5) for the sample. Calculating the *minimum* number required in a quota sample is relatively straightforward:

Step 1: Calculate the totalled percentage and divide it by the highest common factor of the cells in that row.

Step 2: Add together the totals.

Returning to the example of the matrix entries of Figure 4.3 for computer use, row one would appear thus:

$$\frac{50 + 50 + 50 + 20 + 30 + 60}{10} = \frac{260}{10} = 26$$

Row two would appear thus:

$$\frac{30 + 30 + 30 + 60 + 40 + 70}{10} = \frac{260}{10} = 26$$

Row three would appear thus:

$$\frac{10 + 10 + 10 + 10 + 10 + 80}{10} = \frac{130}{10} = 13$$

This process would continue until all the rows were completed. Totalling the first three rows gives us a required sample size of sixty-five (26 + 26 + 13), and that only ensures a frequency of one in each cell, which, as was suggested in the section *above* about random stratified samples, would be inadequate to carry out powerful statistics, as these would require a cell frequency of at least five in 80% or more of the cells. If one were to continue this process, it is easy to see that very quickly a massive sample would be necessary. In fact, in the example of Figure 4.3 the minimum sample size would be 381. This is the price of having too many different characteristics, i.e. too many rows and columns. The rule for quota sampling, therefore, is that unless you are prepared to have a very large sample, keep to the minimum the number of categories for the matrix. The larger the sample, the more categories you can have, the larger the number of categories the greater the sample size has to be.

However, just as in the stratified random sample discussed *above*, the evaluator may not wish to sample every cell of the matrix of Figure 4.3, choosing, rather, to sample those cells which contain what she believes to be data of particular importance; in this case the construction of a sampling matrix exposes clearly the various permutations of the sample categories so that the evaluator can make an appropriate selection.

One way of reducing the problem of sample size in quota sampling is to opt for dimensional sampling. Here the evaluator identifies the group of dimensions or factors to be represented and then obtains one respondent for every *combination* of these factors. For example, the evaluator, being interested in disruptive students, girls and secondary aged students, might be able to find one disruptive secondary aged girl for the sample - i.e. a respondent who is the bearer of all of these characteristics. Combining a range of characteristics (variables) brings vast economy of size of sample and hence time taken to gather data.

A fourth type of non-probability sample is a purposive sample. As its name suggests, the sample has been chosen for a specific purpose, for example, (a) a group of headteachers and senior managers of secondary schools has been chosen because the evaluator is concerned with the incidence of stress amongst senior managers which has been caused by the implementation of government legislation, (b) a group of disaffected students has been chosen because they might indicate *most distinctly* the factors which contribute to students' disaffection, (c) one class of students has been selected to be tracked throughout a week in order to report on the curricular and pedagogic diet which has been offered to them so that other teachers in the school might compare their own teaching to that reported. Whilst it may satisfy the evaluator's needs to take this type of sample, it does not pretend to represent the wider population; it is deliberately and unashamedly biased.

The final type of non-probability sample is the snowball sample. Here the evaluators identify a small sample of respondents who have the characteristics in which they are interested. These respondents then put the evaluators in touch with other respondents who have the same characteristics. This method is useful for sampling a population where access is difficult - maybe because it is a sensitive topic (e.g. teenage solvent abusers) or where communication networks are undeveloped (for example, where an evaluator wishes to interview stand-in supply teachers but finds it difficult to acquire a list of these teachers, or where an evaluator wishes to contact curriculum co-ordinators who have attended a range of in-service courses and built up an informal network of inter-school communication). The task for the evaluators is to establish who are the critical or key informants with whom initial contact must be made.

WHAT GENERAL RULE DO I NEED TO DECIDE ON MY SAMPLING STRATEGY?

The message of this chapter is the same as that of all the others - that every element of an evaluation should not be arbitrary but planned and deliberate, and that, as before, the criterion of planning must be *fitness for purpose*. This chapter has suggested that the selection of a sampling strategy must be governed by the criterion of *appropriacy*. The choice of which strategy to adopt must be mindful of the purposes of the evaluation, the time-scale and constraints on the evaluation, the methods of data collection and the style of evaluation. The sample chosen must be suitable for all of these factors if validity is to be served.

RECOMMENDED READING

Calder, J. (1979) Introduction to Applied Sampling, *Research Methods in Education and the Social Sciences*, Block 3, Part 4, DE304. Milton Keynes: Open University Press.

Cohen, L. and Manion, L. (1985) *Research Methods in Education* (second edition). London: Croom Helm.

Friedman, H. (1982) Simplified Determinations of Statistical Power, Magnitude of Effect and Research Sample Sizes, *Educational and Psychological Measurement*, 42 (2), pp. 521 - 528.

Moser, C.A. and Kalton, G. (1977) *Survey Methods in Social Investigation*. London: Heinemann.

Wiersma, W. (1980) *Research Methods in Education* (second edition), Illinois: F.E. Peacock Publishers.

5   What Can I Do with the Data?

The previous chapters have set out a range of issues in the design and planning of an evaluation and the instruments which are available to the evaluation for gathering data. Just as the design of an evaluation and its instrumentation were premised on the criterion of appropriacy, so the analysis of data must be approached in the same way if validity is to be preserved (discussed in chapter six). There is a variety of different ways of processing of data; which data analysis methods are selected depend on the type of data that have been collected and the evaluation questions which have to be answered. Word-based data will be processed differently from number-based data; quantitative data will be treated differently from qualitative data. The evaluator will have to take an important decision on how to approach the data.

HOW CAN I APPROACH DATA PROCESSING?

One approach is to go to the data with the evaluation questions in mind and see how the data speak to those questions. An analogy for this approach is to regard the evaluation questions as a magnet which attracts pertinent data and does not attract data which are irrelevant. Having collected these data to answer the specific evaluation questions, the evaluator then looks at the remaining data which the magnet did not attract in order to find out if there are other data which might be useful. This approach, then, goes to the data with a sorting frame already set; this could be described as a *pre-ordinate* form of data processing as the framework for analysis was prepared even before the data were collected. This is essentially a 'front-loaded' type of data processing. The data analysis takes much time to prepare (at the instrumentation stage of the evaluation) but little time to analyse.

An alternative approach is to go to the data without a sorting frame; here the evaluator analyses the data without a pre-formed set of categories, reviewing the data to see what issues *emerge* from them. This method, a *responsive* form of analysis, enables the evaluator to be very honest to the data. The evaluator processes the data *and then* sees how the data answer the evaluation questions. This approach is 'end-loaded' in that the categories for analysis have not been pre-formed but only emerge after reviewing the data. The data analysis takes less time to prepare than in the former approach but takes much longer to analyse.

Whichever approach is adopted, the end point of the analysis is the same - the answering of the evaluation questions. Whether this means that a hypothesis is accepted or rejected, or whether this means that the evaluation does not seek to prove or disprove, merely to *illuminate* issues in a particular situation, depends on the style of evaluation. An experimental or survey style of evaluation might seek to confirm or refute a hypothesis, whilst an illuminative evaluation might seek simply to portray a particular set of circumstances or events.

The data themselves will also indicate to the evaluator how they should be processed and presented. Number-based data (quantitative data) will lend themselves to being presented in tables and figures, whereas word-based data (qualitative data) will be processed and presented as written-up accounts or as written responses to particular issues. This chapter will first outline ways in which simple number-based data can be processed and will then discuss how word-based data might be processed. The account here should be regarded as introductory only; further details will have to be gained by looking at texts on research methods in the social sciences.

HOW CAN I PROCESS NUMERICAL DATA?

The processing of numerical data is not only for mathematicians but can be undertaken very quickly, correctly and painlessly by non-specialist statisticians. Indeed there is a certain thrill to be gained by the successful calculation of a given statistic. In many ways there is greater satisfaction in achieving a final figure than in the processing of verbal data where an identifiable final point is far less ascertainable, quite simply because words are capable of infinite meaning.

This section takes the reader step-by-step through a range of statistical treatments which can be applied to numerical data. It tells the reader what the statistics are, what they will do, how they can be used, what they might show. There are very many computer packages which will process statistics for the evaluator rather than the evaluator having to work through formulae and do the calculations by hand. This section of the chapter will not deal with every statistic available to the evaluator but will introduce straightforward statistics, since it is expected that it is these which will be of greatest use to the novice evaluator, particularly as questionnaires, structured observation and interviews - the stuff of some evaluations - will use non-parametric statistics. Further, the statistics used and suggested will ensure that the most can be made of the numerical data gathered, be it small scale or large scale. The explanation of specific statistics breaks off at relevant points in order to discuss some background knowledge which is necessary if the evaluator is to understand the capability and meaning of certain statistics. Care is taken to avoid overloading the reader with too many facts and processes at a particular point in the discussion.

WHAT ARE THE FOUR SCALES OF DATA?

The first step in processing numerical data is to ascertain what *level of data* is being processed. There are four types of scaling or levels of data: nominal data, ordinal data, interval data and ratio data.

A nominal scale is the most elementary scale, giving categories a name or label. These categories are mutually exclusive, for example male or female, numbers on a football shirt (one to eleven), categories of personality (e.g., introvert or extravert), number plates on a car, insurance policy numbers, membership of a political party. Take the example of numbers on a football shirt; we cannot say that a player wearing the number 10 on his shirt is twice as good as the player wearing the number 5 on his shirt, they are simply *different*. The numbers in this scale serve merely to denote *categories*. This scale of data is often found in those questionnaires where factual information is requested - e.g. gender, class in school, which subjects students are following.

An ordinal scale can be used when we are able to put items in a rank order or where we can say that one person or some people display a characteristic *greater than* or *lesser than* another person or persons, for example, degrees of leadership, degrees of fair-mindedness. We cannot assume equal intervals between these degrees, therefore we cannot say, for example, that the degree of leadership of one person is twice that of another or that the difference between the degree of leadership between person A and person B is the same as between person C and person D, because we are dealing in non-standard units. An ordinal scale is that which can be seen in Likert scales and rating scales of various types (*see* chapter three).

The nominal and ordinal scales are used for non-parametric data and are often those scales which feature in evaluations which collect survey data. Parametric data use statistics for interval and ratio scales and are often used in the experimental or the objectives models of evaluation. Both models involve a measure of testing - either using published tests or using 'home-grown' tests. Both scales assume a normal distribution of the characteristic (variable) in the population.

In an interval scale the distance between intervals is both even and known, for example a temperature scale, and the intervals are measured in standard units, so, for example, in this scale we would know whether the difference between person A and person B on a specified characteristic was the same as the difference between person C and person D on the same given characteristic.

In this scale the ratio of two intervals is known but it is still not possible to declare the exact ratio of values, because this scale does not assume an absolute zero; in the example of temperature scaling it would be incorrect to say that a temperature of 40°F was twice as hot as a temperature of 20°F, because this scale does not begin at zero for a freezing point. Similarly in many scholastic tests (e.g. IQ, verbal reasoning, non-verbal reasoning) there is no assumed zero point so we are unable to say that a score of 120 IQ points is twice as high as a score of 60 IQ points.

By contrast, a ratio scale not only has all the properties of an interval scale, but, additionally, it assumes a true zero, e.g. weight, age, height, length, time, money in the school bank. This is more powerful than any of the three previous scales, for it permits us, for example, to say that a particular score is twice as high as another score or three times less than another, or that one object weighs twice as heavy as another object.

Using these scales evaluators have to select the statistic which is both appropriate to the scale and appropriate to their purposes. The following sections outline such statistics.

WHICH STATISTICS DO I USE WITH NOMINAL SCALE DATA?

There are three main ways of handling data in this scale: the modal score, the frequency score and the chi-square statistic. The modal score is simply that score which is achieved by the greatest number of people, so, for example, in the data *below* the modal score is 20:

	N
Males aged seventeen or less	20
Males aged eighteen or less	16
Females aged seventeen or less	18
Females aged eighteen or more	12

N = the number of cases

When presenting nominal data the evaluator would record not only the modal score but the other frequencies observed. (This method is also used for the analysis of data from structured observations). This is usually recorded in bar chart, histogram, or pie chart form.

WHAT CAN I LOOK FOR IN GRAPHED NOMINAL DATA?

Graphed nominal data enable the evaluator to see at a glance:

(a) which are the highest and lowest frequencies;
(b) whether there is an even distribution across all the categories;
(c) whether there is a clear 'front runner' that receives the highest score (the modal score) with low scoring in the other categories, or whether the modal score is only narrowly leading the other scores;
(d) whether there are two scores which are vying for the highest score (i.e. a bi-modal graph, sometimes the case when graphing data for males and females);
(e) whether the frequencies are generally high or generally low.

If more than one graph is being used, then the evaluator can begin to determine patterns of response across the graphs.

The chi-square statistic - a very frequently used statistic - measures the difference between an expected and actual result to see if there is a significant difference between them, i.e. to see if the frequencies observed are significant; it is a measure of 'goodness of fit' between an *expected* and *actual* result or set of results. The expected result is based on a statistical process discussed *below* and set out in Appendix C. To use the chi-square statistic (and other statistics identified *below*) the evaluator will need to understand the concept of statistical significance which is based on notions of probability.

For a chi-square statistic data are set into a contingency table, an example of which can be seen in Figure 5.1 which is a 2×3 contingency table, i.e. two horizontal rows and three vertical columns (contingency tables may contain more than this number of variables). The example in this figure presents data concerning sixty students' entry into science, arts and humanities in a sixth form, and whether the students were male or female. The lower of the two figures in each cell is the numbers of

	Science subjects	Art subjects	Humanities subjects	
Males	7.6 14	8 4	8.4 6	24
Females	11.4 5	12 16	12.6 15	36
	19	20	21	60

Figure 5.1 A Contingency Table 2×3

actual students who have opted for the particular subjects (sciences, arts, humanities). The upper of the two figures in each cell is what might be expected under normal circumstances to be the number of students opting for each of the particular subjects. This figure is arrived at by statistical computation (*see* Appendix C), hence the decimal fractions for the figures. What is of interest to the evaluator is whether this distribution of subject choice by males and females differs significantly from that which could occur by *chance variation* in the population of sixth formers.

WHAT IS STATISTICAL SIGNIFICANCE?

The evaluator begins with the hypothesis that there is *no significant difference* between the *actual* results noted and what might be expected to occur by chance in the wider population. This is called the null hypothesis. When the statistic is calculated, (*see* Appendix C), if the observed, actual distribution differs from that which might be expected by chance alone, then the evaluator has to determine whether that difference is statistically significant, i.e. to *refute* the null hypothesis.

There are two main areas of significance. If the results observed could not have occurred simply *by chance* in 95% of the cases, i.e. that chance only accounted for 5% of the difference, then the evaluator has established statistical significance at the 0.05 level. If the results observed could not have occurred *simply by chance* in 99% of the cases, i.e. that chance only accounted for 1% of the difference, then the evaluator has established statistical significance at the 0.01 level, i.e. a higher level of significance. These two levels, 0.05 and 0.01 are the two main levels of significance. The evaluator would say that the null hypothesis had been refuted and that the level of significance observed (p) was either at the 0.05 or 0.01 level.

Returning to the example of the sixty students with Figure 5.1 and using the formula for chi-square in Appendix C yields a final chi-square figure of 14.6391; this was the figure computed from a sample of 60 sixth form students. The evaluator goes to tables of the distribution of chi-square (given in most books on social science statistics) and looks up the figure to see if it indicates a statistically significant difference from that occurring by chance. Part of the chi-square distribution table is shown here:

Degrees of Freedom	Level of Significance	
	0.05	0.01
3	7.81	11.34
4	9.49	13.28
5	11.07	15.09
6	12.59	16.81

The evaluator will see that the 'degrees of freedom' have to be identified for the result; to establish the degree of freedom, simply take one away from the total number of rows of the contingency table and one away from the total number of columns; in this case it is $6 - 2 = 4$ degrees of freedom. The evaluator looks along the table from the entry for the 4 degrees of freedom and notes that the figure calculated of 14.6391 is statistically significant at the 0.01 level, i.e. is higher than the required 13.28, indicating that the results obtained could not have occurred simply by chance. The null hypothesis is refuted at the 0.01 level of significance. Interpreting the specific figures of the contingency table in educational rather than statistical terms, noting (a) the low incidence of females in the science subjects and the high incidence of females in the arts and humanities subjects, and (b) the high incidence of males in the science subjects and low incidence of males in the arts and humanities, the evaluator would say that this distribution is significant - suggesting, maybe, that the school needs to take action to steer females into science subjects and males into arts and humanities.

What has been described here (and in Appendix C) is a method of calculating the statistic by hand. However, there are very many simple-to-use statistical packages available for computers which will process all the calculations for the evaluator - the evaluator simply enters the raw data and the computer processes the data and indicates the level of statistical significance of the distributions. A much used package is the Statistical Package for the Social Sciences (SPSS) which will process these data using the CROSSTABS command sequence.

The chi-square test requires at least 80% of the cells of a contingency table to contain at least five cases. This means that it may not be feasible to calculate the chi-square statistic if only a small sample is being used. Hence the evaluator would tend to use this statistic for survey data. (The binomial test could be used if the problem of low cell frequencies obtained).

Non-permissible operations for nominal data are those which derive from the other three scales, e.g. means, medians, standard deviations, correlations, t-tests.

WHICH STATISTICS DO I USE WITH ORDINAL SCALE DATA?

The statistical operations which are permissible to the evaluator in ordinal scaling are the mode, rank order correlations (the Spearman rank ordering statistic), the Mann-Whitney U test and the Kruskal-Wallis analysis of variance. The evaluator can also employ the chi-square statistic here to find out whether the distribution of nominal data in relation to ordinal data is statistically significant or not. Non-permissible statistics are the mean, standard deviations and treatments from the interval and ratio scales.

Like the nominal scale the modal score can be calculated for ordinal scale data. Additionally, the median score can be calculated; the median score is that score which is gained by the middle person in a ranked group of people. Let us say that the evaluator has some test scores for five people:

Simon   50%
David   30%
Susan   70%
Alice   65%
Alison 40%

The evaluator firstly places the sample in a rank order:

Susan   70%
Alice   65%
Simon   50%
Alison 40%
David   30%

The median score is that which is scored by the middle person - here it is Simon with 50%. In the event of there being no middle score (i.e. when the number of cases is an even number), then the evaluator will set a score which is midway between the highest score obtained in the lower half of the cases and the lowest score obtained in the upper half of the cases.

Many evaluations used ordinal data because they use some form of rating scale (e.g. in a questionnaire).

WHAT CAN I LOOK FOR IN GRAPHED ORDINAL DATA?

In addition to the four ways of analysing graphed data as set out for nominal data *above*, the evaluator can also determine the following on graphed data:

(a) whether the responses cluster around one or other end of a rating scale. For example, in a scale which had categories of 'strongly agree' to 'strongly disagree' it would be important to know whether responses featured highly for the category or categories which allowed *strong* feelings to be expressed;

(b) whether the graphs are skewed to one end or the other in any consistent way, for example whether respondents who have been asked to rate similar items have responded similarly on these items. The patterning across items is an important feature of an evaluation, for it highlights clusters of response or perception;

(c) whether the frequencies of responses are generally high or generally low (i.e. whether respondents feel strongly about issues);

(d) whether there is a clustering of responses around the central categories of the rating scale (e.g. respondents perhaps not wishing to appear to be too extreme);

(e) whether the spread of the graphed data is generally even or generally steep to a peak (a measure of kurtosis);

(f) whether there is a pattern of rising or falling scores towards one or the other end of the graph;

(g) whether the data are presented in raw scores or percentages.

WHAT DO I MEAN BY CORRELATION?

Ordinal data also allow the evaluator to see if there is any *measure of association* or *correlation* between sets of data - say, for example, the ratings on one set of variables and the ratings on another equal number of variables.

Let us imagine that I noticed that many people with large feet also had large hands and that many people with small feet also had small hands. I decide to conduct an investigation to see if there is any correlation or degree of association between the size of feet and the size of hands or whether it was just chance that led some people to have large hands and large feet. I measure the hands and the feet of one hundred people and observe that 99 times out of a 100 those people with large feet also had large hands. That seems to be more than just coincidence; it would seem to me that I could say with some certainty that if a person has large hands she will also have large feet. How do I know when I can make that assertion? When do I know that I can have confidence in this prediction?

For statistical purposes if I can observe that relationship occurring 95 times out of a 100, then I could say with some confidence that it would not occur in only five people in every hundred, reported as 0.05 level of significance. If I can observe that relationship occurring 99 times out of a 100 (as in the example of hands and feet above) then I could say with even greater confidence that it would not occur only once in every 100, reported as 0.01 level of significance (*see* the previous discussion about significance). I begin with a null hypothesis which says that there is no relationship between the size of hands and the size of feet. My task is to disprove or refute that hypothesis. If I can show that the hypothesis is untrue for 95% or 99% of the population, then I have demonstrated that there is a statistically significant relationship between the size of hands and the size of feet at the 0.05 and 0.01 levels of significance respectively. These two levels of significance - the 0.05 and 0.01 - are the levels at which statistical significance is normally achieved.

Let us take a second example. Let us say that I have devised a scale of 1 - 8 which can be used to measure the sizes of hands and feet. Using the scale I make the following calculation for eight people. I could set out the results thus:

	Hand Size	Foot Size
Subject A	1	1
Subject B	2	2
Subject C	3	3
Subject D	4	4
Subject E	5	5
Subject F	6	6
Subject G	7	7
Subject H	8	8

We can observe a perfect correlation between the size of feet and the size of hands, the person who has a size one hand has a size one foot and the person who has a size eight hand has a size eight foot. There is a perfect *positive correlation*. Using a mathematical formula (*see* Appendix D) I would calculate that this perfect correlation yielded an index of association - a co-efficient of correlation - which is +1.00.

Suppose that this time I carried out the investigation on a second group of eight people and reported the following results:

	Hand Size	Foot Size
Subject A	1	8
Subject B	2	7
Subject C	3	6
Subject D	4	5
Subject E	5	4
Subject F	6	3
Subject G	7	2
Subject H	8	1

This time the person with a size one hand has a size eight foot and the person with the size eight hand has a size one foot. There is a perfect *negative correlation*. Using the same mathematical formula (*see* Appendix D) I would calculate that this perfect negative correlation yielded an index of association (a correlation co-efficient) which is −1.00.

Now, clearly it is very rare to find a perfect positive or negative correlation; the truth of the matter is that looking for correlations will yield co-efficients of correlation which lie somewhere between −1.00 and +1.00. How do we know whether the co-efficients of correlation are statistically significant or not?

Let us say that I take a third sample of eight people and undertake an investigation into their hand and foot size. I enter the data case by case (Subject A to Subject H), indicating their rank order for hand size and then for foot size. This time the relationship is less clear because the rank ordering is more mixed, for example, Subject A is second for hand size and first for foot size, Subject B is first for hand size and second for foot size etc:

	Hand Size	Foot Size
Subject A	2	1
Subject B	1	2
Subject C	3	3
Subject D	5	4
Subject E	4	5
Subject F	7	6
Subject G	6	7
Subject H	8	8

Using the formula in Appendix D, I find that the co-efficient of correlation for the eight people is 0.7857. Is it statistically significant? From a table of significance (commonly printed in appendices to books on statistics or research methods) I read off whether the co-efficient is statistically significant or not for a specific number of cases, for example:

Number of Cases	Level of Significance	
	0.05	0.01
6	0.93	0.96
7	0.825	0.92
8	0.78	0.875
9	0.71	0.83
10	0.65	0.795
20	0.455	0.595
30	0.36	0.47

I see that for eight cases of my investigation the correlation co-efficient has to be 0.78 or higher, if it is to be significant at the 0.05 level, and 0.875 or higher, if it is to be significant at the 0.01 level of significance. As my correlation co-efficient for my third experiment with eight subjects was 0.7857 I see that it is higher than that required for significance at the 0.05 level (0.78) but not as high as that required for significance at the 0.01 level (0.875). I am safe in stating that the degree of association between the hand and foot sizes of the eight subjects in the third of my eight-subject experiments refuted the null hypothesis and demonstrated statistical significance at the 0.05 level.

The first example *above* of hands and feet is very neat because it has 100 people in the sample; if I have more or less than one hundred people how do I know if a relationship between two factors is significant? Let us say that I have data on thirty people; in this case, because my sample size is so small, I might hesitate to say that there is a strong association between the size of hands and size of feet if I observe that in twenty seven people (i.e. 90% of the population). On the other hand, let us say that I have a sample of 1,000 people and I observe the association in 700 of them. In this case, even though only 70% of the sample demonstrated the association of hand and foot size, I might say that because the sample size is so large I can have greater confidence in the data than on the small sample. *Statistical significance varies according to the size of the population in the sample.* In order to be able to determine significance I need to have two facts in my possession, the *size of the sample* and the *co-efficient of correlation*. From here it is simply a matter of reading off the significance level from a table or processing data on a computer program to yield the appropriate statistic.

If I wish to ascertain whether the correlation co-efficients are statistically significant, then, I go to a table of significance levels and read off the results. In the table for the third example *above* concerning hand and foot size, the first column indicates the number of people in the sample and the other two columns indicate the correlation co-efficients required for statistical significance at each of two levels. Hence, if I have thirty people in my sample then, for the correlation to be significant at the 0.05 level, I would need a correlation co-efficient of 0.36, whereas, if there were only ten people in the sample, I would need a correlation co-efficient of 0.65 for the correlation to be significant at the same 0.05 level.

Because the data are ordinal, the evaluator is restricted to using the Spearman rank order correlation statistic. This means that the evaluator has to arrange the two sets of data subject by subject (e.g. person by person), entry by entry (e.g. school subject by school subject) etc.; for example, it could be a list of the positions in a class of students as a result of a termly test, it could be the scoring totals of a rating scale which runs from 'never' to 'always' in its categories, it could be the ranking of frequencies entered for a set of aggregated data - for example, the numbers of students studying maths, language, physics and music in a school sixth form. Further, it could be used to see if there was any relationship between attitude to school and success at school, extroversion and popularity, disruptive behaviour and degrees of bullying (e.g. using a set of rating scales), or a relationship between intelligence (as measured by non-verbal reasoning) and reading ability.

In addition to these purposes, the calculation of a correlation co-efficient is also used in determining item discriminability of a test (*see* chapter three) - e.g. using a point bi-serial calculation - and in determining split-half reliability in test items (*see* chapter six) using the Spearman rank order correlation statistic.

Whilst correlations are widely used in evaluations - and rightly so because they are straightforward to calculate and to interpret - the evaluator must be aware of three *caveats* in undertaking correlational analysis:

(1) Do not assume that correlations imply *causal* relationships (e.g. simply because having large hands appears to correlate with having large feet does not imply that having large hands *causes* one to have large feet);
(2) Be alert to a Type I error - rejecting the null hypothesis when it is in fact true;
(3) Be alert to a Type II error - accepting the null hypothesis when it is in fact not true.

Identifying and resolving issues (2) and (3) can be found by consulting texts on statistical methods.

WHAT OTHER STATISTICS CAN I USE FOR ORDINAL DATA?

There are two more statistics commonly available to the evaluator who is using ordinal data, the Mann-Whitney U-test and the Kruskal-Wallis one-way analysis of variance. The Mann-Whitney U-test is used to see if there is any statistically significant difference between *two* independent samples (it is the non-parametric equivalent of the parametric t-test). In many respects, then, it is similar to a chi-square test, requiring a computation of the relationship between a dichotomous nominal variable and an ordinal variable. Hence this statistic is useful, for example, for seeing if there is a gender-differentiated response to rating scale items, or if the results of a test in the experimental model of evaluation are statistically significant between the control and the experimental group, or comparing students from a rural area with students from an urban area, or comparing the scores of students in two parallel classes in a school, or calculating whether the responses to a 'yes'/'no' question are significantly distributed in relation to responses to a rating scale (for example, to determine whether children who do or do not have other siblings give significantly different responses to a rating scale which asks their liking for group activities in physical education). Once calculated, the Mann-Whitney statistic has to be used in conjunction with frequencies to provide the detail about the significance of those frequencies, i.e. the actual figures. In this statistic, too, formulae and tables to interpret the formulae are generally available in many books on research methods.

Whereas the Mann-Whitney U-test can be used to compare two samples (e.g. male/female, urban/rural, control group/experimental group), the Kruskal-Wallis one-way analysis of variance (the non-parametric equivalent of the parametric analysis of variance) enables the evaluator to see if there are any statistically significant differences between two or more independent samples. For example, if the evaluator wishes to see whether students in four different history classes in a school perform in a statistically-significantly different way from each other in a history examination, the Kruskal-Wallis statistic may yield some data to shed light on this, provided that the groups are drawn from the same wider population of history students so that there is some parity between the groups in the first instance. This statistic could also be used if, for example, the evaluation was a large scale survey which was carried out in five different schools in one area to see, for instance, if enjoyment of science waxed or waned as students grew older. On a larger scale still it could be used in different regions of a country to see if there was any significant difference between, say, each of five regions of a country (for example, rural, urban, suburban, northern, southern) in the estimation of the importance of learning a foreign language. As with the Mann-Whitney statistic the Kruskal-Wallis statistic has to be taken in conjunction with the frequencies to provide the detail about the significance of the frequencies. The formulae and tables for interpreting the indices yielded by those formulae are generally available in several books on research methods.

If the evaluator is computing the Mann-Whitney and Kruskal-Wallis statistics on a commercially available statistical package (e.g. SPSS), then the computer will yield two results - one for a one-tailed test and another for a two-tailed test. Broadly speaking a one-tailed test applies to data which have been acquired from a non-probability sample (*see* chapter four) whereas a two-tailed test applies to data which have been acquired from a probability sample. If the sample has been deliberately selected to represent only a specified fraction of the population or variable (for example, students with a measured IQ of above 120), then a one-tailed test is probably more suitable; if the sample makes no assumptions about the distribution of a population or the distribution of a variable, i.e. is a form of probability sample (e.g. students whose measured IQ might cover the complete range of scores), then a two-tailed test is appropriate.

This chapter will not dwell on the Mann-Whitney U-test nor on the Kruskal-Wallis one way analysis of variance test, as these statistics are usually computed using commercially available statistical packages or a mainframe computer package for analysing data, for example, SPSS (the Statistical Package for the Social Sciences). It is not difficult for the novice evaluator to enter this large statistical program. It is well worth novice evaluators spending a few hours acquainting themselves with a computer package to process statistical data as this could save many days or even weeks in processing numerical data by hand (and without human error entering the process of calculation).

Unless the small scale evaluator intends to use published tests (i.e. those which are parametric), it will probably turn out that the scales used for data collection will be nominal and ordinal. This chapter has so far set out the tests which are available to the evaluator using these types of data; it is important to select the appropriate statistics for the level of data being used. One common error in evaluations is that they blithely use means and standard deviations on ordinal data; this is inappropriate and invalid, they are the stuff of interval and ratio data.

WHICH STATISTICS DO I USE WITH INTERVAL AND RATIO DATA?

Permissible operations in an interval scale (in addition to those used in the previous two scales) are the mean, standard deviation, z-scores, Pearson product moment correlations and t-tests (discussed *below*). Permissible operations in the ratio scale are all those available to the interval scale but with the addition of ratios, e.g. twice as large as, three times smaller than etc.

Once evaluators move into these two scales of data they are entering a world of parametric data where powerful statistics are able to be computed. The mean allows comparisons to be made between groups of scores, calculated by totalling the scores and dividing it by the number of cases. This statistic is usually the first statistic to be included on a hand-held calculator. However, the mean alone will only yield crude data.

For example, let us look at the three sets of numbers at the top of the following page.

(1)	1	2	3	4	20	mean = 6
(2)	1	2	6	10	11	mean = 6
(3)	5	6	6	6	7	mean = 6

If we were to plot these points on three separate graphs we would see very different results.

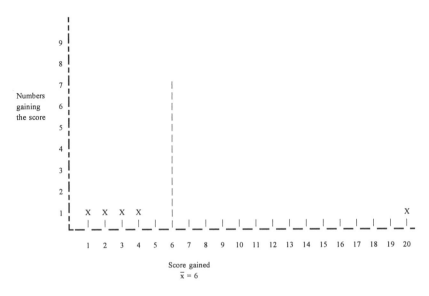

Figure 5.2 A First Graph Indicating Position of the Mean and Distributions

Figure 5.2 shows the mean being heavily affected by the single score of 20; in fact, all the other four scores are some distance below the mean. The score of twenty is exerting a disproportionate influence on the data and on the mean.

Figure 5.3 shows one score actually on the mean but the remainder some distance away from it.

Figure 5.4 shows the scores clustering very tightly around the mean. The point at stake is this; it is not enough simply to calculate the mean; for a fuller picture of the data we need to look at the *dispersal* of scores. For this we require the statistic of the standard deviation; the standard deviation will indicate the range and degree of dispersal of the data. Some scores will be widely dispersed (Figure 5.2), others will be dispersed evenly (Figure 5.3), others will be bunched together (Figure 5.4).

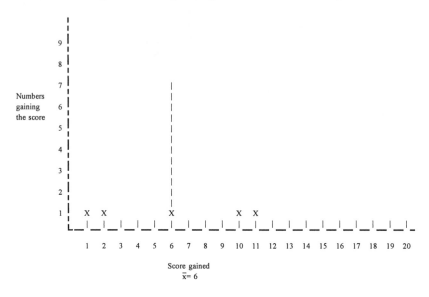

Figure 5.3 A Second Graph Indicating Position of the Mean and Distributions

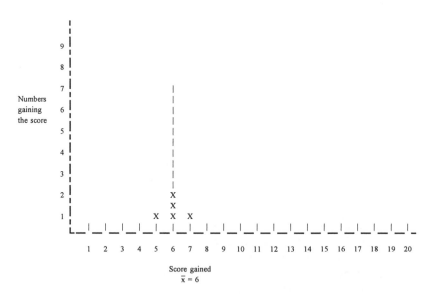

Figure 5.4 A Third Graph Indicating Position of the Mean and Distributions

A high standard deviation will tend to indicate a wide dispersal of scores, a low standard deviation will indicate clustering or bunching together of scores. Whilst the standard deviation is usually the second or third statistic to be included on a hand-held statistical calculator, the formula for its calculation is included in Appendix E.

The standard deviation is necessary for comparing test scores. For example, suppose I wished to compare the performance of twelve children on a maths and language test. I could list the results as follows:

	Maths Score	Language Score
Subject A	7	27
Subject B	6	25
Subject C	5	15
Subject D	4	12
Subject E	2	5
Subject F	8	27
Subject G	7	14
Subject H	4	7
Subject I	9	28
Subject J	3	2
Subject K	1	4
Subject L	4	8

How do I know how well the students have done on their tests? Is a mark of 8 for maths better than a mark of 8 for language? Does the fact that Subject C received three times as many marks for language than for maths mean that he is three times better at language? Does the fact that Subject L received twice as many marks for language than for mathematics indicate that she is twice as good at language? Certainly not. We have not been told whether the tests are being marked on the same totals, for example the mathematics mark might only be scored out of ten whereas the language marks might be scored out of thirty. If that is the case, then Subject E, for instance, seems to have done comparatively less well in language than in mathematics even though he received an apparently higher mark in language, whilst Subject C has done equally well in mathematics and language even though the scores are different. We need to be able to standardize the scores so that we have a correct and fair basis for comparison. To be able to do this requires us to be able to calculate z-scores (*see* Appendix F for the formula for this calculation); this requires the use of the standard deviation. A z-score translates marks from a test into a form which will enable these to be fairly compared to marks from another test (similarly converted to z-scores).

A fourth statistic, a t-test, is available to the evaluator who is using parametric data for the evaluation. Though it does not require the use of standard deviations, it does require an understanding of the concept of deviation.

Suppose an experimental form of evaluation were being undertaken and the evaluator wished to see whether test scores obtained on the post-test (using a parametric test) differed statistically from the scores obtained on the pre-test (using the same parametric test or an alternative form of the same test). In this case the t-test could be employed (*see* Appendix G for the formula). The t-test for interval and ratio data can be used to compare one sample on two separate occasions; alternatively it can be used to compare two samples on one occasion (particularly useful, for example, in the experimental model of evaluation to see if the two groups - the control and the experimental group - are fairly matched).

As with the chi-square statistic the evaluator will need to consult statistical tables under the appropriate degrees of freedom (in this statistic this is taken as the total of the cases minus one) to see if the differences between either the single sample on two occasions or two matched samples on one occasion are statistically significant. As with the chi-square and the Spearman rank order correlation statistics outlined so far, so this statistic begins with the null hypothesis; in the case of the t-test the null hypothesis asserts that there is no statistically significant difference between the two sets of scores. The intention of calculating the t-test statistic is to confirm or refute the null hypothesis, and if that null hypothesis is refuted, then to indicate at what level it is refuted (e.g. the 0.05 or the 0.01 level of significance).

The t-test is not only a fairly powerful statistic but it is one which is frequently used, its calculation being straightforward and applicable to teachers and other evaluators who are dealing with test scores or results. For example, a teacher could use a t-test to chart progress of a class over a school term or year, to see if measured progress was statistically significant or not.

As with correlational data the evaluator must be alert to Type I and Type II errors. For a t-test a Type I error would be committed where a putative significant difference was held to exist between the two scores when in fact this was not the case; a Type II error would be committed where the results failed to find a significant difference between the two scores when such a difference in fact existed. As with correlational data the way in which an evaluator can address Type I and Type II errors can be found in texts on statistical methods.

It was shown when dealing with non-parametric, ordinal data that a correlation co-efficient could be calculated using the Spearman test of association between two ranks of data. The parametric equivalent of this is the Pearson product moment correlation statistic (the formula for this appears in Appendix H). As with the other tests of association and statistical significance the Pearson product moment correlation statistic enables the evaluator to compute the difference between two sets of interval or ratio data to investigate whether the differences between the two sets of data are statistically significant (e.g. test scores on a norm-referenced test). Hence it is a more sophisticated and more sensitive test of association than the Spearman rank order correlation statistic, though the three *caveats* which were signalled for the Spearman correlation statistic apply also to the Pearson correlation statistic (viz assumption of causality, Type I and Type II errors).

WHAT CAN I DO TO SAVE TIME IN CALCULATING STATISTICS?

In using quantitative data the evaluator might use either a hand-held calculator or a commercially available statistical package - either for a stand-alone computer or for a mainframe computer. There are numerous cheap commercial statistical packages which can be used on stand-alone computers which will calculate means, standard deviations, correlations, chi-squares, t-tests and medians, and will print out data in a variety of numerical forms - tables, lists, correlation co-efficients, statistical computation - and a variety of graphical forms - bar charts, histograms, scattergrams, pie charts, exploded pie charts, three-dimensional block graphs, whilst for a mainframe computer the SPSS computer package will not only process vast quantities of data extremely quickly but will print out the significance levels for different types of data as appropriate. As with stand-alone computer programs the SPSS computer package will print out bar charts and a whole array of different types of statistical data. The time taken to learn to use this package will be repaid richly in time saved. At the time of writing there are SPSS computer packages produced for stand-alone computers which have large memories. Using computer packages will not only save hours of time but will not make computational errors - often a risk when evaluators are calculating formulae, even the simple formulae such as those produced in the Appendices here.

WHAT CAN I DO TO SAVE SPACE IN PRESENTING QUANTITATIVE DATA?

It has been suggested here that evaluations which are quantitatively based should seek to present their data in tables, scattergrams, graphs of all kinds, matrices, figures, lists of data, or even a single sentence to tell the reader what have been correlated and with what result. A written commentary will tell the reader which statistics have been computed, why the particular statistics chosen have been selected, what they are designed to show, what are their parameters and what the results of the computation turn out to be, what are the significance levels and whether or not statistical significance has been demonstrated. For quantitative data the actual amount of space taken to present the data might well be slight, there is an attractive economy of words in presenting this type of data.

The evaluator will have to remember that the purposes of using quantitative data are usually to indicate amounts, frequencies, the significance of certain scores, to be able to compare, to look for patterns and trends within a particular group of people or issues or between particular groups of people or issues, to look for common traits and responses, to notice similarities and differences, to suggest generalizations and common threads, to identify interesting relationships between data, to suggest associations between data, to answer questions which require a 'more than' or 'less than' type of response. Hence quantitative data will need to be accompanied by a commentary from the evaluator on what he or she takes the data to indicate, what are the areas of interest in the data, what are the main features of the data, and, of *crucial importance*, how the data answer the evaluation questions.

WHICH STATISTICS DO I USE TO ANSWER WHICH EVALUATION QUESTIONS?

So far this chapter has indicated how to calculate certain statistics and the uses to which they can be put. We can summarize these uses by listing some evaluation questions and then indicating the type of statistic which can be used on data in order to answer these evaluation questions (*see* Figure 5.5). The type of evaluation question will determine the choice of statistic; the choice of statistic must be appropriate for the type and level of data gathered.

HOW CAN I PROCESS WORD-BASED DATA?

It was mentioned earlier in this chapter that one could approach data analysis in two ways. Either one could go to the data with a series of categories already worked out for which relevant data are selected (i.e. a deductive process), or one could go to the data cold, i.e. without a series

Evaluation Question	Statistic
Do I want to see which is the mean (average) score for interval or ratio data?	Mean
Do I want to see if the frequencies of one set of nominal variables (eg age groups) is significantly related to a set of ordinal variables (e.g. the points on a rating scale)?	Chi-square
Do I want to see if the results of one rating scale correlate with those of another rating scale?	Spearman Rank Order Correlation
Do I want to see if the rank order positions in one subject for one class correlate significantly with their rank order positions in another subject?	Spearman Rank Order Correlation
Do I want to see if the scores on a parametric test are evenly distributed?	Standard Deviation
Do I want to see which score on a rating scale is the highest?	Mode
Do I want to see which is the score of the middle person in a list of scores?	Median
Do I want to see voting patterns on a rating scale?	Frequencies
Do I want to see if there is a significant difference in the results of a rating scale for two independent samples (e.g. males and females)?	Mann-Whitney U-test Chi-square
Do I want to see if there is a significant difference between three or more nominal variables and the results of a rating scale (ordinal data)?	Chi-square Kruskal-Wallis
Do I want to be able to compare scores on a test which was marked out of 20 with scores on a test which was marked out of 50?	z-scores
Do I want to see if the frequencies of one set of nominal variables is significantly related to the frequencies of another set of nominal variables? (e.g. subject specialists with the popularity of school subjects)?	Chi-square
Do I want to see if the frequencies of three or more nominal variables is significantly related to the frequencies of three or more other nominal variables (e.g. school subjects and qualifications sought)?	Kruskal-Wallis Chi-square
Do I want to see if there is a correlation between one set of interval data and another set of interval data with the same number of cases (e.g. the test scores of one group of children in French and German)?	Pearson Product Moment Correlation
Do I want to see if a control and experimental group are matched in their scores in a parametric pre-test?	t-test
Do I want to see if there is a significant difference between pre-test and post-test scores using a parametric test?	t-test

Figure 5.5 Using Statistics to Answer Particular Evaluation Questions

of pre-determined categories and, by reviewing the data, generate a series of categories which emerge from the data themselves (i.e. an inductive process). When applied to word-based data this problem takes on greater significance than for numerical data.

Whichever approach is used to process word-based data which have been gathered from open-ended interviews, field notes, semi-structured or unstructured observations, the fundamental problem remains the same: how does the evaluator glean the relevant data from what can often be a massive amount of written material? How can the evaluator cut through the mass of written data which can quickly be generated if field notes, transcripts of interviews, documents and conversational data have been collected? The issue is made more tricky by the fact that very often the data are specific to a particular institution, i.e. they are context-bound. The word data capture perspectives and opinions on a situation through the eyes of the participants; it is important that the uniqueness of each situation is not lost in an attempt to pattern responses. Word data are the stuff of illuminative and decision-making models of evaluation.

A further issue exists in words data in that interview data and oral data operate in two dimensions: not only are there the actual words which have been spoken and which can be transcribed from audio-cassette but there are also all the other factors which obtain in a face-to-face situation - the tone of voice, the cadence of the sentence, the emphasis on a word or words, the non-verbal communication, the background noise (often a feature of interviewing in schools!), side-conversations in a group interview, problems of students' understanding of what is being asked, nervousness or inarticulateness of respondents, distractors of all sorts. A transcript rarely captures these features, yet they might be the very points which influence the course of the data collection. There are several ways in which analysing word data can be approached:

(a) through the identification of key issues;
(b) through coding of responses or field notes;
(c) through content analysis of responses or field notes;
(d) through cognitive mapping of responses or field notes.

These techniques can be applied to most written forms of data. Essentially these four approaches constitute an attempt to tackle two issues, the first is of *data reduction* without loss of meaning or context, the second is of *data display*, similarly without loss of meaning or context.

HOW CAN I IDENTIFY KEY ISSUES IN WORD-BASED DATA?

If the evaluator has already established the issues which are to be investigated in the evaluation, then they can be listed quite simply and data found which will illuminate these issues. If there are, say, five people who have been interviewed in connection with the issue, then the five responses could be listed individually; alternatively, if the five respondents gave basically the same response to each issue, a global response could be given to the issue, maybe incorporating some transcribed comments made about the issue. If the issues which will be of interest in the evaluation have not been already established, then the data will have to be read, read again, read as many times as are necessary to identify which issues appear to be emerging. These are then presented issue by issue or respondent by respondent. If the evaluator is proceeding in this way, then a further step in the evaluation will have to be undertaken which is seeing how the emergent issues answer the evaluation questions.

WHAT IS A CODE IN PROCESSING WORD DATA?

In chapter three the term 'coding' was used to indicate the ascription of a number to each variable in a survey questionnaire. This was undertaken in order to identify the column number within a data file into which the appropriate piece of data could be entered for future processing with a mainframe computer; the program recommended for this was the SPSS program. The coding system was worked out in advance and entered onto the right hand side of each page of the questionnaire. In this section the term 'coding' means something completely different; it is the ascription of a category label to a piece of data, with the category label or code either decided in advance or once the data have been collected. Though coding has been the subject of frequent discussion, there is a key text on coding (Miles and Huberman, 1984) which deals with its complexity and usage. The following remarks are an attempt to identify the main principles which are set out in their work. Coding can be undertaken of interview transcripts, field notes, documents, diaries and observational data. A code is simply a word, label or abbreviation that can be attached to a particular piece of data.

HOW CAN I CODE RESPONSES AND FIELD NOTES?

Look at the following fourteen lines which are taken from an interview transcript. The evaluator is asking the respondent how she feels about the move away from a content-driven view of science and towards a process-driven view of science:

1. Evaluator: It has been suggested that a move towards a process-
2.   driven view of science is more suited to low ability
3.   students rather than to high ability students. How
4.   do you feel about this?
5. Respondent: I don't think that this is so because a lot of the

6.   problem-solving experiments that the students will
7.   undertake depend on what the students make of them,
8.   what they do depends on their abilities, the higher
9.   ability students will be able to perform at their own
10.   level in this. We have always believed that
11.   practical work was essential for students of all
12.   abilities though we would have to ensure that this
13.   did not mean the end of some important scientific
14.   content.

To work a pre-ordinate coding system, let us imagine that the evaluator
had already generated codes as follows:

PROC refers to process-driven science
PROB refers to problem-solving
EXPT refers to experiments
ABIL refers to the abilities of students
PRAC refers to practical work
CONT refers to content-driven science

The evaluator would then go through the fourteen lines and by the side of
each piece of datum as appropriate write the codes which are suited to it.
In the example *above*, line one would be coded PROC, lines two to five
ABIL, line six PROB and EXPT, line seven ABIL, lines eight to ten
ABIL, line eleven PRAC, line twelve ABIL, lines thirteen to fourteen
CONT. Note that the codes are often abbreviations. They are easily
identified with the issue that they are describing because even in
abbreviated form they resemble the issue being described - they are close
to the issue. The advice here is to keep codes as abbreviations rather than
as numbers in order to make recognition of the issue straightforward.
Having coded the data the evaluator can then examine frequencies or
issues which seem to receive much coverage.

In the example *above,* clearly the issue of ability appears to be important. We are also to see that problem-solving appears to be mentioned
alongside experiments, as though the two things are often considered together (a feature which perhaps may be noticed in future instances in the
interview).

The evaluator is also able to detect any *patterns* of coding or emergent
themes. In data which draw on several respondents or several institutions
then clearly this is significant, for it enables generalizations to be made
from qualitative data. A further code can then be generated which defines
a pattern across people or institutions. Of course in this latter case of

attempts at generalization care must be taken to ensure that the context-specificity of data is not lost or surrendered to a crude generalization.

If the evaluator were to go to the interview data *above* and generate codes *responsively*, then not only might he fortuitously generate the same codes but instead of using ABIL might have generated a code named LOWABIL for low-ability students in line two and a code named HIGHABIL for the high-ability students in the same line. Line ten might have a code entitled PHIL to indicate that the teacher's philosophy or belief in science is an issue, and lines thirteen to fourteen might have a code entitled IMPORTCONT to indicate 'important content'.

It is possible to keep very many codes in mind as one goes through word data - Miles and Huberman (1984) suggest that as many as ninety codes can be held in the working memory at any one time. Clearly there could well be a case for recording data on a second or third reading, as codes which were used early on in the data might need to be refined in light of codes generated later in the data, either to make initial codes more discriminating or to conflate codes which are unnecessarily specific. There is also a danger that early codes might influence the coding of later parts of the data. Miles and Huberman (1984) suggest that codes be kept as discrete as possible, that they should capture the complexity and comprehensiveness of the data upon which they are being used. They recommend that coding data should start sooner rather than later as later coding enfeebles analysis.

WHAT DO I DO WHEN I HAVE CODED THE DATA?

Once the codes have been generated then patterns, links, key features, emphases and side issues can be identified, all of which in turn have their own codes. Using the interview data *above* one code might for instance be used to describe a pattern (for example, PATTABIL, to describe a pattern code which concerns ability, or PATTPRAC, to describe a pattern code which concerns practical work). Another code might be used to describe an emphasis (for example, EMPHPRAC to describe an emphasis on practical work or EMPHEXPT to describe an emphasis on experiments). Another code might be used to describe a side issue (for example, SIDECONT might be used to indicate that content-driven science is a side issue).

The evaluator can then look to see if there are clusters of codes which can be grouped together under the umbrella of another main code; this will enable salient points and themes and their sub-issues to be identified, i.e. to create domain codes and their elements. The evaluator can then look at the main codes to see if, in turn, they themselves can be grouped together under a more over-arching code. The evaluator, then, is engaged in a system of generating hierarchies of codes. This abides by the view set out in Miles and Huberman (1984) that codes are astringent, pulling together a wealth of material. A further analysis of data might suggest not only using codes as descriptors of data but using codes which begin to *explain* or *to make inferences*. If an illuminative evaluation is being undertaken over time it is more likely that these over-arching category codes will become clearer.

There is an expanding list of computer programs which will enable evaluators to codify and process word data, for example, the program Ethnograph can be used on a stand-alone computer provided it has a reasonably good-sized memory. Given that word data are very time-consuming not only to transcribe (for example, one hour's taped interview often takes as much as five hours to transcribe) but also to process, as many ways as possible should be employed to shorten the time spent on data handling. In this respect computer analysis might save the evaluator many hours.

WHAT ARE THE ADVANTAGES AND DISADVANTAGES OF PRE-ORDINATE AND RESPONSIVE CODING?

Coding is a major quick way of cutting a swathe through word data. The evaluator can approach the data with a series of codes already drawn up and then the data can be looked at to see how those codes have been addressed. The attraction of this pre-ordinate method is that the codes can derive directly from the evaluation questions and can be used quickly to select relevant data to answer the evaluation questions. On the other hand this method may miss key issues or clusters of issues, which are there in the data but which the sorting frame has failed to capture. It is essential, therefore, that the evaluator, having used a pre-ordinate set of codes, then goes back into the data to see if other data might be useful or whether clusters of data are present.

Alternatively, the evaluator might go straight to the data and operate responsively, generating codes for the particular pieces of data or combinations of data under scrutiny. Whilst the attraction of this approach lies in its honesty to the data, being 'strong on reality' it requires the evaluator to undertake the supplementary exercise of relating the codes and responses to the evaluation questions.

One way is not better than another, they are simply different; the former requires evaluators to generate codes in advance of the data processing, the latter requires them to generate codes once the data have been examined.

HOW CAN I PERFORM A CONTENT ANALYSIS OF RESPONSES, DOCUMENTS OR FIELD NOTES?

Content analysis can take a variety of forms. It can be, for instance, simply a count of the number of times a particular word or phrase or mention of an issue appears in the transcript or field notes - i.e. using word data to generate numerical data. If key words are identified (maybe from the evaluation questions), then this simple form of frequency count might be useful. Alternatively, the evaluator can identify the key issues which are being addressed (solicited or unsolicited) in the interview.

If data are derived from interviews, then the evaluator might wish to add a second element to this content analysis, which is sometimes an indication of the other factors at play in the interview which a simple word transcript fails to capture - tone of voice, the non-verbal communication, the setting of the interview (physical and emotional) and the emotion expressed in the interview. By combining these two elements - the substantive content of the interview and the style of the interview (e.g. those aspects of the interview which are lost in a simple written transcript) - a third element might then be addressed: the inferences the evaluator can make about the issues under discussion (Fox, 1969).

To undertake this form of content analysis the evaluator will have to undertake not only the coding and categorizing of responses (discussed *above*) in order to summarize the word data but also develop a coding and categorizing of those aspects of the interview which a transcript does not capture - aspects of the style of the interview. This second element might require the evaluator to consider the degree of animation or intensity with which a particular item is discussed, or the positive or negative tone adopted (or a mixture of these two), or the apparent level of engagement with the issue, or the length of time which was devoted to a particular issue, or the willingness of respondents to reveal deeply held beliefs, or the general state of the respondent (nervous, forthcoming, relaxed etc.), or how the respondent answers (one word answers or complex and convoluted responses), or willingness to elaborate on an issue, a whole range of factors.

By combining these two elements the evaluation then is able to go further - to indicate the emphasis which was placed on particular issues, either by the evaluator or the respondent. In this way a priority of issues may be generated. Moreover this combination of content and style will enable the evaluator to identify how the respondent *feels* about a particular issue, to determine any regularity of feelings or strength of feelings either in the respondent or towards one or more of the issues. For the former this might indicate that the respondent generally was a positive, lighthearted, animated, morose, introverted, negative person; for the latter it would enable the evaluator to establish whether the same issue aroused the same emotion in more than one respondent. Such an analysis would clarify the seriousness or importance attached to an issue either by one respondent or by many respondents.

This style of analysis can be taken further with the evaluator looking at the interview data to see if issues are discussed in isolation, in tandem with other issues (i.e. to see if the respondent consistently or inconsistently puts issues in pairs, triads etc.) and whether mention of one issue triggers off the mention of another issue. In this way the evaluator can establish links between the data, by commenting on either the links between content or links between style. For the former these would be cognitive links (*see below* on cognitive mapping); for the latter it would involve seeing whether a particular emotion which was evoked then led on to the respondent identifying another issue which evoked the same emotion. An example of the latter would be the respondent who begins to comment on a positive opinion which is held about one aspect of her institution and who then goes on to list all the other positive opinions that she has about the institution.

The linking or separation of issues in interviews has its equivalent in the written record of observational data where the evaluator would be looking to see whether one particular behaviour observed by the evaluator was consistently demonstrated in tandem with another particular behaviour or whether one behaviour triggered another. For example, field notes might indicate that whenever Jane was cross she refused to work, or that whenever Jane was in a good mood she still refused to work, preferring to chat to her friends.

WHAT IS COGNITIVE MAPPING OF RESPONSES AND FIELD NOTES?

In many ways cognitive mapping (Jones, 1987) is an attempt to fuse together the notion of coding and the notion of content analysis. It was suggested at the beginning of this section that the twin issues which the evaluator faces with word-based data are data reduction and data display. The two are connected, for the process of data reduction is enacted through careful data display. So far the data display has taken the forms of coding, categorizing and content analysis. In cognitive mapping the display element features more graphically, as the evaluator attempts to display the linkages between the constructs that are elicited from the respondent, as will be seen in Figure 5.6 opposite.

This is a graphic presentation of data from a semi-structured interview which was held to solicit attitudes to and opinions of a piece of curriculum

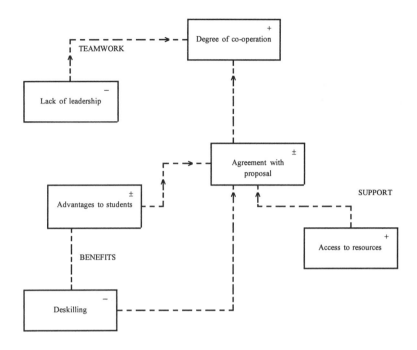

Figure 5.6 The Early Stages of a Cognitive Map

innovation in a school. The words in boxes indicate the substantive issues which emerged during the interview; the capitalized words outside the boxes indicate the evaluator's own categorical headings which he or she might use later in reporting the findings; the plus signs (+), minus signs (−) and plus or minus signs (±) indicate the degrees of positive feelings about the issues under discussion, i.e. whether the respondent feels that this issue is safe for the innovation. The arrow signs indicate some causal relationships which the respondent articulated in the interview. Seen like this a cognitive map displays clearly significant issues and their interrelationships.

Figure 5.6 has resonance with Miles' and Huberman's (1984) forms of data reduction and data display, for they attempt to show how displaying data in the form of boxes with arrows indicating the direction of effects on other boxes can clearly illustrate how key features link, how one feature impinges on, or affects, another. In this cognitive mapping the processes of coding and categorizing data are undertaken in order to identify the key factors or constructs in the respondent's perspective and then the 'thick description' - the rich contextual detail - is interrogated in order to try to put in the linkages, clusters of constructs, the positive and negative relationships, the strong or weak links, any causal links, the relative emphases of different constructs as articulated by the respondents, whether some constructs are subsumed by others, and similarities and differences between relationships and constructs.

WHEN CAN I USE COGNITIVE MAPPING?

Though Jones (1987) suggests that cognitive maps may be of use primarily for evaluators, to help them acquire an overall picture of a situation, nevertheless the similarity between Jones' cognitive mapping and Miles' and Huberman's (1984) causal pathways and networks suggests that these can be used as part of the formal evaluation rather than the background work on assembling the results of the data and the production of the evaluation report.

HOW CAN I ENSURE THAT MY INTERPRETATION OF WORD DATA IS ACCEPTABLE?

There are two main ways of validating the interpretation of evaluation data. Firstly the evaluator can simply take back the interpretation he or she has made to those respondents who yielded the data in the first place. The evaluator will ask the respondents to indicate whether they agree with the interpretation, a process known as respondent validation. Whilst this might be eminently desirable it does raise the question of what can be done in the event of disagreement between the evaluators and the *evaluands*. For example, the evaluator might give a different meaning to events from the *evaluands* - who is correct in that situation? This might lead to the need for the reporting of disagreement or multiple perspectives (the latter maybe involving the preparation of a lengthy evaluation report). One way of approaching this is to anticipate it in the planning stage of evaluation where the problem of whose interpretation will be accepted is ironed out in advance.

A second approach to the validation of the evaluator's interpretation is to submit the data without comment to a 'critical friend' in order that the data might be analysed. If the analysis which the 'critical friend' performs matches that of the evaluator, then this could well demonstrate a measure of validity through triangulation of evaluators (or maybe that both interpretations are invalid!). The notion that the data can be submitted to scrutiny by a disinterested party who is ignorant of the existing interpretation of those data is a standard and fairly powerful form of validation.

HOW DO I PRESENT THE ISSUES THAT I HAVE ANALYSED?

Whether numerical data or word data are being presented, the evaluator will have to decide on the most appropriate format for presenting the results. One way is simply to use the evaluation questions for each sub-heading, noting, if appropriate, the sources of particular comments - for example, person by person, school by school, group by group, or a more collective presentation if that is appropriate. This is essentially a pre-ordinate form of data presentation, as the evaluation questions have already been decided in advance.

A second way for the data to be presented is issue by issue in what could well be a more responsive mode of presentation, the issues *deriving from* rather than determining the analysis. Here the issue would be presented in a sub-heading and the relevant data assembled for it, maybe giving, as before, the source of the data - for example, person by person, school by school, group by group, or a collective interpretation if appropriate.

A third way is for the evaluator to present the material respondent by respondent, or case by case (if it is a school for example, or a group of students or teachers). In this way there could well be some duplication of responses (which would need to receive comment) which might result in a wordy report. This way could well be the only one available to the illuminative evaluator, for the uniqueness and individuality of the context of each person, situation or case being studied might render it impossible to draw out any generalizations. This is the essence of the case study approach which does not seek to make generalizations. If the situation accords with a reader's own situation, then, maybe, that reader might gain some insights into his or her own situation, but that is not the expressed intention of a case study; the case study is a deliberate attempt to portray the specific context or a unique instance and it is perhaps invidious to try to determine patterns and make generalizations.

SHOULD I BE TRYING TO GENERALIZE FROM QUALITATIVE DATA?

This last point of the previous paragraph strikes at the very heart of some of the issues raised so far in discussing the analysis of word-based data. So far it has been assumed that it is desirable for an evaluator to try to look for themes, general issues, clusters of issues, emerging patterns of response and generalizations across different individuals, groups and schools. That has not been questioned.

There is a powerful argument against this view which states that to seek generalizations, themes and patterns is to try to apply to qualitative data the criteria for quantitative data. Quantitative data analysis deliberately seeks to make generalizations, to derive frequencies and patterns, to generate law-like positivist accounts of whatever is being measured. To bring this approach to qualitative data is to violate the very essence of qualitative data analysis; qualitative data analysis should rather seek to present the richness and uniqueness, ideography and context-specificity of the very particular situation which it is describing or investigating, quite simply to accord uniqueness, individuality, non-generalizability a central and crucially important position rather than to regard it as an encumbrance whose effects have to be minimized. Further, if illuminative and decision-making models are to be true to themselves, they will need to chart the *change* and *development* of issues *over time*, a feature which a single snapshot approach to data collection will overlook.

WHAT CAN I DO WITH NON-GENERALIZABLE DATA?

If the points in the previous section are accepted, then the implications are several. Firstly, it will mean that the evaluation will have to be written up case by case as a series of case studies. Secondly, it will mean that a much more stringent approach to coding has to be adopted, where codes are very specific to specific institutions, people or contexts and where the attempt to develop main codes or over-arching codes stops short of becoming too general. Thirdly, it will mean that an important place in the evaluation will be given to multiple accounts which could well end up by being written in narrative form. Fourthly, it will mean that the case study might be unrepresentative of anything but itself caught in a particular socio-cultural, geographical and temporal moment and that the presentation of the richness of that situation will be sought. Finally, it will mean that the negotiation stage in planning an evaluation will have to agree on the style of reporting (for example, to agree that executive summaries are inappropriate). This is to say that the agenda for the evaluation will have to be agreed very carefully in the planning stages.

As in all discussions so far the overwhelming criterion for the evaluation is appropriacy - goodness of fit. This chapter has set out a range of issues in and techniques for data analysis. The decision of which to employ is not an arbitrary one but one which sets the analysis in the context of being faithful to the methodology, instrumentation, design of the evaluation which enable the evaluation questions to be answered appropriately and fully.

RECOMMENDED READING

Bryman A. and Cramer, D. (1990) *Quantitative Data Analysis for Social Scientists*. London: Routledge.

Cohen, L. and Holliday, M. (1979) *Statistics for Education and Physical Education*. London: Harper & Row.

Fitz-Gibbon, C.T. and Lyons Morris, L. (1987) *How to Analyze Data*. Beverly Hills: Sage Publications.

Hammersley, M. (1979) Analysing Ethnographic Data, Unit 1, Block 6, DE304, in *Research Methods in Education and the Social Sciences*. Milton Keynes: Open University Press.

Hopkins, D. (1989) Analysing Data and Enhancing Validity, in D. Hopkins *Evaluation for School Development*. Milton Keynes: Open University Press.

Hopkins, D., Bollington, R. and Hewett, D. (1989) Growing Up with Qualitative Research and Evaluation, in *Evaluation and Research in Education*, 3 (2), pp. 61 - 80.

Hopkins, K.D. and Glass, G.V. (1978) *Basic Statistics for the Behavioral Sciences*. Englewood Cliffs, New Jersey: Prentice Hall.

Kemmis, S. (1982) Seven Principles for Programme Evaluation in Curriculum Development and Innovation, *Journal of Curriculum Studies* 14 (3) pp. 221 - 240.

Miles, M. and Huberman, M. (1984) *Qualitative Data Analysis*. Beverly Hills: Sage Publications.

Siegel, S. (1956) *Nonparametric Statistics for the Behavioral Sciences*. New York: McGraw-Hill.

Spradley, J.P. (1979) *The Ethnographic Interview*. New York: Holt, Rinehart and Winston.

Steadman, R. (1982) Evaluation Techniques, in R. McCormick (ed.) *Calling Education to Account*. London: Heinemann.

6 Achieving Reliability and Validity

Mention has been made throughout the previous chapters about reliability and validity. This chapter will clarify the twin concepts of reliability and validity and then indicate not only how bias might enter into every stage of an evaluation but also what the evaluator can do to minimize bias.

The concepts of reliability and validity are multi-faceted, there are many different types of reliability and different types of validity. Hence there will be several ways in which they can be addressed. It is unwise to think that threats to reliability and validity can ever be erased completely, rather the effects of these threats can be attenuated by attention to reliability and validity throughout an evaluation.

WHAT IS RELIABILITY?

Reliability is essentially a synonym for consistency and replicability over time, over instruments and over groups of respondents. For an evaluation to be reliable it must demonstrate that if it were to be carried out on a similar group of respondents in a similar context (however defined), then similar results would be found. There are three principal types of reliability: stability, equivalence and internal consistency.

Reliability as Stability

In this form reliability is a measure of consistency over time and over similar samples. A reliable instrument for an evaluation will yield similar data from similar respondents over time. A leaking tap which each day leaks one litre is leaking reliably whereas a tap which leaks one litre some days and two litres on others is not. In the experimental, survey and objectives models of evaluation this would mean that if a test and then a re-test were undertaken within an appropriate time span, then similar results would be obtained. The evaluator has to decide what an appropriate length of time is; too short a time and respondents may remember what they said or did in the first test situation, too long a time and there may be extraneous effects operating to distort the data (for example, maturation in students, outside influences on the students). An evaluator seeking to demonstrate this type of reliability will have to choose an appropriate time scale between the test and re-test. Correlation co-efficients can be calculated for judging the reliability of pre- and post-tests, using formulae which are readily available in books on research methods and test construction; the formulae for Spearman and Pearson correlations are reproduced in Appendices D and H respectively, whilst the t-test of significance is reproduced in Appendix G.

In addition to stability over time reliability as stability can also be stability over a similar sample. For example, we would assume that if we were to administer a test or a questionnaire simultaneously to two groups of students who were very closely matched on significant characteristics (e.g. age, gender, ability etc. - whatever characteristics are deemed to have a significant bearing on the responses), then similar results (on a test) or responses (to a questionnaire) would be obtained. The correlation co-efficient on this form of the test/re-test method can be calculated either for the whole test (e.g. by using the Pearson statistic or a t-test) or for sections of the questionnaire (e.g. by using the Spearman or Pearson statistic as appropriate or a t-test). The statistical significance of the correlation co-efficient can be found (*see* chapter five) and should be 0.05 or higher if reliability is to be guaranteed. This form of reliability over a sample is particularly useful in piloting tests and questionnaires.

Reliability as Equivalence

Within this type of reliability there are two main sorts of reliability. Reliability may be achieved firstly through using equivalent forms (also known as alternative forms) of a test or data-gathering instrument. If an equivalent form of the test or instrument is devised and yields similar results, then the instrument can be said to demonstrate this form of reliability. For example, the pre-test and post-test in the experimental model of evaluation are predicated on this type of reliability, being alternate forms of instrument to measure the same issues. This type of reliability might also be demonstrated if the equivalent forms of a test or other instrument yielded consistent results if applied simultaneously to matched samples (e,g, a control and experimental group or two random stratified samples in a survey). Here reliability can be measured through a t-test, through the demonstration of a high correlation co-efficient and through the demonstration of similar means and standard deviations between two groups.

Secondly, reliability as equivalence may be achieved through inter-rater reliability. If more than one evaluator is taking part in an evaluation then, human judgement being fallible, agreement between all evaluators must be achieved through ensuring that each evaluator enters data in the same way.

It was mentioned in chapter three that this would be particularly pertinent to a team of evaluators gathering structured observational or semi-structured interview data where each member of the team would have to agree on which data would be entered in which categories. For observational data reliability is addressed in the training sessions for evaluators where they work on video material to ensure parity in how they enter the data.

Reliability as Internal Consistency

Whereas the test/re-test method and the equivalent forms method of demonstrating reliability required the tests or instruments to be run twice, to demonstrate internal consistency requires the instrument or tests to be run once only through the split-half method of demonstrating reliability. Let us imagine that a test were to be administered to a group of students. Here the test items are divided into two halves, ensuring that each half is matched in terms of item difficulty and content. Each half is marked separately. If the test is to demonstrate split-half reliability, then the marks obtained on each half should be correlated highly with the other. Any student's marks on the one half should match his or her marks on the other half. This can be calculated using the Spearman-Brown formula:

$$\text{Reliability} = \frac{2r}{1+r}$$

where r = the actual correlation between the halves of the instrument.

This calculation requires a correlation co-efficient to be calculated (discussed in the previous chapter - e.g. a Spearman rank order correlation or a Pearson product moment correlation).

Let us say that using the Spearman-Brown formula the correlation co-efficient is 0.85, in this case the formula for reliability is set out thus:

$$\text{Reliability} = \frac{2 \times 0.85}{1+0.85} = \frac{1.70}{1.85} = 0.919$$

Given that the highest co-efficient will be 1.00 we can see that the reliability of this instrument, calculated for the split-half form of reliability, is very high indeed.

This type of reliability assumes that the test administered can be split into two matched halves; many tests have a gradient of difficulty or different items of content in each half. If this is the case and, for example, the test contains twenty items, then the evaluator, instead of splitting the test into two by assigning items one to ten to one half and items eleven to twenty to the second half may assign all the even numbered items to one group and all the odd numbered items to another. This would move towards the two halves being matched in terms of content and cumulative degrees of difficulty.

WHAT IS VALIDITY?

Whilst validity is essentially a demonstration that a particular instrument in fact measures what it purports to measure, validity takes many forms. For example, in qualitative data validity might be addressed through the honesty, depth, richness and scope of the data achieved, the participants approached, the extent of triangulation and the disinterestedness or objectivity of the evaluator. In quantitative data validity might be approached through careful sampling, appropriate instrumentation and appropriate statistical treatments of the data. It is impossible for an evaluation to be 100% valid, that is the optimism of perfection. In quantitative evaluations there is a measure of standard error which is in-built and which has to be acknowledged; in qualitative data the subjectivity of respondents, their opinions, attitudes and perspectives all build in a measure of bias. Validity, then, should be seen as a matter of degree rather than as an absolute state (Gronlund, 1981). Hence at best we strive to minimize invalidity and maximize validity. Internal validity seeks to demonstrate that the explanation of a particular event, issue, set of data which an evaluation provides can actually be sustained by the data. External validity refers to the degree to which the results can be general-ized to the wider population, cases or situations. There are, however, many more types of validity.

Content Validity

To demonstrate this form of validity the instrument must show that it fairly and comprehensively covers the domain or items that it purports to cover. It is unlikely that each issue will be able to be addressed in its entirety simply because of the time available or respondents' motivation to com-plete, for example, a long questionnaire. If this is the case, then the evaluator must ensure that the elements of the main issue to be covered in the evaluation are both a fair representation of the wider issue under investigation (and its weighting) and that the elements chosen for the evaluation sample are themselves addressed in depth and breadth. Careful sampling of items is required to ensure their representativeness. For example, if the evaluator wished to see how well a group of students could spell 1,000 words in French but decided only to have a sample of 50 words for the spelling test, then that test would have to ensure that it represented the range of spellings in the 1,000 words - maybe by ensuring that the spelling rules had all been included or that possible spelling errors had been covered in the test in the proportions in which they occurred in the 1,000 words.

Criterion-Related Validity

This form of validity endeavours to relate the results of one particular instrument to another external criterion. Within this type of validity there are two principal forms: predictive validity and concurrent validity.

Predictive validity is achieved if the data acquired at the first round of evaluation correlate highly with data acquired at a future date. For example, if the results of examinations taken by sixteen year-olds correlate highly with the examination results gained by the same students when aged eighteen, then we might wish to say that the first examination demonstrated strong predictive validity.

A variation on this theme is encountered in the notion of concurrent validity. To demonstrate this form of validity the data gathered from using one instrument must correlate highly with data gathered from using another instrument. For example, suppose I wished to evaluate a student's problem-solving ability. I might observe the student working on a problem, or I might talk to the student about how she is tackling the problem, or I might ask the student to write down how she tackled the problem. Here I have three different data-collecting instruments - observation, interview and documentation respectively. If the results all agreed - concurred - that, according to given criteria for problem-solving ability, the student demonstrated a good ability to solve a problem, then I would be able to say with greater confidence (validity) that the student was good at problem-solving than if I had arrived at that judgement simply from using one instrument.

Concurrent validity is very similar to its partner - predictive validity - in its core concept (i.e. agreement with a second measure); what differentiates concurrent and predictive validity is the absence of a time element in the former; concurrence can be demonstrated simultaneously with another instrument.

Construct Validity

A construct is an abstract; this separates it from the previous types of validity which dealt in actualities - defined content. In this type of validity agreement is sought on the 'operationalized' forms of a construct, clarifying what we mean when we use this construct. Hence in this form of validity the articulation of the construct is important; is my understanding of this construct similar to that which is generally accepted to be the construct? For example, let us say that I wished to evaluate a child's intelligence (assuming, for the sake of this example, that it is a unitary quality). I could say that I construed intelligence to be demonstrated in the ability to sharpen a pencil. How acceptable a construction of intelligence is this? Is not intelligence something else (e.g. that which is demonstrated by a high result in an intelligence test)?

To establish construct validity I would need to be assured that *my construction* of a particular issue agreed with other constructions of the same issue, e.g. intelligence, creativity, anxiety, motivation. This can be achieved through correlations with other measures of the issue or by rooting my construction in a wide literature search which teases out the meaning of a particular construct (i.e. a theory of what that construct is) and its constituent elements. Demonstrating construct validity means not only confirming the construction with that given in relevant literature, but requires me to look for counter examples which might falsify my construction. When I have balanced confirming and refuting evidence I am in a position to demonstrate construct validity. I am then in a position to stipulate what I take this construct to be. In the case of conflicting interpretations of a construct I might have to acknowledge that conflict and then stipulate the interpretation that I shall use.

HOW MIGHT I ENSURE VALIDITY IN MY EVALUATION?

It is very easy to slip into invalidity; it is both insidious and pernicious as it can enter at every stage of an evaluation. The attempt to build out invalidity is essential if the evaluator is to be able to have confidence in the elements of the evaluation plan, data acquisition, data processing, analysis, interpretation and its ensuing judgement.

At the design stage threats to validity can be minimized by,

(a) choosing an appropriate time scale;
(b) ensuring that there are adequate resources for the required evaluation to be undertaken;
(c) selecting an appropriate methodology for answering the evaluation questions;
(d) selecting appropriate instrumentation for gathering the type of data required;
(e) using an appropriate sample (e.g. one which is representative, not

too small or too large);

(f) demonstrating internal, external, content, concurrent and construct validity;

(g) 'operationalizing' the constructs fairly;

(h) ensuring reliability in terms of stability (consistency, equivalence, split-half analysis of test material);

(i) selecting appropriate foci to answer the evaluation questions;

(j) devising and using appropriate instruments (for example, to catch accurate, representative, relevant and comprehensive data (King, Morris and Fitz-Gibbon, 1987); ensuring that readability levels are appropriate; avoiding any ambiguity of instructions, terms and questions; using instruments that will catch the complexity of issues; avoiding leading questions; ensuring that the level of test is appropriate - e.g. neither too easy nor too difficult; avoiding test items with little discriminability; avoiding making the instruments too short or too long; avoiding too many or too few items for each issue);

(k) avoiding a biased choice of evaluator or evaluation team (e.g. insiders or outsiders as evaluators).

In addition to the specific issues in data-gathering outlined in chapter three, there are areas where invalidity or bias might creep into the evaluation at the stage of data gathering; these can be minimized by,

(a) reducing the Hawthorne effect (*see* chapter three);

(b) minimizing reactivity effects (respondents behaving differently when subjected to scrutiny or being placed in new situations, for example, the interview situation);

(c) trying to avoid drop-out rates amongst respondents;

(d) taking steps to avoid non-return of questionnaires;

(e) avoiding having too long or too short an interval between pre-tests and post-tests;

(f) ensuring inter-rater reliability;

(g) matching control and experimental groups fairly;

(h) ensuring standardized procedures for gathering data or for administering tests;

(i) building on the motivations of the respondents;

(j) tailoring the instruments to the concentration span of the respondents and addressing other situational factors (e.g. health, environment, noise, distraction, threat);

(k) addressing factors concerning the evaluator (particularly in an interview situation); for example, the attitude, gender, race, age, personality, dress, comments, replies, questioning technique, behaviour, style and non-verbal communication of the evaluator.

At the stage of data analysis, in addition to the issues outlined in chapter five, there are several areas where invalidity lurks; these might be minimized by,

    (a) using respondent validation;
    (b) avoiding subjective interpretation of data (e.g. being too generous or too ungenerous in the award of marks) i.e. lack of standardization and moderation of results;
    (c) reducing the halo effect, where evaluators' knowledge of the person or knowledge of other data about the person or situation exerts an influence on subsequent judgements;
    (d) using appropriate statistical treatments for the level of data (e.g. avoiding applying techniques from interval scaling to ordinal data or using incorrect statistics for the type, size, complexity, sensitivity of data);
    (e) recognizing spurious correlations and extraneous factors which may be affecting the data (i.e. tunnel vision);
    (f) avoiding poor coding of qualitative data;
    (g) avoiding making inferences and generalizations beyond the capability of the data to support such statements;
    (h) avoiding the equating of correlations and causes;
    (i) avoiding selective use of data;
    (j) avoiding unfair aggregation of data (particularly of frequency tables);
    (k) avoiding unfair telescoping of data (degrading the data);
    (l) avoiding Type I and/or Type II errors (*see* p. 140).

At the stage of data reporting invalidity can show itself in several ways; the evaluator must take steps to minimize this by, for example,

    (a) avoiding using data very selectively and unrepresentatively (for example, accentuating the positive and neglecting or ignoring the negative);
    (b) indicating the context and parameters of the evaluation in the data collection and treatment, the degree of confidence which can be placed in the results, the degree of context-freedom or context-boundedness of the data (i.e. the level to which the results can be generalized);
    (c) presenting the data without misrepresenting its message;
    (d) making claims which are sustainable by the data;
    (e) avoiding inaccurate or wrong reporting of data (i.e. technical

errors or orthographical errors);
(f) ensuring that the evaluation questions are answered;
(g) releasing evaluation results neither too soon nor too late.

Having identified the realms in which invalidity lurks, the evaluator can take steps to ensure that, as far as possible, invalidity has been minimized in all areas of an evaluation.

A great problem in using evaluations is to make unrealistic claims from the data. *Below* are four examples of this feature, selected to indicate the range of problems which surround the use made of data.

Example One: improving secondary school mathematics performance

A secondary school is anxious to determine and evaluate a range of factors which affect the level of achievement of mathematics in its sixteen-year-old students. Students in two of the school's mathematics classes take a commercially produced test of mathematical ability, then the classes follow the mathematics curriculum for six months. After this time the students take a similar test (or equivalent form) of mathematical ability. Students in class A score more than students in class B. The evaluator reports that teacher quality is a significant factor in improving mathematics performance and that the teacher of class A is better than the teacher of class B.

Comment: In an age of accountability this conclusion might be very welcome to some audiences. However, the conclusion drawn here is fundamentally flawed. We have no knowledge of how the two groups were matched other than by age, for example, one group might contain students whose abilities in mathematics were naturally higher than the other, one group might contain thirty students and the other contain only ten students. We have no knowledge of what treatment took place in the mathematics lessons during the year or whether that treatment was the same for both groups, for example, one group might have received specific instruction in one aspect of mathematics whilst the other had not. We have no indication of what extraneous variables might have been operating on the students (for example, the effect of maturation, motivation to learn mathematics, the mathematics diet outside the school, parental pressure to succeed). We do not know whether the measured increase in mathematics ability in one group was statistically significant or not, we do not know the reliability scales being used, the standard deviations of the results, the standard error in the two tests and we do not know whether the two groups were taught by the same teacher, teachers with similar characteristics or teachers with very different characteristics. The evaluator is confusing correlation with cause.

The claims made by the evaluator have been wildly fanciful. Beware the evaluator who does not understand the boundaries of her data!

Example Two: improving children's use of history texts

Concern has been expressed about children's poor ability to select relevant material from history text books. It is decided to try to remedy this problem, so a small project is planned which will be designed to improve this ability. An evaluation is undertaken to see if this project is a success. Some of the eleven-year-old children take a diagnostic test on selecting relevant information from a history book. The group is then given an intensive morning's work on how to extract relevant material from a history text book. In the afternoon the group is given a post-test on selecting relevant information from a history book; 10% of the children score more highly on this second test. The evaluator reports that the morning's intensive work has increased the children's ability to select information from history books and that the project is a success.

Comment: Though this example appears to be a pre-test/post-test experimental type of evaluation, this is in fact a masquerade, for there is no control group; we have no insights into the reliability and validity of the test items, no analysis is given of other extraneous variables which might be exerting an influence (i.e. variables have not been isolated and held steady or controlled); we have no knowledge of the group size and therefore are unable to say whether the 10% difference is significant or not; we have no idea of any long-term benefits of the intensive programme - the post-test being carried out on the same afternoon of the project; we have no idea on the statistical analysis of the results; we have no data on the possible differences of performance by some children on the post-test. We are confusing correlation and cause. We are asked to believe that the project is a success based on one evaluation alone - i.e. on very limited, short-term results.

Beware the claims made by this evaluator! They far exceed the capability of the data to support her evaluation.

Example Three: science in secondary schools

A pilot project has been undertaken in science teaching. All the science teachers in ten secondary schools have been invited to participate in the project which is being funded by local industries. However, only three schools decide to participate in the project. The project runs for three years and is then evaluated. The local evaluator is asked to analyse the results in national examinations of all the students in the ten schools to see if there is a difference between the results of those in the three project schools and the results of those in the other seven. He finds that the students in the three schools who *had* participated in the project have achieved generally better than those in the other seven in the three year period of the project. Because the evaluator has been asked to suggest whether the project should continue, he recommends that it should continue and that all ten schools should participate in the funded science project.

Comment: In this example we know nothing about the nature of the schools involved or uninvolved in the scheme. It might well be that the three schools who opted into the scheme contained students who were already destined to achieve more highly than those in the other schools (for whatever reason - e.g. catchment, parental support, teacher enthusiasm). It might have been that the three schools opted into the scheme because they believed that it would confirm what was already a local belief - that these schools always performed well on public examinations.

We know nothing about the process variables - the nature of the teaching, the nature of the treatment (the science project) - the attitudes of the students, the perceived benefits of the project, the size of classes, the size of schools, the age of the students. Quite simply we have no indication of how well the sample of three schools represents all the ten schools. The three schools might have creamed off the high ability students from the local school population, leaving the other seven schools to teach the remainder. We do not know how many students were taking part in the new scheme and how many were not.

There was no pre-test so it is unclear how valid the post-test (the national examination) was as a measure of the success of the project. A national examination might have borne no relation at all to the project, i.e. the students in the three schools might have scored highly in spite of the project. The evaluator has made a potentially spurious correlation between an examination and the success of a particular project. If we had tested all ten schools at the start of the three year period, we might have found that the three schools who involved themselves in the project began it already ahead of other students in performance in science and that their rate of improvement might in fact have turned out to be less when using the project material than if they had not used it. We have no understanding of how the project worked - whether it operated in the same way in the three experimental schools.

Beware the evaluator who has not paid sufficient attention to sampling, pre-testing and post-testing in an experimental mode, and who uses tests whose validity for the task is uncertain.

Example Four: using learning support teachers in school

The governing body of a school is anxious to use its financial budget to best effect. It wishes to evaluate the effectiveness of its part-time learning support teachers to see if money is being spent wisely on this aspect of the school. Learning support teachers are placed with a group of seven year-olds whose performance in mathematics is poor. After two terms the class teacher administers a mathematics test to all the children who have been working with the learning support teachers. She discovers that these children perform better on the test than other children in the class. The class teacher is then able to recommend to the governors that the learning support teachers improved children's mathematical ability and that funding here should improve.

Comment: Here again we have no real insight into the make-up or matching of the control or the experimental groups by size or other significant features. The evaluator assumes that because an alleged correlation could be observed between the results of one group's mathematical work this would imply a causal relationship, i.e. that working with learning support teachers had improved the children's mathematical ability. There is no indication of what the significant variables might be, no isolation and control of variables.

We have no indication of whether the group who did not work with the learning support teachers might have achieved equally well if they had worked with the learning support teachers, or whether they might have been better or worse than the other group. Because we have no indication of the key characteristics of the two groups we have no indication whether the children who showed an improvement might have improved anyway. We have no details on the test used, so that we are unable to say with any certainty whether the test was reliable and valid, whether the differences between the groups were actually measured or simply seemed to be better, or whether they were statistically significant. We have no indication of whether other process variables were held constant or whether the treatments meted out to the alleged experimental group were the same on a variety of criteria. We cannot be clear on whether any improvement in the experimental group was due to the support teachers' personality or to the work undertaken.

Beware the evaluator who believes that correlation implies causality! We can only make crude judgements from crude data. We cannot make huge claims from invalid evaluations.

CONCLUSION

The four examples *above* should cause the evaluator to hesitate before making any great claims for the evaluation. The golden rule is never to make claims that are unsupportable by the evidence collected. To do otherwise is to court danger, however politically attractive those claims might or might not be.

The list of sources of bias is legion. Though validity and reliability have been touched on throughout this book, this chapter has attempted to draw them together for convenience. No evaluation is completely clean or free from unreliability or invalidity. The task of the evaluator is to ensure that the biases, invalidities and unreliabilities that can distort an evaluation are kept to a minimum. The evaluator has to be very vigilant for sources of bias and in light of these declare the degree of confidence which can be placed in the evaluation.

RECOMMENDED READING

Carmines, E.G. and Zeller, R.A. (1979) *Reliability and Validity Assessment*. Beverly Hills: Sage Publications.

Gronlund, N.E. (1981) *Measurement and Evaluation in Teaching* (4th Edition). New York: Collier Macmillan.

Hutchinson, B., Hopkins, D. and Howard, J. (1988) The Problem of Validity in the Qualitative Evaluation of Categorically Funded Curriculum Development Projects, *Educational Research*, 30 (1) pp. 54 - 64.

Oppenheim, A.N. (1966) *Questionnaire Design and Attitude Measurement*. London: Heinemann.

7 How Do I Report an Evaluation?

The previous chapters have suggested that each element of the evaluation needs to be planned in advance - to be negotiated where necessary and agreement found between all participants. The same holds true for the reporting of the evaluation, it needs to be planned and agreement must be sought on the form and audience of the evaluation report.

HOW CAN I APPROACH THE REPORTING OF AN EVALUATION?

In approaching the reporting of an evaluation there are seven main questions which have to be addressed:

(1) What must be reported to different audiences?
(2) Who must receive a report?
(3) Who might be interested in a report?
(4) What forms will the reporting take for different audiences?
(5) When will the summative reporting take place?
(6) When will the formative reporting take place?
(7) How can the reporting be made user-friendly?

With regard to question (1) *above*, there are several sub-issues which the evaluator will need to consider:

(a) some audiences will require a full report, other audiences will require an executive summary (a summary of the main features of the programme and the main findings of the evaluation together with a brief synopsis of the purposes, context and methodology and instrumentation of the evaluation, the whole summary totalling no more than two or three sides of paper);
(b) some audiences will be interested in the evaluation design, others only interested in the outcomes;
(c) the evaluator will need to decide what the minimum contents of an evaluation report must contain in order to do justice to the evaluation.

With regard to questions (2) and (3) *above* the evaluator will need to differentiate between those who *must* receive a report and those who *might be interested* in the report. An example of the former might be the headteacher, the local authority education officers, the participants in the evaluation and the stake-holders in the evaluation (those whom the evaluation might affect). An example of the latter might be the institutions, other teachers, curriculum planners known to the participants and a university department.

With regard to (4) *above* the reporting might be:

(a) written;
(b) oral;
(c) a combination of written and oral presentation of the findings to a selected group, to all the stake-holders, to all interested parties in an open meeting;
(d) a prior circulation of a written report followed by a discussion between agreed audiences and the evaluator or evaluators.

Given that different audiences might be receiving different reports, the evaluator will have to decide on the form of dissemination of the evaluation findings and the opportunities to be given to various audiences to discuss the findings with the evaluators and the stake-holders. If a full report were to be given to the governors of a school or to a local authority inspector, then it might be more appropriate for these parties to disseminate the evaluation findings rather than for the evaluator to undertake that dissemination, i.e. the evaluator hands over a written report and the recipients do with it what they will. The degree of formality of the reporting will also have to be considered; for some audiences a very formal reporting might be appropriate, for others a more informal, perhaps discussion-based, form of reporting might be more appropriate. This would probably be the case, for example, if teachers were presenting to their colleagues at a staff meeting the results of an evaluation of a particular issue, set of practices, curriculum innovation or management structures. Depending on the formality appropriate, a combination of these might be deemed desirable.

With regard to (5) and (6) *above* the timing of an evaluation report must be appropriate. A summative report should not be released so long after the event that the whole episode has been bleached from the mind of the participants or where the release of the report coincides with what might be a more pressing issue so that the importance of the evaluation report is lost (for example, where the results of an innovation of school and community links are presented to a staff on the same occasion as an announcement that the school will be fully inspected in a month's time!).

In a formative evaluation the reporting of the evaluation must take place before each successive stage of the development of, for example, a curriculum innovation, a series of in-service days for teachers, a restructuring of a school management team, the development of a school management plan, a whole school approach to preventing bullying - in short, anything which takes place *over time*. In a formative evaluation the reporting might be oral rather than written, or a written report might take the form of an executive summary with the full report available on request. It is important that a formative evaluation report takes place in a carefully planned time sequence so that participants have the opportunity to reflect on its findings before moving to the next stage of the development, since the intention of the formative evaluation is that it helps to shape each stage of a development.

With regard to (7) *above*, the appearance and presentation of a written report is important. It is only the evaluation fanatic who will read a lengthy report; most participants will probably only read a summary or that section of the report which applies to them, or that section of the report which they can understand. For example, an evaluation might be presented deliberately in the form of graphs, tables, statistics, a profusion of jargon, an over-emphasis on methodology, a battery of figures with little explanation of what these might mean. Further, a written report might place critical comments deliberately at the end in the knowledge that many readers will not reach the end!

Many hard working teachers will not wish to receive lengthy documentation but an oral report, perhaps accompanied by one or two sides of paper. This would be an appropriate format for, say, a staff meeting.

An oral presentation must be clear (overhead projection slides might be useful here to accompany a executive summary), yet sufficiently full in order to do justice to the context, methodology and instrumentation of the evaluation, i.e. it must be accessible to the audience.

For both a written or oral report opportunities must be provided for discussion and questioning of the evaluation. The evaluator must be sufficiently primed to be able to answer questions clearly and honestly.

WHAT NEEDS TO APPEAR IN A WRITTEN EVALUATION REPORT?

In order to be user-friendly the layout of a report is important. For a full formal report the language of that report must be comprehensible and the ordering of contents must be clear. Headings and sub-headings should be liberally used and sections and sub-sections clearly numbered (e.g. 1.1, 1.2,

2.1, 2.2, 2.3.1, 2.3.2, 2.4, etc.) Tables, figures, diagrams, graphs, bar charts, etc. which might be useful for clarity of exposition or summary need titles and comment to clarify what they demonstrate. Emboldened, italicized and capitalized letters should be used to highlight particular features. Spacing between sections should be clear; jargon should be avoided where possible. Brevity and clarity are cardinal virtues in an evaluation report. A written report might contain:

- a cover page with a title - probably including the name of the project, the names of the evaluators and/or institution to which they belong, the people/party who requested the evaluation, the dates when the project was being evaluated and the date of the report;
- acknowledgements;
- an abstract of maybe two paragraphs at most which outlines very briefly the context, purposes, methodology, instrumentation and findings of the evaluation;
- a contents page (which includes reference to lists of tables and figures and appendices);
- a summary of the main findings of the evaluation;
- a description of the evaluator or evaluators, the purposes of the evaluation, the brief given to the evaluators (and from whom it was received), the constraints on the evaluation, the context of the evaluation, the costs of the evaluation, the main evaluation questions asked;
- a summary of the project being evaluated, its purposes, content, organization, resourcing, implementation, significance;
- the technical details of the evaluation which indicate the style of the evaluation, sampling, methodology, timing and time scales, instrumentation, methods of data processing and presentation, management of the evaluation, ethics of release of data, validity and reliability, piloting etc.; references here should be made to appendices which give blank examples of the instruments (e.g. questionnaires, interview schedules, tests, observation schedules, documents etc.); the scope and parameters of the evaluation need to be clarified here;
- the findings of the evaluation, what the evaluation shows - reported as word data, lists of findings, tables, figures, graphs, histograms etc., with clear comment and interpretation of such data and statistics used; reference might be made here to appendices which present raw data; the parameters of the data and their application need to be clarified here, outlining the degree of generalizability (or its lack), degree of representativeness of the

data (particularly important if the evaluation is concerned only to report critical moments or incidents), spheres of applicability to a wider audience and limitations of the scope of the evaluation. A summary of key findings might be included here, maybe at the start of this section in order to catch the eye of the reader; *this section must answer the evaluation questions*;

● a discussion of the significance of the findings and their implications for:

(a) appropriate parties (e.g. headteacher, senior management, local authority officers, budget holders, curriculum co-ordinators, subject specialists, liaison teachers - either between schools or home/school liaison, governors, in-service providers);

(b) substantive content (e.g. curricula, teaching and learning, management styles, course organization, content of in-service), and

(c) future investigation, i.e. outlining areas where further investigation is needed if a fuller picture is required; recommendations for the future development, implementation, organization, resourcing, evaluation etc. of the project might be included here if they are within the brief of the evaluation;

● summary conclusions;
● references to published literature used;
● appendices, suitably titled.

It is important to recognize that the evaluation report must do justice to the scope of the evaluation and the styles of the evaluation. Selective reporting can allow bias and invalidity to enter the evaluation; an illuminative or word-based evaluation might necessarily take more space than an evaluation whose findings can be reported through numbers, tables and graphs. There is a tension here between a lengthy report which does full justice to the scope of the evaluation and a report that is so long that it is seldom read. If an executive summary is being prepared, then clear reference must be made to the full report and the parameters of an executive summary need to be clearly stated. Reporting, therefore, needs to be planned and agreed in advance of the evaluation.

RECOMMENDED READING

Bell, J. (1987) *Doing Your Research Project.* Milton Keynes: Open University Press.

Brinkerhoff, R., Brethower, D. O., Hluchyi, T., Nowakowski, J. R. (1983) *Program Evaluation.* Boston: Kluwer-Nijhoff.

Lyons Morris, L., Fitz-Gibbon, C.T., Freeman, M.E. (1987) *How to Communicate Evaluation Findings.* Beverly Hills: Sage Publications.

Miles, M. and Huberman, M. (1984) *Qualitative Data Analysis.* Beverly Hills: Sage Publications.

Wilcox, B. (1992) "Developing Trustworthy Conclusions", in B. Wilcox *Time-Constrained Evaluation.* London: Routledge.

8 The Management and Ethics of Evaluation

This chapter discusses two important areas in the conduct of evaluation:

- decisions on who the evaluator or evaluators will be;
- ethical issues involved in planning, implementing and reporting an evaluation.

Their appearance towards the end of this book belies their importance, for they are issues of central concern in planning an evaluation. The debates which they generate amongst evaluators, participants, those who have asked for the evaluation to be done, stake-holders, must be resolved before the evaluation begins. Resolutions might well be a compromise since they engage the politics of evaluation, as will be revealed in the course of this chapter.

WHO WILL THE EVALUATOR BE?

There are three main areas which need to be resolved here:

(1) whether the evaluator will be drawn from within the institution in which he or she works or drawn from outside (i.e. insider or outsider evaluation respectively);

(2) whether the evaluation will be undertaken by an individual or a team (Brinkerhoff, *et al.* 1983);

(3) whether the evaluation will be undertaken by a 'professional' or an 'amateur' evaluator (Brinkerhoff, *et al.* 1983).

SHOULD I USE AN INSIDER OR AN OUTSIDER TO DO THE EVALUATION?

There are many powerful arguments for evaluators evaluating their own institutions (indeed it is anticipated that many readers of this publication will be doing just this either for a named educational award or at the request of the senior management of a school, or simply for their own benefit).

On the one hand an internal evaluator might be less threatening than an external evaluator because the participants are already known to each other. The staff-member-as-evaluator already knows the context of the institution, its dynamics, personalities in it, its subtleties, complexities, ethos and organization, and so will not need to spend time on becoming familiar with this. Moreover, an insider-as-evaluator might have a greater commitment to the institution and the evaluation than an outsider (Morrison and Ridley, 1988). Knowing the personalities in the institution might enable the insider to elicit more sensitive information than could have been gathered by an external evaluator. The insider as evaluator will be well placed:

(a) to capture the processes of teaching and learning;
(b) to know the biographies of participants and the evolution of the situation in the institution;
(c) to generate wide, deep and detailed data;
(d) to disseminate information easily to all parties;
(e) to balance formal and informal evaluation and dissemination;
(f) to engage the school's declared needs, areas of interest and areas of decision-making;
(g) to operate formatively;
(h) to protect colleagues, e.g. from unwarranted accountability.

Against this it must be stated that having insiders as evaluators might be very dangerous if they have little credibility in the institution or if they are likely to use an evaluation for their own ends (e.g. for promotion) or to promote or put down identified members of staff. Questions of power or appraisal might arise if the evaluator is a senior member of staff who has to evaluate a junior member of staff or if the evaluator is a junior member of staff who, in turn, has to evaluate a senior member of staff. The charge of spying might also be made against certain insider evaluators, i.e. that they are less concerned with the evaluation than with gaining intelligence about what is happening and reporting it back to a senior member of the institution.

The very fact that the evaluators are already inside the institution might cause them to miss significant aspects of the school simply because they are too familiar with the institution; key factors have become so sedimented in day-to-day practices that they have been assigned to the unconscious. What is required here is to 'make the familiar strange' (Delamont, 1981) in order to avoid any unconscious bias in the evaluation, i.e. to be as disinterested as possible and to examine the norms, principles, key practices and roles of the institution.

The insider-as-evaluator must be very thorough in attempts not only to disclose possible biases but to build them out in the evaluation. This can be undertaken (a) by triangulation - where data and their interpretation are re-worked by a 'critical friend' or an external evaluator; (b) by careful piloting and examination of instruments - to expose any biases that might be built into the instrumentation, e.g. leading questions, selective and narrow choices in a multiple-choice questionnaire.

If the evaluator is to be an insider, then it is vital that objectivity be sought in the evaluation. Objectivity might be difficult to achieve, for example the evaluator might not wish to sour relations with colleagues or stir up discord amongst colleagues. Furthermore, the insider-as-evaluator might have a vested interest in the evaluation; for example, if the evaluator were in the history department of a school and the history teaching was being evaluated, then it might be in her interests either to present a favourable or unfavourable report on the history teaching. A favourable report might be self-congratulatory whilst an unfavourable report might have the effect of causing an early retirement from the head of department whom the evaluator does not like or might ensure that more resources are brought into the department. The insider-as-evaluator might become a very powerful figure in the institution.

The alternative to insider evaluation is to have an outsider as evaluator who may be more objective and less caught up in the dynamics of the institution and who may be perceived by the participants as having no particular 'axe to grind' (i.e. being able to ask questions which might be very sensitive if they issued from the insider evaluator). Against this must be set the difficulty that an external evaluator might be seen as very threatening to some participants, maybe being seen as an 'inspector'. Moreover, the complexity, dynamics, ethos and personalities of a particular institution or programme might well be missed by an evaluator from outside. However, the use of an outsider might be desirable as it makes for less work for hard-pressed teachers. Teachers who might also welcome an outsider's potential clarity of vision.

It can be seen that arguments can be advanced both for and against insider or outsider evaluation. One resolution of the problem might be to choose one of the two alternatives in the knowledge that there will be drawbacks to the single choice. Another resolution of the problem might be to plan an evaluation in which internal and external evaluators can complement each other. Of course this would have to be agreed with the participants.

SHOULD THERE BE ONE OR SEVERAL EVALUATORS?

The previous paragraph sets the scene for the next question in this section - whether the evaluation will be undertaken by a team of evaluators or by an individual evaluator. A team approach might be formidable and threatening if it is constituted of a range of externals who are perceived to have a measure of power (for example, a team of local authority inspectors). Alternatively, a team which has been drawn from within the institution might be desirable, practicable and a useful way of developing collegiality, a shared approach to problem-solving and a means of building support structures in the school.

A team of evaluators will enable the various foci and tasks of the evaluation to be shared out, thereby reducing the burden on any one member, or, if a limited range of foci has been selected for evaluation, a team will be able to triangulate data and perspectives. Moreover, a team approach can enable a great deal of data to be gathered in a short time, which is particularly useful and feasible if the team is drawn from within the institution. If a team approach has been decided, then there is a need for inter-rater reliability to be established before and during the evaluation (*see* chapter six) and maybe for a team building programme to be followed before the evaluation is undertaken. Planning a team approach which uses outsiders will have to weigh carefully the costs of bringing in, say, a team of five evaluators for two days (i.e. ten days' costings) against the costs of having one evaluator involved for, say, eight days. A team approach which uses insiders may require teachers to be released from teaching, it may take place in a series of staff meetings, or it may be able to utilize non-contact time by teachers.

Having a single evaluator will probably mean that the evaluator will necessarily have to be in the institution for longer than if a team were employed. This has its advantages, for as an external evaluator he or she will be able to become familiar with people and situations. This is particularly important in illuminative and decision-making models of evaluation as these two types are very sensitive to specific contexts. On the other hand it places the whole burden of evaluation on the shoulders of one person. Here again the relative advantages and disadvantages of the issue have to be weighed and resolved.

SHOULD I USE AN AMATEUR OR A PROFESSIONAL EVALUATOR?

The credibility or legitimacy of the evaluation might depend on whether it is undertaken by an amateur or a professional. This is problematic, for it is unclear what these terms mean in the context of an evaluation. For example, in the case of using a teacher as evaluator he or she may have several years' experience and might have developed a degree of connoisseurship about teaching which a professional evaluator who comes to the institution armed with tests, schedules and statistics might easily miss. The task is to harness the strengths of the professional teacher to the strengths of the professional evaluator, with the recognition that both of these strengths might be found in one person either within or outside the school.

A professional evaluator will have experience of undertaking evaluations and hence will have an insight into technical considerations in undertaking evaluations - sampling, instrumentation, data processing etc. The outsider, however, may have a particular way of working which he or she prefers to adopt - for example, a numerical type of evaluation or an experimental mode of evaluation. This may be inimical to the particular situation being evaluated. On the other hand the teacher as evaluator may need to develop specific technical skills of evaluation.

WHAT ETHICAL ISSUES ARE RAISED IN UNDERTAKING AN EVALUATION?

Because evaluation is a high profile activity (argued in the first chapter of this book) there are important ethical issues which need to be addressed in planning, implementing and releasing evaluation findings. At the heart of the issues lies a fundamental tension: the right of the public or stake-holders to have access to evaluation data and the right of the individual to privacy.

It is impossible to lay down hard and fast rules for addressing this tension, rather it is a matter which has to be agreed with reference to every individual evaluation. It is a tension which raises huge questions of ownership of data; it was argued in chapter one that this is so fundamental that it must be clarified, indeed, negotiated at every stage of the evaluation. It must be established *when* ownership of the data passes from the respondents to the evaluator, when the ownership passes from the evaluator to the recipients of the evaluation and beyond. Many evaluations are never released to a wide public, many items of data which were initially given to an evaluator are subsequently held back by the respondents.

It might be the case, for example, that a report which is condemning of a particular member of staff has to be presented by the evaluator to a senior manager; does that particular member of staff have the right of veto or right of redress? It might also be the case that data have been given by that person in confidence in the certain knowledge that they will never see the light of day; what does the evaluator do with that type of data, particularly if they contain some jewels of information? This is especially the case when sensitive or even taboo issues are being dealt with by the evaluations.

The evaluator has to agree on protection for respondents, indeed the Data Protection Act (1984) in the United Kingdom requires this to be done. For example, if data about a named person are held on computer, then that person has a right to see such data. In respecting confidentiality it might not be adequate for the data to be reported anonymously, for an individual might still be able to be identified from them. Wilcox (1992) suggests that this problem can be made more tractable by the evaluator writing a general rather than person-specific account, though whether this is feasible is subject to the nature of the evaluation. Anonymity can apply to individuals, groups and institutions.

HOW CAN I ADDRESS ETHICAL ISSUES INVOLVED IN EVALUATION?

Pring (1984) sets out five criteria which can be used to protect participants in an evaluation:

(1) The evaluator establishes the kinds of knowledge being sought.
(2) The evaluator provides interim reports and is open to cross-examination on these by participants.
(3) The evaluator is open to questioning by those involved as the evaluation is being planned.
(4) Information is treated as confidential until clearance has been obtained from the respondent for its release.
(5) The interpretation which the evaluator has made of the data is open to scrutiny by the respondents.

Pring is attempting to establish a protocol which can be used in the planning, implementing and reporting of an evaluation. Whilst this set of criteria attempts to reconcile the respondent's right to control the data with the public's right to be informed of important data, it needs to be amplified.

In Pring's point (1) not only would the purposes of the evaluation need to be made clear but also it would need to be made clear how these data were to be collected and permission obtained for such data collection procedures. This is particularly important if data are going to be gathered from personal files, from a lengthy stay in a particular classroom and from interviews. It implies also that permission must be sought from parents if minors are going to be involved in an evaluation. Pring's point also implies that the respondent would not be expected to reveal information which would not normally be made public (with the usual appropriate safeguards), i.e. to act unprofessionally. This can be extended to embrace any unprofessional behaviour (Fox, 1969), morally questionable behaviour or behaviour which might be damaging or dangerous.

In Pring's point (2) it would need to be clarified who the participants in the evaluation were - simply those who yielded data or those whom the data mentions? It would also point to the need for respondents to receive draft written reports rather than solely the finished document. If one were to extrapolate point (2) the issue which would be raised would be the freedom of the respondent either to refuse to take part in an evaluation or come out of an evaluation at any stage. If this is the case, then prior agreement should have been reached on what to do with the data which might already have been gathered from that respondent (i.e. to use them or to destroy them). This latter point is particularly troublesome if the data had been particularly useful.

In Pring's point (3) it would need to be clarified whether this was simply a dissemination of an agenda which was not mutable or whether, in fact, the participants could effect changes in the evaluation design in these planning stages.

In Pring's point (4) it would need to be clarified that here were several levels of release which had to be negotiated - release to other participants (but not to those who had asked for the evaluation to be done or the wider public), release to those who requested the evaluation but not the wider public, and release to anybody who is interested. This would necessitate either different reports being made available to different audiences or the deletion of certain parts of a single report if it were going to different audiences. This might be particularly important if data were going to be released which might adversely affect those who yielded them. If the evaluation enables the respondent to profit from the exercise rather than be damaged by it, then respondents might be more amenable to giving permission for data to be used. Pring's point requires respondents to be made aware of all the anticipated uses to which the data might be put.

In Pring's point (5) it would need to be clarified whether this concerns respondent validation of data or the right of the respondent to veto the publication or circulation of these data. It is similar to the qualification to point (3) outlined *above*, viz whether the participants could decide or simply receive the agenda. This is an important point because the situation might arise where the evaluator makes an interpretation of a particular issue or set of issues which had not been identified by the respondents, or whether the evaluator's interpretation of a situation differs from, or is in conflict with, that made by the respondents. Pring's point can be taken to mean that agreement needs to be made on the rights to report different interpretations of the same data.

WHAT ARE THE ETHICAL ISSUES IN UNDERTAKING A COVERT EVALUATION?

It must also be stated that Pring's criteria might apply very well to evaluations where the evaluator is undertaking an overt evaluation. However, if the evaluator is an 'undercover', *covert* evaluator (maybe necessitated by the need to catch sensitive, threatening or data about taboo areas) this set of criteria may have to be rewritten. Here the evaluator might not only fail to reveal the purposes of the evaluation but might deliberately conceal the fact of being an evaluator, or, further still, might undertake activities deliberately to divert attention from the real motives in the situation.

Considering the ethics of covert research is daunting. One school of thought would put it in the same league as doctors operating on patients without their permission (Hitchcock and Hughes, 1989); another school of thought would regard it as a necessary evil, compromising the evaluator in the interests of gathering important but sensitive data; yet another school of thought would regard it as innocuous, being simply one out of a battery of techniques available to an evaluator. This is a matter which can be decided only with reference to specific planned evaluations.

WHAT ARE THE RIGHTS OF RESPONDENTS IN AN EVALUATION?

Pring has attempted to encapsulate one of the rights of respondents in an evaluation - to make a *fully informed* choice about and to give fully *informed consent* (Sammons, 1989) to which data to yield and to whom. Once the evaluation has been undertaken, it takes on a life of its own and can effect changes, either anticipated or unanticipated, in the lives of respondents. For example, it could be devastating to one person if the evaluation showed that he or she was held in low regard by colleagues, or the same could be used to promote a particular philosophy in the school in the face of disagreement by certain colleagues. The task of evaluators, if they are to enable the respondent to make a fully informed choice, is to point out the anticipated effects of the evaluation and to try to unravel some previously unanticipated effects.

The ethical conduct of the evaluation should not be treated lightly but should feature as importantly in the planning of the evaluation as the other issues which have been discussed in this book. This chapter has suggested that this is a problematic issue which is not capable of a simple decision but, rather, should be decided by negotiation. The ethical conduct of an evaluation should be decided on the criterion of appropriacy. This echoes the recurring theme of this book and underlines the double message upon which that theme was predicated - that evaluation issues have to be exposed and that any problems contained in these issues should take place before the evaluation begins.

RECOMMENDED READING

Adelman, C. (1984) *The Politics and Ethics of Evaluation*. London: Croom Helm

Brinkerhoff. R., Brethower, D. O., Hluchyi, T., Nowakowski, J. R. (1983) *Program Evaluation*. Boston: Kluwer-Nijhoff.

Burgess, R.G. (ed.) *The Ethics of Educational Research*. Lewes: Falmer.

Praise, N. (1987) Ethical Guidelines, in R. Murphy and H. Torrance (eds.) *Evaluating Education: Issues and Methods*. London: Paul Chapman Publishing.

Pring, R. (1987) "Confidentiality and the Right to Know", in R. Murphy and H. Torrance (eds.) *Evaluating Education: Issues and Methods*. London: Paul Chapman Publishing.

Simons, H. (1981) Process Evaluation in Schools, in C. Lacey and D. Lawton (eds.) *Issues in Evaluation and Accountability*. London: Methuen.

9 Conclusion

This book has contained several *leitmotivs*. From the very beginning evaluation was seen to be a high profile activity which had much to offer in a range of educational and political contexts. Education is inescapably political, it is contestable and indeed is contested; that is its delight as well as its danger. Evaluation has a significant contribution to make to the on-going debate about education and values in education. Evaluation serves education and politics simultaneously; certain types of evaluation (e.g. survey, objectives and experimental models) might serve macro-political decisions whilst other types of evaluation (e.g. illuminative evaluation and decision-making modes of evaluation) might serve micro-political decision-making.

Teachers-as-evaluators can draw on the whole range of types of evaluation within political and educational decision-making. With regard to the importance of teachers developing skills of evaluation this book has attempted to raise issues in evaluation and to provide a step-by-step guide to evaluation for novice evaluators. One message throughout has been that evaluation is an exciting activity, that it should involve teachers, and that teachers, by developing skills of evaluation, can feed directly into decision-making at an institutional or supra-institutional level. Such expertise is the province of teachers and other educationists.

The politics of education suffused its constituent elements - methodology, timing and time scales, instrumentation, sampling, validity and reliability, data processing and reporting, choice of evaluator and ethics of evaluation. Recognizing this has meant that throughout the book care has been taken to indicate that this places on the evaluator a responsibility to negotiate and agree in advance of an evaluation the interpretation and application of its constituent elements.

If a fully informed decision is to be made about how an evaluation will take place, then the evaluator will have to be aware of the dimensions of each element of evaluation. Each element has been explored in turn in order to expose the issues contained in it and how evaluators - teachers or other educationists - might address them. By exploring issues in each area of evaluation design, the intention has been to offer some insights into evaluation not only in order to ensure that evaluation planners go into evaluation with their eyes open - fully aware of the areas and issues which need to be negotiated - but also to provide an outline of how each area of evaluation might be addressed so that a robust evaluation can be managed.

The exhortation here is to become involved in an evaluation but to know what such involvement entails.

Evaluations need to be planned; every element needs to be planned and agreed in advance with the relevant parties or individuals. To leave the implementation to chance is to risk real problems occurring once the evaluation has begun. Making up 'the rules of the game' once the evaluation has started is not only bad practice but very dangerous because it is to invite conflict, dissension and breakdown into the evaluation. This book has attempted to indicate those elements of an evaluation which must be addressed if these risks are to be minimized and how those elements can be addressed.

Implicit in the term 'evaluation' is the judgement of *value*; this can be addressed in two ways: firstly, by looking carefully at the mechanisms of undertaking an evaluation - the technical questions - so that procedural and internal validity are addressed; secondly, by looking at what happens when the evaluation has taken place - i.e. how it serves decision-making and judgements of worth or value, i.e. external validity. Throughout the book questions of validity have been addressed. Internal validity enters the arena of evaluation from the moment when the crude or overall purposes of an evaluation are 'operationalized' into evaluation questions, turning a series of objectives into a series of concrete questions upon which data can be collected, for example, from a series of observed behaviours, a range of opinions, a table of test scores, an analysis of documentary evidence.

Validity was defined in terms of *fitness for purpose* and of 'appropriacy' to the element of evaluation under scrutiny. Hence:

- the model of evaluation had to be appropriate to the evaluation purposes and the 'operationalized' evaluation questions;
- the methodology had to be appropriate to the model of evaluation and to the evaluation questions;
- the instrumentation had to be appropriate to the methodology and to the evaluation questions;
- the instrumentation had to be appropriate to the technical details of types of validity and reliability;
- the sampling had to be appropriate to the model, purposes, methodology and instrumentation of the evaluation;
- the process of data gathering had to be appropriate to the sampling and instrumentation;
- the data processing and presentation had to be appropriate to the instrumentation, methodology, sampling and technical details (e.g. levels of data);
- the reporting had to be appropriate to the purposes, questions and audiences of the evaluation, it had to answer the 'operationalized'

evaluation questions and onwards to serve the overall purposes of the evaluation.

Addressing internal validity was seen to involve setting very carefully the parameters of the evaluation design, of the processing and interpretation of the data gathered and of the generalizability (or otherwise) of the results. On the one hand detailed evaluation questions can lead to subtle designs, sensitive choice of methodology and sampling, careful instrumentation, carefully bounded interpretation, specific answering of specific evaluation questions, detailed responses to detailed purposes of the evaluation. On the other hand crude designs only yield crude data, crude data can only support crude interpretation, crude interpretation can only answer crude evaluation questions; the utility value of such crudity is low.

If an evaluation is to be externally valid, if it is to have *value*, then the *significance* of the results need to be considered, weighed and judged; a process of deliberation needs to follow the evaluation. Perhaps we should heed the poet Pasternak's (1969) words:

How shameful, when you have no meaning,
To be on everybody's lips!

or the caution spelled out in the *dictum* 'everything has meaning, nothing has value' in order to remind us that an evaluation is only an early stage in the process of decision-making, educational improvement and development. The evaluation is simply an instrument or implement which informs decision-making. The process of educational improvement does not cease once the evaluation has been undertaken, rather it commences or recommences. Evaluation informs decision-making rather than replaces it. In this sense evaluation is part of an action research cycle of feedback and development, retrospect and prospect. The invitation in this book is to become involved in evaluation because that brings involvement in decision making.

Correctly undertaken evaluation is a powerful tool for innovation, reform and school improvement. That we should all be participants in these areas is a message which this book advocates; to gain understanding of how evaluation can be undertaken is to be part of this process. Knowledge is both powerful and empowering. Be part of this empowerment, become an evaluator!

Appendix A:
Costing an Evaluation

When calculating costs the following list of items might be useful.

PRINTING AND POSTAGE

*   Postage
      Stationery
      Photocopying
      Reprographics for producing reports
*   Headed notepaper
*   Reprographics for data gathering instruments (e.g. questionnaires, interview schedules, observation schedules, record sheets for content analysis of documents)

TECHNOLOGY SOFTWARE

Commercially available computer software (e.g. for processing data, graphic designs of reports, desk-top questionnaires, word processing)

TECHNOLOGY HARDWARE

Computer(s)
Audio Cassette Players
Video Cassette Players and Monitors
Tape Transcription Machine

TIME

Evaluator's time to plan, implement, process and report evaluation
Secretarial time
Transcriber's time (1 hour of taped interview can take up to 5 hours)
*   Use of consultants
      Stand-in cover for absent colleagues
      Computer time (if using a mainframe computer)

TRAVEL

*   To and from evaluation sites and relevant meetings
*   Journey expenses for evaluators and consultants

ADDITIONAL COSTS

*   Telephone charges
*   Hire of rooms
*   Hire of Office Equipment
*   Petty cash
*   Subsistence (including subsistence for those attending meetings)

N.B. Items marked * will usually only be incurred in more 'formal' evaluations, i.e. those for which contracts are prepared between evaluators and sponsors. The remainder will be incurred if teachers are the evaluators.

Appendix B:
A Sample Interview Schedule

1. What has been happening in the innovation? Why has it been happening in the way that it has? What factors have caused it to happen in the way that it has?
2. How well or how badly do you think the innovation is going? Why?
3. Which aspects of the innovation have been particularly successful or unsuccessful? Why?
4. What problems have arisen in the implementation of this innovation?
5. What unexpected factors caused the innovation to happen in the way that it has? What are your feelings about this?
6. From the list of factors which facilitate or impede change (supplied to the respondent before the interview) could you identify which factors have been significant in the course of the innovation in your institution? Can you put them in order of priority? What have been their main effects on the innovation?
7. Are there any other factors which apply in your institution which do not appear on the lists?
8. Which aspects of the innovation have taken longer or shorter to implement than you anticipated?
9. How easy or difficult has the implementation of the innovation been to date? Why?
10. What deviations from your original plans for the innovation have you had to make? Why?

Appendix C:
Calculating the Chi-Square (χ^2) Statistic

The formula for calculating the chi-square (χ^2) statistic for nominal or nominal with ordinal data is given as:

$$\Sigma \left(\frac{(O-E)^2}{E} \right)$$

where
Σ = 'the sum of';
O = the observed (actual) score;
E = the expected score.

The χ^2 is calculated once a contingency table has been drawn. Let us imagine that we wished to see if the distributions of boys and girls were statistically significant. We could set up a contingency table thus:

	Enjoy maths	Do not enjoy maths	
boys	20	15	35
girls	14	26	40
	34	41	75

This is a 2 × 2 contingency table. The expected score (E) for each cell the formula is:

$$E = \frac{\text{row total} \times \text{column total}}{\text{grand total}}$$

Working out the formula for each cell will yield scores as follows:

For the top left hand cell $\quad E = \dfrac{35 \times 34}{75} = 15.8667$

For the top right hand cell $E = \dfrac{35 \times 41}{75} = 19.1333$

For the bottom left hand cell $E = \dfrac{40 \times 34}{75} = 18.1333$

For the bottom right hand cell $E = \dfrac{40 \times 41}{75} = 21.8667$

If we were to enter these scores into the contingency table we could present it thus:

	Enjoy maths	Do not enjoy maths	
boys	15.8667 20	19.1333 15	35
girls	18.1333 14	21.8667 26	40
	34	41	75

Now for each cell we can work out $O - E$ as follows:

For the top left hand cell this is:	20 − 15.8667 =	4.13333
For the top right hand cell this is:	15 − 19.1333 =	−4.13333
For the bottom left hand cell this is:	14 − 18.1333 =	−4.13333
For the bottom right hand cell this is:	26 − 21.8667 =	4.13333

Now square these figures for each cell:

For the top left hand cell: $(4.1333)^2 = 17.0842$
For the top right hand cell: $(-4.1333)^2 = 17.0842$
For the bottom left hand cell: $(-4.1333)^2 = 17.0842$
For the bottom right hand cell: $(4.1333)^2 = 17.0842$

Now divide each of these totals by the expected frequency of that cell:

For the top left hand cell: $17.0842 \div 15.8667 = 1.0767$
For the top right hand cell: $17.0842 \div 19.1333 = 0.8929$
For the bottom left hand cell: $17.0842 \div 18.1333 = 0.9421$
For the bottom right hand cell: $17.0842 \div 21.8667 = 0.7813$

Now add these four totals: $1.0767 + 0.8929 + 0.7813 = 3.693$.

Now look up 3.693 on a table of χ^2 (usually found in the appendices of most books on statistics or on educational research methods). The table for χ^2 will require you to look up the score at the appropriate degree of freedom. A contingency table 2×2 only has one degree of freedom. Looking up the figure of 3.693 with one degree of freedom we notice that this figure is statistically significant at the 0.10 level. This tells us that the distribution which we have observed of boys' and girls' enjoyment of mathematics is statistically significant. The interpretation that we can make from this is: (a) that the high numbers of boys who do enjoy maths is significant; (b) that the low numbers of boys who do not enjoy maths is significant; (c) that the low numbers of girls who enjoy maths is significant; (d) that the high numbers of girls who do not enjoy maths is significant. Overall we can suggest that there is an important gender differentiation at work in the enjoyment of mathematics.

In the example here of the 2×2 contingency table both the rows and the columns were dealing with nominal data. Chi-square can operate for nominal with ordinal data. For example if we wished to calculate the significance of boys' and girls' voting on a Likert scale of, say, 'strongly agree', 'disagree', 'neither agree nor disagree', 'agree', 'strongly agree' this would be a 2×5 contingency table where the nominal data (boys and girls) would be the row headings and the ordinal data (the five ratings from 'strongly disagree' to 'strongly agree') would be the column headings.

The calculation of chi-square is time-consuming. There are numerous statistical packages for computers - both stand-alone and mainframe - which will do this very quickly.

Appendix D:
Calculating the Spearman Rank Order Correlation Co-efficient

The formula for calculating a Spearman Rank Order Correlation Co-efficient to be used for ordinal data is given as:

$$r = 1 - \frac{6\Sigma d^2}{N(N^2 - 1)}$$

where
Σ = 'the sum of';
d^2 = the difference between the two scores of each case squared;
N = the size of the population in the sample.

Imagine that thirteen cases (people) had been ranked on a scale of 'degree of leadership' and 'degree of co-operativeness' and the evaluator wished to see if there was any correlation between the two sets of results. The data could be set out thus:

	Rank order of Degree of Leadership	Rank order of Degree of Co-operativeness	Difference d	d^2
Subject A	1	1	0	0
Subject B	3	2	2	1
Subject C	3	3	0	0
Subject D	3	4	1	1
Subject E	5	5	0	0
Subject F	6	7.5	1.5	2.25
Subject G	7	7.5	0.5	0.25
Subject H	8	7.5	0.5	0.25
Subject I	9	7.5	1.5	2.25
Subject J	10	10	0	0
Subject K	11	11	0	0
Subject L	12	12	0	0
Subject M	13	13	0	0

$$r = 1 - \frac{6\Sigma d^2}{N(N^2-1)} = 1 - \frac{6 \times 7}{13 \times 168} = 1 - \frac{42}{2184} = 1 - 0.01923 = 0.98077$$

Note in this example how equal rankings have been calculated. For example, in the rank ordering on 'degree of co-operativeness' there were four people tying in sixth position. The way of calculating what to put into the appropriate place is to total the numbers of the rank occupied by the ties; in this case they are positions 6, 7, 8 and 9 in the rank order. Add these numbers together $(6 + 7 + 8 + 9 = 30)$ and divide by the number of places occupied by the ties. Here four places are tied. Divide 30 by 7 equals 7.5. The four places are given the rank order of 7.5 each.

Note that the difference (d) is entered as a positive number. Even if it were to be entered as a negative number d^2 would cancel the negative. Looking up 0.98077 in a table of significance we see that the correlation co-efficient for the two ranks of scores is statistically significant at the 0.01 level of significance, i.e. a high correlation exists.

Appendix E:
Calculating the Standard Deviation
of a Set of Scores

The formula for calculating the Standard Deviation for interval and ratio data is given as:

$$SD = \sqrt{\left(\frac{\Sigma d^2}{N}\right)}$$

where
Σ = 'the sum of';
d^2 = the difference between (also known as the 'deviation from' or 'dev') the score recorded and the mean for the whole set of scores;
N = the number of scores (cases).

Let us work this out for a set of 8 scores as follows:

Score	difference between the score obtained and the mean	d^2
25	−3	9
24	−4	16
27	−1	1
31	3	9
32	4	16
35	7	49
21	−7	49
29	1	1

This mean has been calculated as the total of the scores divided by the number of cases (224 ÷ 8 = 28). Hence the statistic is calculated thus:

$$SD = \sqrt{\left(\frac{\Sigma d^2}{N}\right)} = \sqrt{\frac{150}{8}} = \sqrt{18.75} = 4.33$$

Appendix F:
Calculating Z-Scores

The formula for calculating z-scores for interval and ratio data is given thus:

$$z\text{-score} = \frac{dev}{SD}$$

An example of this would be where we wish to compare the two sets of scores from twelve cases (subjects A - K). The data could be set out and calculated thus:

	Maths Score	dev	d^2	z-score	Language Score	dev	d^2	z-score
Subject A	7	2	4	0.8528	27	12.5	156.25	1.3672
Subject B	6	1	1	0.4264	25	10.5	110.25	1.1485
Subject C	5	0	0	0	15	0.5	0.25	0.0547
Subject D	4	−1	1	−0.4264	12	−1.5	2.25	−0.1641
Subject E	2	−3	9	−1.2792	5	−9.5	30.25	−1.0391
Subject F	8	3	9	1.2792	27	12.5	156.25	1.3672
Subject G	7	2	4	0.8528	14	−0.5	0.25	−0.547
Subject H	4	−1	1	−0.4264	7	−7.5	56.25	−0.8203
Subject I	9	4	16	1.7056	28	13.5	182.25	1.4766
Subject J	3	−2	4	−0.8528	2	−12.5	156.25	−1.3672
Subject K	1	−4	16	−1.7056	4	−10.5	110.25	−1.1585
Subject L	4	−1	1	−0.4264	8	−6.5	42.25	−0.7109

where
dev = deviation from the mean;
SD = Standard Deviation (*see* Appendix E for the formula to calculate this).

Mean of Maths score = 5   Mean of Language score = 14.5
Standard Deviation   = 2.3452   Standard Deviation   = 9.1424

$$\text{To calculate } z\text{-score for each entry} = \frac{\text{dev}}{\text{SD}}$$

The z-score enables *fair comparison* to be made between two sets of scores whose means and standard deviations are different.

Appendix G:
The T-Test of Significance

This is a statistic which is used very widely in evaluation; it is used with interval and ratio data which means that it can be used with the results of test scores. It enables two sets of scores to be compared to see if there is any statistically significant difference between the two scores. Hence it can be used with control and experimental groups and with pre- and post-tests. There are two formulae for calculating the t-test; the first is used with matched samples and the second is used with independent samples.

The t-test for matched samples is used where pairs of cases are matched (for example, students with the same IQ, reading ability, etc.). The formula is given thus:

$$t = d \div \sqrt{\frac{\Sigma d^2 - (\Sigma d)^2 / N}{N(N-1)}}$$

where
Σ = 'the sum of';
d = the difference between each pair of scores;
N = the number of pairs of scores.

Let us imagine that there were two sets of scores received from six pairs of subjects as follows:

	Score 1	Score 2	Difference (d)	d^2
Subject 1	17	20	3	9
Subject 2	15	19	4	16
Subject 3	23	30	7	49
Subject 4	20	24	4	16
Subject 5	18	24	6	36
Subject 6	19	27	8	64

Work out $\Sigma d = 3 + 4 + 7 + 4 + 6 + 8 = 32$

Now work out $\dfrac{\Sigma d}{N} = \dfrac{3+4+7+4+6+8}{6} = \dfrac{32}{6} = 5.333$

Now work out $\Sigma d^2 = 9+16+49+16+36+64 = 190$

Now work out $(\Sigma d)^2 = (32)^2 = 1024$

Now work out $\dfrac{(\Sigma d)^2}{N} = \dfrac{1024}{6} = 170.667$

Now work out $\Sigma d^2 - \dfrac{(\Sigma d)^2}{N} = 190 - 170.667 = 19.333$

Now work out $\dfrac{\Sigma d^2 - (\Sigma d)^2/N}{N(N-1)} = \dfrac{19.333}{6 \times 5} = 0.644$

Now work out $\sqrt{0.644} = 0.8025$

The t-score would work out thus:

$$t = d \div \sqrt{\dfrac{\Sigma d^2 - (\Sigma d)^2/N}{N(N-1)}} = \dfrac{5.333}{0.8025} = 6.645$$

There are 5 degrees of freedom (total number of pairs minus $1 = 6 - 1$).

When we look up 6.645 with 5 degrees of freedom in the tables of the t-distribution we find that the 0.01 significance level requires a t-value of 4.032 and that the 0.05 significance level requires a t-value of 2.571. As our t-value which we have calculated is 6.645 we conclude that there is a statistically significant difference between the two scores at the 0.01 level of significance.

Where the t-value is being calculated for independent samples the formula is different. This statistic is used when the two sets of scores are not matched, for example, where subjects are allocated to the two groups randomly. Again this could be used with the experimental model of evaluation. The formula is given thus:

$$ t = \frac{(\bar{x}_1 - \bar{x}_2)}{\sqrt{\left[\left(\frac{\Sigma d_1^2 + \Sigma d_2^2}{N_1 + N_2 - 2}\right)\left(\frac{1}{N_1} + \frac{1}{N_2}\right)\right]}} $$

where
$\bar{x}_1$ = the mean for the first group;
$\bar{x}_2$ = the mean for the second group;
Σd_1^2 = the sum of the squared deviations from the mean of the first group;
Σd_2^2 = the sum of the squared deviations from the mean of the second group;
N_1 = the number of cases in the first group;
N_2 = the number of cases in the second group.

Let us imagine the following sets of scores:

	Score 1	Score 2
Subject 1	31	19
Subject 2	23	20
Subject 3	36	30
Subject 4	32	26
Subject 5	29	24
Subject 6	39	26

(Note that the highest scores are set out to be the first column rather than the second column, thereby avoiding minus numbers when the formula is calculated).

The formula would work out thus:

$$t = \frac{(\bar{x}_1 - \bar{x}_2)}{\sqrt{\left[\left(\dfrac{\Sigma d_1^2 + \Sigma d_2^2}{N_1 + N_2 - 2}\right)\left(\dfrac{1}{N_1} + \dfrac{1}{N_2}\right)\right]}}$$

$$= \frac{(31.667 - 24.167)}{\sqrt{\left[\left(\dfrac{155.3335 + 84.8334}{6 + 4}\right)\left(\dfrac{1}{6} + \dfrac{1}{6}\right)\right]}}$$

$$= \frac{7.5}{\sqrt{[(24.0167)(0.333)]}} = \frac{7.5}{\sqrt{8.0048}}$$

$$= \frac{7.5}{2.8293} = 2.6508$$

There are 10 degrees of freedom because there are two sets of scores. When we look up 2.6508 with ten degrees of freedom in a table of t-values we see that for the 0.05 level of significance we would need a t-value of 2.228 and for the 0.01 level of significance we see that we would need a t-value of 3.169. Hence we see that the difference between the two scores this time is statistically significant at the 0.05 level but not at the 0.01 level.

Appendix H:
Calculating the Pearson Product Moment Correlation Co-efficient

The formula for calculating the Pearson Product Moment Correlation Co-efficient for interval and ratio data is given thus:

$$r = \frac{\Sigma xy - \frac{(\Sigma x)(\Sigma y)}{N}}{\sqrt{\left[\left(\Sigma x^2 - \frac{(\Sigma x)^2}{N}\right)\left(\Sigma y^2 - \frac{(\Sigma y)^2}{N}\right)\right]}}$$

where
Σ = 'the sum of';
x = the first score (in the example this is the mathematics score);
y = the second score (in the example this is the language score);
N = the number of cases (in the example this is twelve).

	Maths Score x	Language Score y	x^2	y^2	xy
Subject A	17	20	289	400	340
Subject B	16	16	256	256	256
Subject C	15	13	225	169	195
Subject D	4	3	16	9	12
Subject E	2	3	4	9	6
Subject F	18	14	324	196	252
Subject G	7	10	49	100	70
Subject H	4	7	16	49	28
Subject I	13	12	169	144	156
Subject J	3	2	9	4	6
Subject K	1	4	1	16	4
Subject L	4	4	16	16	16
	104	108	1374	1368	1341

$$r = \frac{\Sigma xy - \dfrac{(\Sigma x)(\Sigma y)}{N}}{\sqrt{\left[\left(\Sigma x^2 - \dfrac{(\Sigma x)^2}{N}\right)\left(\Sigma y^2 - \dfrac{(\Sigma y)^2}{N}\right)\right]}}$$

$$= \frac{1341 - \dfrac{(104)(108)}{12}}{\sqrt{\left[\left(1374 - \dfrac{10816}{12}\right)\left(1368 - \dfrac{11663}{12}\right)\right]}}$$

$$= \frac{405}{\sqrt{[(472.667)(396)]}} = \frac{405}{\sqrt{187176}}$$

$$= \frac{405}{432.639} = 0.9361$$

When we look up 0.9361 in the tables of significance for the product moment statistic we see that for significance at the 0.05 level we need a co-efficient of 0.65 and for significance at the 0.01 level we need a co-efficient of 0.795. As our co-efficient is 0.9361 we see that this is significant at the 0.01 level. This tells us that a statistically significant correlation exists between the two sets of scores.

Bibliography

Adams, R.S. (1970) Duration and Incident Frequencies as Observation Indices. *Educational and Psychological Measurement* 30 pp. 669 - 674.

Bell, J. (1987) *Doing Your Research Project*. Milton Keynes: Open University Press.

Bennett, S.N., Desforges, C., Cockburn, A., Wilkinson, B. (1984) *The Quality of Pupil Learning Experiences*. London: Lawrence Erlbaum Associates.

Bloom, B. (ed.) (1956) *Taxonomy of Educational Objectives. Handbook 1: Cognitive Domain*. London: Longman.

Bobbit, F. (1918) *The Curriculum*. Boston, Mass.: Houghton Mifflin.

Brinkerhoff, R., Brethower, D. O., Hluchyj, T., Nowakowski, J. R. (1983) *Program Evaluation*. Boston: Kluwer-Nijhoff.

Brown, T. and Morrison, K.R.B. (1990) *The Curriculum Handbook*. Harlow: Longman.

Cohen, L. and Holliday, M. (1979) *Statistics for Education and Physical Education*. London: Harper & Row.

Cohen, L. and Manion, L. (1985) *Research Methods in Education* (second edition). London: Croom Helm.

Delamont, S. (1981) All too Familiar? A Decade of Classroom Research. *Educational Analysis*, 3 (1) pp. 69 - 83.

Eisner, E. (1985) *The Art of Educational Evaluation*. Lewes: Falmer.

Fox, D.J. (1969) *The Research Process in Education*. New York: Holt, Rinehart and Winston.

Frisbie, D. (1981) The Relative Difficulty Ratio - a Test and Item Index. *Educational and Psychological Measurement*. 41 (2), pp. 333 - 339.

Galton, M. and Simon, B. (1980) *Progress and Performance in the Primary Classroom*. London: Routledge and Kegan Paul.

Gronlund, N.E. (1981) *Measurement and Evaluation in Teaching* (fourth edition). New York: Collier Macmillan.

Hargreaves, D. and Hopkins, D. (1991) *The Empowered School*. London: Cassell.

Harrow, A.J.A. (1984) Taxonomy of the Psychomotor Domain, cited in J.C. Bondi *Curriculum Development: a Guide to Practice* (second edition). Columbus, Ohio: Charles E. Merrill Publishing.

Hitchcock, G. and Hughes, D. (1989) *Research and the Teacher*. London: Routledge.

Huberman, M.A. and Miles, M.E. (1984) *Innovations Up Close*. New York: Plenum Press.

Jones, S. (1987) The Analysis of Depth Interviews, in R. Murphy and H. Torrance (eds.) *Evaluating Education: Issues and Methods*. London: Paul Chapman Publishing.

King, J.A., Lyons Morris, L. and Fitz-Gibbon, C.T. (1987) *How to Assess Program Implementation*. Beverly Hills: Sage Publications.

Krathwohl, D., Bloom, B. S. and Masia, B. (1956) *Taxonomy of Educational Objectives Handbook 2: Affective Domain*. London: Longman.

Krejcie, R.V. and Morgan, D.W. (1970) Determining Sample Size for Research Activities. *Educational and Psychological Measurement*, 30, pp. 607 - 610.

McCormick, R. and James, M. (1989) *Curriculum Evaluation in Schools* (Second Edition). London: Routledge.

Miles, M. and Huberman, M.A. (1984) *Qualitative Data Analysis*. Beverly Hills: Sage Publications.

Morris, D. (1977) *Manwatching: a Field Guide to Human Behaviour*. London: Panther.

Morrison, K.R.B. and Ridley, K. (1988) *Curriculum Planning and the Primary School*. London: Paul Chapman Publishing.

Neill, S. and Caswell, C. (1993) *Body Language for Competent Teachers*. London: Routledge.

Nietzsche, F. (1961) *Thus Spake Zarathustra*. Harmondsworth: Penguin.

Norris, N. (1990) *Understanding Educational Evaluation*. London: Kogan Page.

Oppenheim, A.N. (1966) *Questionnaire Design and Attitude Measurement*. London: Heinemann.

Osgood, C.E., Suci, G. S. and Tannenbaum, P. H. (1957) *The Measurement of Meaning*. Urbana: University of Illinois.

Pasternak, B. (1969) *Fifty Poems*. London: Unwin Books.

Pollard A. and Tann, S. (1987) *Reflective Teaching in the Primary School*. London: Cassell.

Pring, R. (1984) The Problems of Confidentiality, in M. Skilbeck (ed.) *Evaluating the Curriculum in the Eighties*. Sevenoaks: Hodder and Stoughton.

Sammons, P. (1989) Ethical Issues and Statistical Work, in R.G. Burgess (ed.) *The Ethics of Educational Research*. Lewes: Falmer.

Southgate, V., Arnold, H. and Johnson, S. (1981) *Extending Beginning Reading*. London: Heinemann (for the Schools Council).

Stake, R.E. (1976) The countenance of educational evaluation. Cited in D. Jenkins, "Six Alternative Models of Curriculum Evaluation", Unit 20, E203, *Curriculum Design and Development*. Milton Keynes: Open University Press.

Stenhouse, L. (1975) *An Introduction to Curriculum Research and Development*. London: Heinemann.

Stubbs, M. and Delamont, S. (1976) *Explorations in Classroom Observation*. Chichester: John Wiley.

Tyler, R.W. (1949) *Basic Principles of Curriculum and Instruction*. Chicago: University of Chicago Press.

Whitehead, F., Capey, A.C., Maddren, W., Wellings, A. (1977) *Children and Their Books*. London: Macmillan Educational.

Wilcox, B. (1992) *Time-Constrained Evaluation*. London: Routledge.

Yeats, W. (1962) News for the Delphic Oracle, in N. Jeffares (ed.) *Yeats: Selected Poetry*. London: Macmillan .

Index

Note: where several references are given, the bold numbers indicate the most important page numbers

access 52, 112, 114-5, 126-7
aggregation 70, 73-4, 78, 140, 169
alternative forms 105, 163-4, *see* reliability
anchor statements 69-70
anonymity 61, 70, 97, 186
association 136-140, 146-7, *see also* correlation
attitude measures 60, 68
audio-recording 63, 91-2

bi-modal score 132
binomial test 134

case study 159-160
cell frequencies 119, 125-6, 134
chi-square 69-70, 99, **131-4**, 140, 146, **196-8**
closed questions 39, 59-60, 64, **68-77**, 106
cluster sample 117, 121
coding 70, 77, 83, **151-160**, 169
cognitive mapping 156-8
computing 77, 92, 99, 101, 129, 134, 142, 147, 151, 154, 186
concurrent validity 166-7 *see* validity
confidentiality, *see* evaluation, ethics of
connoisseurship 6
consistency 162-4, 168
construct validity 166-7
content analysis 60, 155-6
content validity 165-7,
context-specificity 37, 40, 67, 70, 80, **88-90**, **92**, 94, 99, 101-2, 113, 150, 159, 168, 169, 177-8, 183
contingency table 132-4, 196-7
control groups 45, 55, 105, 141, 146, 163, 168, 173
control of data 57, 78
convenience sample 122-3,
conversational interviews 66-7, 90, 150
correlation 39, 134, **136-140**, 146, **162-7**, **169-171**
criterion-referencing 60, 98-100

criterion-related validity 166
critical friend 106, 158, 183
critical incidents 68, 87, 92
cross-tabulations 69-70, 121

data, analysis 84, 94, 101, **128-161**, 167,
degradation of 169
display of 147-8, 150-160
interpretation of 26, 70, 101, **158-160** 167, 170-4, 178
levels of 69, **98-9**, 148, 168
ownership of 26, 52, **185-9**
see also evaluation, ethics of
data collection 24, **59-111**, 163-5, 167-9, 184, 186, 191
written forms of 59-61, **68-79**, 90, 92-8
live forms of 60-1, 64-8, ̄ **79-92**, 94-6, 149-160
data handling 16-17, 23-6, 67, 89-90, 93, **130-160**
data presentation 17, 27-8, **147-8**, **150-160**, 177-9, 191
data processing 57, 64, 67-8, 74-9, 84, 89-90, 93, 101, **128-161**, 167, 178, 190-1
approaches to 25, 128-9
numerical data 39, 55, 63, 74-87, 92-4, 98-110, **128-149**
pre-ordinate 35, 80, 148-9, **151-160**
responsive 55, 80, 148-9, **151-160**
word data 51, 56, 60-1, 63-79, 90, 92-4, 96-8, 128-9, **149-160**, 179
Data Protection Act 186
data reduction 51-2, 89-90, 97, 113, **148-160**
data types 24, 69
decision making 9,11, **18-23**, 48, 190, 192
decision-making models 39, **47-50**, **54-6**, 113, 184, 190
deductive methods 148
degrees of freedom 134, 146
Delphi techniques 60-1, **94-8**, 110
descriptive statistics 37, 55

diaries 60, 89, 92-4, 151
dichotomous questions 60, 69, 73, **76-7, 140-1**
dimensional sample 122, 126
dispersal 143-5
distributions 98-9
distributions of chi-square 133
documentary data 51, 60, 89, 92-4, 105, **107-110, 150-1**, 166, 178

equivalence 162-4, 168 *see* reliability
equivalent forms 163-4 *see reliability*
evaluation
  and status 3-4
  approaches to 7-9, 34-58
  as illumination, *see* illuminative evaluation
  as portrayal, *see* portrayal methods
  bias in, *see* reliability, validity
  coherence of 19-20
  contexts of 2-7, 169, 177-8
  control of 57, 77, 97, **186-9**
    see also evaluation, ethics of
  costs of **15-16, 22**, 113, 167, 178, 184, **193-4**
  covert 89, 188
  data, *see* data collection, data presentation, data processing, data reduction, data types
  defined 1-2, 191
  deliberative 5, 192
  descriptions in 50-4
  end loaded 36, 81, 128
  ethics of 26, 29, 46-7, 52, 57-8, 89, 93, 97, 121, 178, **185-190**
  foci of 22, 83, 101, 168, 184
  formative 11, 12, 50, 109, **175-7**
  front loaded 35-6, 81, 83, 128
  information for 2, 8-9
  insider 50, 89, 168, **181-5**
  instrumentation 25, 35-7, 51, 57, **59-111**, 112, 127, 160, 167-8, 177-8, 190-1, *see also* data collection, data handling
  internal validity of *see* validity
  judgements in 2, 9, 11, 49, 167, 173, 191-2
  management of 16-18, 26-7, 163-4, **181-5**, 190-1
  methodologies of **34-7**, 57, 112, 160, 167, 177-8, 190-1
  models of 36-58, 191
  objectivity of 46, 58, 90, 101, 165, 183
  'operationalization' of 31-3, 56-8, 86, 167-8, 191
  orienting decisions 15-23
  outsider 50, 89, 168, **181-5**
  overt 89, 188 *see also* evaluation, ethics
  ownership of 23, 57-8, 93, **185-9**
  parameters of 48-9, 100, 169, 178, 192
  piloting in 39, 50, 57, 64, 79, 82, **101-7**, 124, 163, 178, 183
  planning of 2, **15-34, 56-8**, 158, 160, 167, 179, 186, 188-190
  politics of 2-5, 9, 11, 42, 46, 49, 54-5, 71, 75-6, 183, 190
  pre-ordinate 35, 64, 80, 87, 90, 128, 148-9, **151-160**
  presenting results of 16-18, 27-8, **147-8, 150-160**, 170, **175-180**, 191
  purposes of 19, 22, 31-3, 37, 43-4, 57, 101-2, 127, 178
  qualitative 5, **35-7**, 59, 63, 73, 78, 120, 128-9, **149-161**, 165, 169
  quantitative 5, **35-7**, 59, 63, 74, 78, 120, **128-149**, 160, 165
  reporting of 16, 27-8, 52-3, 57, 109-110, 147-8, 169, **175-180**, 183, **185-191**
  responsive 35, 80, 87-90, 128, 148-9, **151-160**
  scale of 38-40, 52-3, 59, 63, 77, 112-3, 141-2
  stages of 28-30, 47-8
  styles of 57, 127, 179
  subjectivity of 58, 90, 168
  summative 40, 110, 175-6
  time scales of **15-16**, 22, 28, **33-4**, 57, 64, 81, 83, 87-9, 91, 93, 101-2, 106-110, 127, 160, 162, 167-8, 176, 178,186,190
evaluation questions 2,7, **9-10**, 16, 22, **32-3, 56-7**, 128, 148, 154, 160, 168, 170, 178-9, 191-2
evaluator, amateur, professional **181, 184-5**
  choice of 26, 90, 168, 178, **181-5**, 190
  insider/outsider 168, **181-5**
  objectivity of 165
  one or many 181, **183-4**
  powers of 26, 57
  roles of 26-7, 57, 88
event sampling 83-5
executive summary 177-9

experimental group 45, 55, 105, 141, 146, 163, 168, 173
experimental models 36, **44-7**, 54-5, 98, 105, 113, 141, 146, 162, 170, 172, 190
external validity 165, 167, 191

field notes 89, 92, 149, **151-160**
frequencies 70, 74, 83-4, 86, 94, 119, 125, **131-2**, 136, **141**, 148, 155, 160

generalizability 39, 51
generalization 39, 51, **113-6**, 121, 148, **152-3**, **159-160**, 165, 169, 178
goal-free models 43-4
graphs **131-133**, **135-6**, **143-5**, 147, 178-9

Guttman scale 160

halo effect 169
Hawthorne effect 46, 88, 91, 93, **105**, 168
honesty 51, 65-7, 77, 79, 128, 154, 165

illuminative evaluation 36, **50-4**, 56, 80, **87-94**, 113, 129, **150-160**, 179, 184, 190
inductive methods 88, 149, 154-5, 169
inferential statistics 37, 55, 120
internal consistency 19-20, 162, 164-5
inter-rater reliability 82,163-4, 168, 184
interval data 98-9, **130-1**, 135, **142-9**
interval recording 85-6
interviews 31, 36-7, 59, **61-8**, 70, 79, 87, 90-1, 105-6, 107-110, 112, **149-160**, 164, 166, 178, 195
item analysis 102-3
item difficulty 102-6, 164, 168
item discriminability 102-6, 140, 168

journals 60, 89, 92-4

Krustal-Wallis statistic 70, 121, 134, **140-2**

leading questions 66-7, 168, 183
levels of significance *see* statistical significance
Likert scales 60, 72-7, 130
logs 60, 92-4

Mann Whitney U-test 69, 121, 134, **140-2**
matrix planning, evaluation design 18-30

in instrumentation 107-110
in sampling 118-120, 123-6
mean 99, 134-5, **142-9**, 163
median 134-5
modal score 99, 131-2, 134-5
moderation 169
multi-phase sample 117, 122
multiple choice items 39, 60, 64, 69-70, 183
multi-stage sample 121-2

nominal data 69-70, **130-142**
nominal group technique 61, **94-9** ,110
non-parametric data **130-142**, 146
non-parametric statistics, *see* statistics
non-parametric tests 98-9, 102
non-probability sample 115-6, **122-7**, 141-2, *see also* sampling
non-verbal communication 63, **66**, 91, **150**, **155-6**, 169
norm-referencing 60, 98-100, 104
null hypothesis **133-4**, 136, **140**, 146

objectives models **40-4**, 46, 54, 55, 113, 162, 190
observations 36, 51, 59, 61, **79-92**, 106, 110, 149-150, 164, 166, 178
one-tailed test 115, **141-2**
open questions 31-2, 59-60, 65, 68, **77-9**, 87, 106
opportunity sample 122-3, *see* sampling
ordinal data 98-9, **130**, **134-142**, 146

parametric data 142-9
parametric tests 98-9, 101
participant observation 52, 87-90
Pearson correlation statistic 99, 142, 147, **163-5**, **208-9**
perfect correlation 137-8
periodicity 118-9
photographs 91-2
point bi-serial calculation 140
portrayal methods 40, 56, 59, 87-8, 159
positive correlation 137
predictive validity 166
pre-test / post-test 44-5, 98, 105, 110, 146, 163, 168, 170-2
probability sample **115-122**, 141-2
probes 66
product moment correlation, *see* Pearson correlation statistic

progressive focussing 51, 89-90
prompts 66
proportionate sample 123-6
purposive sample 122, 126

questionnaires 31, 36-7, 39-40, 51, 55, **59-61, 68-79**, 87, 105-7, 110, 135, 140-1, 163, 165, 168, 178
quota sample 122-6

randomisation 45
random sample 115, 122, 125-6, 163
rank order correlation *see* Spearman correlation statistic
ratio data 98-9, **130-1**, 135, **142-9**
rating scales 42, 60, 65, **69-78**, 98, 130, 135, 139-140
reactivity 88, 90, 105, 168
see also Hawthorne effect
reliability 3, 24, 33, 57, 63, 65-7, 70-7, 79, 82, 90-1, 94, 98, 101-2, 105-6, 110, 114, 118, 140, 158, **162-5**, 168, 170, 173-4, 178, 183, 190
see also consistency, halo effect, Hawthorne effect, non-verbal communication, reactivity, respondent validation, triangulation
respondents 61-4, 70-2, 77, 79, 87, 96-7, 150-1, 158-9, 165, 168, **185-9**,
see also evaluation, ethics of
respondent validation 26, 51, 64, 89-90, **158** 169, 187
respondent verification, *see* respondent validation
response rate 79, 168
results of evaluation 27-8 *see also* data

sampling 24, 29, 38-9, 55, 98-9, 106-110, **112-127, 139**, 146, 165, 167-8, 172, 178, 190-1 *see also* access, case study, generalizability, matrix planning, randomisation, respondents
sampling error 115, 123-4
sampling frame 114-5, 120, 123
sampling, instantaneous 85
scales of data 68-70, **130-1**
scattergrams 147-8
school development plans 42-3, 92
semantic differential scales 60, 73
significance 45, 49, 192
sign systems 84

snowball sample 122, 126
snowball technique 61, 95-6
sociometry 60
Spearman-Brown formula 164-5
Spearman correlation statistic 99, 134, **139-140**, 146-7, 163-5, **199-200**
split-half reliability 140, 164-5, 168
SPSS 77, **134, 141-2**, 147, 151
spurious correlation 169, 172-3
stability 162-3
stage sampling 117, 121-2
stake-holders 19, 52, 176, 181
standard deviation 99, 134-5, **142-9**, 163, 170, **201**
standard error 105, 165, 170
standardization 98-9, 101, 145-6, 168-9
statistical significance 45, **133-4, 136-142**, 146-7, 163, 170-1, 173
statistics 37, 55, 68-70, 75-7, 92, 98-9, 101-2, 115, **129-150**, 165, 178
stratified sample 119-120, 163,
survey models **36-40**, 55, 59, 60, 113, 162-3, 190

teacher-as-researcher 6-7, 54, 89, 184, 190
test/re-test 106, 162, 164
tests 39, 45, 60, 90, **98-110**, 135, 146, 168, 170, 172-3
thick descriptions 50-1, 59, 88
timing of evaluation, *see* evaluation, time scales of
time sampling 85
t-tests 99, 134, 142, **146**, 163, **204-7**
triangulation **90-1**, 158, 165, 183-4
two-tailed test 115, **141-2**
Type I, Type II errors **140**, 146-7, 169

unstructured interview, *see* interviews
unstructured observation, *see* observations

validity 3, 23, 26, 33, 51-2, 57, 62, 65-7, 70-2, 78, 83, 86, 90-1, 94, 98, 101-2, 106, 108, 110, 113-4, 118, 124, 127, 158, **165-174**, 178-9, 182, **190-2**
see also honesty, illuminative evaluation, respondent validation
variables 39, 44-7, 69-70, 114, 130, 136, 170, 172-3
video recording 63, 82, **91-2**, 164

z-scores 142, **145-6, 202-3**